Mimbres Archaeology of the Upper Gila, New Mexico

ANTHROPOLOGICAL PAPERS OF
THE UNIVERSITY OF ARIZONA
NUMBER 53

Mimbres Archaeology of the Upper Gila, New Mexico

Stephen H. Lekson

THE UNIVERSITY OF ARIZONA PRESS
TUCSON
1990

About the Author

Stephen H. Lekson began his archaeological career by help-ing to lay out grids at the Saige-McFarland Site. He con-tinued to work in southwestern New Mexico, assisting in and eventually directing excavations at eight sites in the Cliff Valley and the Big Burro Mountains, and directing a survey of the Redrock Valley of the Gila River, which was the subject of his Master's thesis. His subsequent research in and around Chaco Canyon produced his doctoral dissertation (University of New Mexico, 1988), several monographs, and a number of journal articles on Chacoan architecture and settlement pattern. He returned to the Mimbres area with a University of New Mexico field school on the east slopes of the Black Range and later directed a survey of the Rio Grande in Sierra County, New Mexico. This work resulted in a monograph and several shorter papers. He has written an overview of the Mimbres for the National Park Service and an archaeological synthesis of southwestern New Mexico for the New Mexico Historic Preservation Division. Lekson is a Research Associate at the Arizona State Mu-seum, University of Arizona.

Cover: Mimbres Transitional (Style II) Black-on-white bowl from Burial 2, Room 4A, Saige-McFarland Site (Vessel 28; rim diameter, 27 cm). Draw-ing by Fel Brunett.

THE UNIVERSITY OF ARIZONA PRESS

Copyright © 1990
The Arizona Board of Regents
All Rights Reserved

This book was set in Linotype CRTronic 10/12 Times Roman
♾ This book is printed on acid-free, archival-quality paper.
Manufactured in the United States of America.

94 93 92 91 90   5 4 3 2 1

Library of Congress Cataloging-in-Publication Data

Lekson, Stephen H.
   Mimbres archaeology of the Upper Gila, New Mexico / Stephen H.
Lekson.
      p.   cm. — (Anthropological papers of the University of
Arizona : no. 53)
   Includes bibliographic references.
   ISBN 0-8165-1164-0 (alk. paper)
   1. Saige-McFarland Site (N.M.) 2. Mogollon culture—New
Mexico. I. Title. II. Series.
E99.M76L43   1990   89-20538
978.9'692—dc20   CIP

British Library Cataloguing in Publication data are available.

Contents

FIGURES

TABLES

Preface

The Saige-McFarland Site is a multicomponent Mimbres site in the Cliff Valley of the Gila River, located less than a mile northeast of Cliff, in Grant County, New Mexico. James E. Fitting excavated the site in 1971 and 1972. A preliminary report was published for the first season's work (Fitting and others 1971), but a final report was never completed. I had an opportunity to study the records and artifacts in the late 1980s, and this monograph represents a description of architecture and stratigraphy of the site and of the artifact analyses completed in 1987.

The importance of the Saige-McFarland Site for Mimbres archaeology became obvious in late 1985, when I was preparing a proposal through the Arizona State Museum for archaeological contract work in the Upper Gila area. I am apparently the only supervisory-level member of the Upper Gila Project who continues to work in Southwestern archaeology, and I decided to reassemble the Saige-McFarland materials. Jim Fitting, who had changed careers, sent me the notes, maps, and photographs from the site. Fel Brunett packed and shipped to Tucson the major part of the collections, which had been stored in Michigan. With the assistance of Jim Judge, I obtained another truck load of material from the site that had been stored at the Fort Burgwin Foundation in New Mexico. In July 1986, with the support of the Arizona State Museum and the A. N. Lindley Foundation of Tucson, Arizona, I began preparing the materials for museum curation and writing this descriptive report.

The major goals of the project at that time were (1) the preparation of the collections for museum curation (they are now in a permanent repository at the Museum of New Mexico in Santa Fe), and (2) the preparation of a descriptive report of the site to assist future analyses of the collections. Architecture and stratigraphy were described first, largely independent of artifact data. Larger items (whole or reconstructible vessels and ground stone artifacts) were noted in the description of specific architectural and stratigraphic proveniences, but no attempt was made to integrate bulk artifacts into their architectural and stratigraphic contexts.

The architectural and stratigraphic proveniences were then compared to the 1971 and 1972 inventories and analyses and finally to the inventory of the artifact collection as it now exists so as to evaluate the completeness of the collection. Compiling and comparing those inventories provided basic data for artifact analyses in Chapter 3. Artifact counts are presented in a series of appendixes. New analyses were undertaken only when changes in typology over the last 15 years made reanalysis necessary (as with ceramics) or to complete unfinished projects (as with chipped stone).

Although a number of observations and conclusions are offered in the course of the descriptions of architecture and artifacts, integration of one with the other remains incomplete. What may appear to be a lack of cohesiveness in this regard results primarily from the nature of available documentation. The limitations imposed by that fragmented record on synthetic analyses and interpretation are fully discussed in Chapter 1.

A primary concern throughout the preparation of this report was the integrity and utility of the data. How much reliance should the reader place on the data included here and on the collections now stored at the Museum of New Mexico in Santa Fe? The site was, for its time, well excavated. The documentation has suffered over the last 15 years, which does detract from the quality of resulting description. On balance, however, better than average field control combined with variable preservation of notes results in a set of data that is reasonably good compared to other Southwestern excavations of the 1970s and is useful even by today's standards. Whatever its flaws, the information salvaged on Saige-McFarland is valuable because the site spans a critical period, the shift from pit house to pueblo, in a virtually unknown portion of the Mimbres region. Saige-McFarland expands the currently restricted scope of the Mimbres to the upper Gila, the major drainage of southwestern New Mexico.

Acknowledgments

This research was made possible by the generous support of Mrs. Agnese N. Lindley and the Lindley Foundation, with additional funding for special analyses from the Arizona State Museum. Dr. R. Gwinn Vivian (Arizona State Museum) encouraged both analysis and publication, and I thank him for his advice and administrative support. Dr. Raymond H. Thompson (Arizona State Museum) provided additional funds for the preparation of graphics. Publication was supported by grants from Mr. Jack W. Keen of the Western New Mexico Telephone Company (which now owns the Saige-McFarland Site) and Dr. James Neely of Archaeological Research, Inc. and the University of Texas, Austin. I am grateful to these individuals and the organizations they represent for their kindness and support.

The 1971–1972 excavations at Saige-McFarland were supported by grants to James E. Fitting from the Wenner-Gren Foundation, the American Philosophical Society, and Case Western Reserve University.

I was allowed to use the excellent facilities of the Arizona State Museum, first as a visiting scholar and later as a research associate, during the preparation of this report. The staff of the Museum helped in many ways. I particularly thank William Deaver, Bruce Huckell, Lisa Huckell, Bruce Masse, and Arthur Vokes for their assistance in artifact identification. Ron Beckworth provided skillful assistance in preparation of the ceramic illustrations and last minute corrections on other graphics. William Gillespie prepared a fine report on the faunal materials from Saige-McFarland that is on file at the Laboratory of Anthropology in Santa Fe (Gillespie 1987). Peter J. McKenna of the National Park Service Southwest Region identified a number of mysterious sherds.

Dr. Jeffrey S. Dean (Laboratory of Tree-Ring Research, University of Arizona) processed the tree-ring samples from Saige-McFarland and produced the first Mimbres tree-ring date from the Upper Gila. I thank Jeff both for that date (which was much later than I wanted) and for his good advice on chronology in general.

The Museum of New Mexico generously agreed to curate the collections from Saige-McFarland. Curt Schaafsma, State Archaeologist, arranged the Museum's acceptance of the collections.

Mr. Jerry Saige and Mr. and Mrs. George L. McFarland allowed and encouraged the original excavations and later graciously transferred title to the collection to the Museum of New Mexico. I appreciate their aid in bringing these materials back to New Mexico.

A number of individuals were important in reassembling the collections and data from Saige-McFarland. Foremost, Fel V. Brunett, who excavated Room Block A, repacked the majority of the materials and shipped them from Michigan to Arizona. This project could not have been completed without Fel's many contributions. Dr. James E. Fitting sent me all his notes and maps from the site. I thank Jim for his assistance in this project and for introducing me to Southwestern archaeology. Dr. W. James Judge of the Fort Burgwin Foundation allowed me to transfer Saige-McFarland materials at Fort Burgwin first to the Arizona State Museum and finally to the Museum of New Mexico. Dr. Patricia Crown of Southern Methodist University discovered, at Dallas, a number of pots from the Saige-McFarland collections and arranged for them to be transferred to the Museum of New Mexico. Kenneth Brown, Jim Fitting, Thomas Gray, Chuck Mobley, and Timothy Klinger were all remarkably calm when confronted by the ghost of field seasons past and by my questions about twenty-year-old trivia.

Portions of this report were reviewed by Roger Anyon, Fel Brunett, Dr. Patricia Gilman, Curtis Schaafsma, Dr. Harry J. Shafer, and Dr. Michael B. Schiffer. Their many fine comments improved both style and content. Needless to say, these scholars do not agree with all my opinions and conclusions, and they are not liable for my odd ideas.

Carol Gifford, editor of the *Anthropological Papers*, turned a fragmented manuscript into a coherent text. Carol made this potentially burdensome process very pleasant (at least for me). Carmen Prezelski of the Southwest Center (University of Arizona) kindly provided the Spanish translation of the Abstract. Catherine Cameron, of the University of Arizona, helped greatly with the final revisions.

The excavations at Saige-McFarland were under the overall supervision of James E. Fitting. Site directors and crew chiefs included Kenneth Brown, Fel Brunett, Carolyn Farndell, B. Thomas Gray, James Ross, and myself. The lab director was Timothy C. Klinger, who converted me to Motown music. The crew consisted of Chris Anderson, Paul Bloch, Jake B. Jackson, Charles Brilvitch, Lynn Cohen, Ronnie Davis, Sarah Dinsmore, Pat Draine, Doug Elliott, Jerry Galm, Adrian Levi, Larry Louka, Chuck Mobley, Debby Nichols, Debby Pavilovis, Fran Pergericht, Amy Rubin, Kerry Shears, Claudia Smith, Valerie Stephens, Ann Viront, Kim Waldron, Don Weir, John Weiner, and Ralph Zimak. These were the friends of my first wide-eyed days in archaeology, and every archaeologist knows how special those friends can be.

I would be remiss if I did not acknowledge my debt to Dr. Steven A. LeBlanc and Dr. Harry J. Shafer. Their contributions to modern Mimbres studies are fundamental. We often disagree, but I never fail to benefit from those exchanges (won or lost). Finally, I thank Dr. Emil Haury for his pioneering work in the Mimbres Mogollon and his good counsel in more recent days.

CHAPTER ONE

The Saige-McFarland Site and Mimbres Archaeology

The Mimbres area of southwestern New Mexico has long been famous for its Classic Black-on-white pots, familiar today from motifs on T-shirts, calendars, notecards, and trivets. Indeed, the first major research in the Mimbres area consisted of catalogues of pots from private collections (Fewkes 1914). A series of early excavations at large Classic Mimbres pueblos (Bradfield 1929; Cosgrove and Cosgrove 1932; Nesbitt 1931) produced an archaeological context for the Classic Black-on-white pots, and the pioneering work of Haury (1936) defined the outline of the archaeologica! sequence that preceded Mimbres.

After this initial burst of activity, archaeological interest in the Mimbres area waned for some thirty years. Not until the 1970s did major research projects return to the Mimbres area, with the Upper Gila Project (Fitting 1972b), the Mimbres Foundation (LeBlanc 1983) and the NAN Ranch Research Project (Shafer and Taylor 1986) being perhaps the most productive of those efforts. Nearly all of the early and most of the recent work in the Mimbres area was restricted to sites in the Mimbres River valley, but the Upper Gila Project expanded the geographic scope of Mimbres studies to the Gila River, an important but largely unknown area within the Mimbres region (Fig. 1.1). The Upper Gila Project's work at Saige-McFarland was by far the largest and archaeologically the most productive excavation of a Classic Mimbres site on the Gila River.

The 1970s renaissance of Mimbres studies produced (and continues to produce) a quantity of data that we have only begun to assimilate. The Mimbres Foundation (Anyon and others 1981; LeBlanc and Whalen 1980; LeBlanc 1983), adding new data to the previously defined sequence (Haury 1936), established the chronology that currently guides Mimbres research (Table 1.1). Although I argue with details of this synthesis in later sections, I gladly acknowledge here the debt Mimbres studies owe to the Mimbres Foundation for developing this baseline for Mimbres prehistory.

THE CLIFF VALLEY

The Cliff Valley (Fig. 1.1) is a straight, 9-mile long segment of the Gila River. The 1-mile wide valley begins at about 4,700 feet (1,435 m) elevation, where the river emerges from its narrow course through the Mogollon Mountains (the Gila's Upper Box) and ends at about 4,430 feet (1,350 m), where the river enters a much shorter narrows at Fort West Hill. Below Fort West Hill, the Gila flows through a series of alternating narrows and small open bottoms until it reaches the rugged Middle Box, about 11 miles below Cliff.

Three major tributaries join the river in the Cliff Valley. At the upper end, Mogollon Creek enters the Gila just below the mountain scarp. At the lower end of the valley, Duck Creek joins the river from the west and, immediately opposite it, Bear Creek joins the Gila from the east.

The Saige-McFarland Site, at 4,585 feet (1,395 m) elevation, is located on a terrace point that separates the Gila and Duck Creek, just above their confluence. The site is on the Gila side of the point, directly opposite the mouth of Bear Creek, a location at the confluence of the Gila and its two major tributaries in the lower Cliff Valley, Duck and Bear creeks.

Precipitation records for more than 90 years (with short gaps) are available from stations at Cliff and Buckhorn. Both are within 8 miles of the site and at approximately the same elevation. Annual rainfall at these two stations averages about 13.75 inches (34.9 cm) with slightly more than half of the total coming in July, August, and September thunderstorms. The growing season (consecutive days without a killing frost) currently averages about 170 days.

The Cliff Valley is a riparian oasis through the northern reaches of the Chihuahuan Desert; vegetation away from the river is Chihuahuan desert scrub. The valley floor is excellent farmland, with over 4,000 acres of the Cliff Valley irrigable by simple gravity (nonpump) ditch systems (Lekson 1986b). Besides the river itself, one of the most notable aspects of the Cliff Valley is its close proximity to the Mogollon Mountains. Within 10 miles of the site are peaks rising to over 7,500 feet (2,285 m) and extensive pinyon-juniper and ponderosa forests.

THE SAIGE-McFARLAND SITE

The site was named Saige-McFarland for its joint owners, Mr. and Mrs. Jerry L. Saige and Mr. and Mrs. George C. McFarland, Mrs. Saige's parents. Numbered LA 5421 in the Museum of New Mexico system, it is also known as MC–146, a designation from the 1967 Mimbres Area Survey of the University of Michigan directed by Dr. Arthur Jelinek, the historical predecessor of the Upper Gila Project.

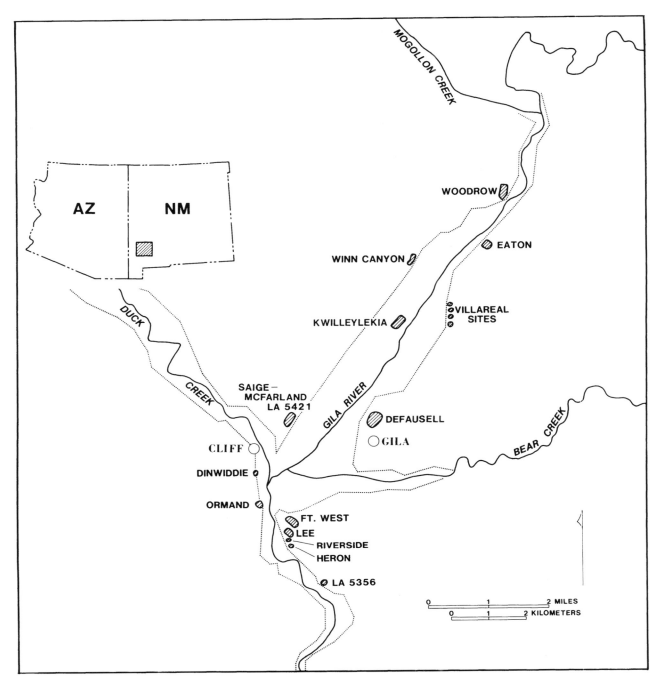

Figure 1.1. Location of Cliff Valley.

Geology

The Saige-McFarland Site sits on the edge of an alluvial terrace, about 90 feet (27 m) above the present bed of the Gila River. The terrace was cut in the vast southern pediment of the Mogollon Mountains, which fills the wide Mangas Trough between the Mogollons and the smaller Burro and Redrock mountains.

The precise nomenclature for the surface geology at the site was a bit of a mystery during the excavation, and remains unclear. We sometimes referred to the consolidated gravels that underlay the terrace surface as "Gila Conglomerate"; in notes, it was more often termed hardpan or caliche. "Gila Conglomerate" is clearly incorrect, and the other two terms are not accurate.

Table 1.1. Mimbres Valley Chronological Sequence

Period	Phase	Date A.D.	Architecture	Diagnostic Ceramics
Pueblo	Cliff	1375–1450	Adobe pueblos	Gila Polychrome
	Black Mountain	1180–1300	Adobe pueblos	El Paso Polychrome, Chupadero Black-on-white
	Mimbres	1000–1150	Cobble masonry pueblos	Mimbres Classic Black-on-white
Late Pit House	Three Circle	750–1000	Rectangular pit structures	Three Circle Red-on-white, Boldface Black-on-white
	San Francisco	650–750	Rectangular pit structures	Mogollon Red-on-brown
	Georgetown	550–650	Circular and D-shaped pit structures	San Francisco Red
Early Pit House	Cumbre	200–550	Circular and oval pit structures	Red-slipped ware

Note: Simplified, after Anyon and others 1981, LeBlanc and Whalen 1980, and Nelson and LeBlanc 1986.

Prehistoric construction at the site was either preceded by stripping the thin topsoil and clearing slightly into the consolidated gravels (for above-grade building), or by excavating into the gravels (for below-grade building). The consolidated gravels consist of alluvial cobbles in a distinctive red clay matrix. With topsoil and the uppermost portion of the subsoil removed prehistorically, the difference between the cultural deposits and the red substrate beneath them was dramatic and impossible to miss.

The red-clay-and-cobble horizon was the sterile base level for our excavations. I use the term "substrate" throughout this report to refer to it. The terms hardpan and caliche, used in the field notes, are not used here. Well-defined caliche layers were observed in the walls of deeper pit structures, but in general the substrate, where excavations were terminated, was well above the developed caliche.

Archaeology

The Saige-McFarland Site (Fig. 1.2) consists of three or four Mimbres phase (A.D. 1000 to 1150) masonry room blocks, a large "Great Kiva" of the Three Circle phase (A.D. 750 to 1000), and at least 25 pit house depressions, which probably date to the Three Circle phase or earlier. Fitting (1972b: 22) estimated that "the site originally contained 150 rooms, including both pit structures and surface rooms." Fitting and Richard C. Ellison, a local archaeologist, "feel that there might be a ballcourt at the site" (Fitting and others 1982: 75). Although it is possible that ballcourts will someday be identified at Mimbres sites, I doubt that one exists at Saige-McFarland. I know of no feature identified in the field work of the 1970s or during my examination of aerial photography and the site itself in the 1980s that is a likely candidate for a ballcourt.

Three of the masonry room blocks (A, B, and C) were located in, around, and partially under a complex of telephone company offices and outbuildings along the edge of a terrace. A fourth room block was located under a trailer at the north end of the site (the building immediately north of Pit House 3 on Fig. 1.2).

The "Great Kiva" (Pit House 1) was located about 50 feet (15 m) southwest of Room Block B, away from the terrace edge. Numerous depressions were noted in the area north and northwest of Pit House 1; some of these, at least, indicate other pit structures. The "pit house area," as it was called at the time of excavation, was farther back from the terrace edge than Room Blocks A and C (several pit structures were found beneath Room Block B, but not under either of the other two excavated room blocks). Possible pit structures shown as depressions on Figure 1.2 were identified from small-scale aerial photography taken in 1965. Both the locations and sizes of these features are approximate.

A single masonry-lined pit structure (Pit House 3) was excavated at the northern end of the site.

A variety of modern structures impacted parts of the site in 1971. A paved road (State Route 293) cut through the southeastern quadrant of the site and destroyed most of Room Block C. A bladed dirt spur road (a driveway to the telephone company offices) ran between Room Blocks A and B, and over the northern end of the latter. As noted, a mobile home at the northern end of the site may have been sitting on a small fourth room block. Fences crisscrossed the site (one fence ran along the crest of the Room Block B mound) and telephone and power poles for the various offices and homes were occasionally located in cultural features (as in Pit House 3).

Despite all this modern construction, the site was in relatively good condition in 1971. Vandalism was largely avoided by the careful attention of the owners, who protected the site from pothunters. Room Block C, the farthest from the telephone company offices, was the most badly disturbed unit. It had been largely destroyed by the highway cut, and vandals had repeatedly dug into the rooms thus exposed. Potholes and disturbances in Room Blocks A and B are discussed in later sections.

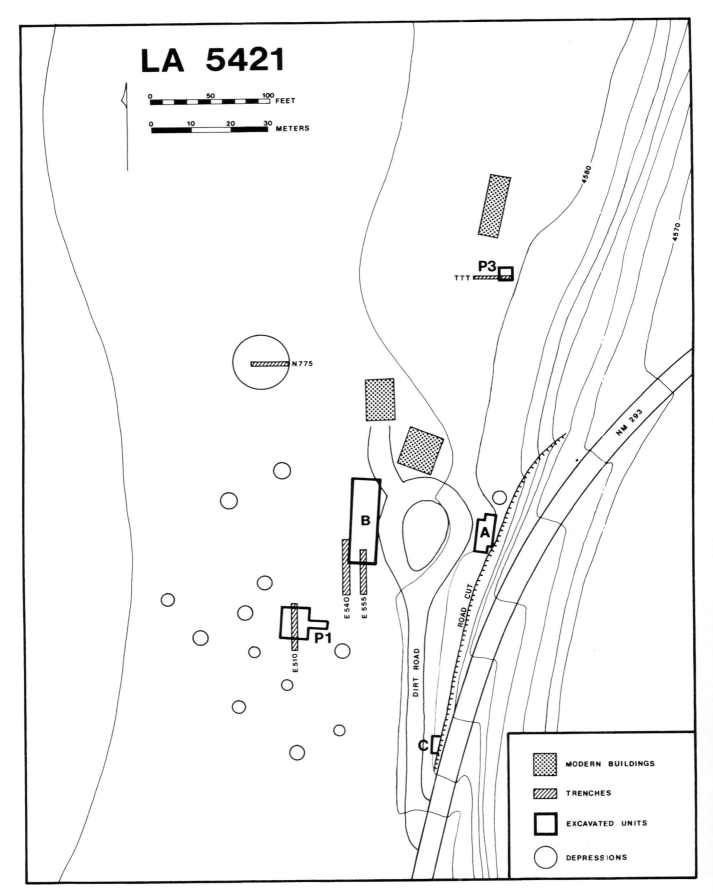

Figure 1.2. Plan of the Saige-McFarland Site.

Today, almost all of Saige-McFarland is gone. The telephone company operation expanded considerably: a garage now sits on top of Room Block B, and Room Blocks A and C are lost beneath a bladed, gravel-paved parking lot. Pit House 1 has been backfilled, and most of the "pit house area" has been leveled for equipment storage or subdivided into lots for homes.

Excavations, 1971–1972

The Saige-McFarland Site was investigated as part of the Upper Gila Project (Fitting and others 1971). The excavations, undertaken as a field school of Case-Western Reserve University, spanned three separate field seasons: a four-week session in January of 1971, a six-week session during the Summer of 1971, and another four-week session in January of 1972. Although the overall direction of the project was managed by Fitting, immediate field supervision was the responsibility of several graduate students: for the first season, James Ross and Fel Brunett; for the second season, Kenneth Brown, Carolyn Farndell, and B. Thomas Gray; and for the last season, Tom Gray and me. Timothy Klinger joined the project as field laboratory director and ceramic analyst during the Summer 1972 session. Between 10 and 12 students were ordinarily engaged in excavation.

During the January 1971 season, Room Blocks A and C were completely uncovered, and Room Block B was begun with the excavation of Rooms 8 and 9. Initial testing in the pit house area was discontinued after only a few days because of problems with frozen ground. Excavations in Room Block B were completed during the Summer 1971 season (with the exception of Room 12, which was cleared only to the uppermost floor). Initial trenching in the pit house area (the N775 trench) failed to define a pit structure in that section, and efforts were moved to the E510 trenches at Pit House 1. About three-fourths of the fill in Pit House 1 was removed during the Summer 1971 season. Pit House 1 was completed during the January 1972 season, along with the subfloor deposits of Room 12 and Pit House 3. That concluded field work at the site.

The excavations were an uneasy hybrid of Midwestern archaeological tactics and Southwestern masonry architecture. Architectural features were approached by trenches, generally segmented in 5-foot by 10-foot (1.5-m by 3.1-m) units. Almost no data survive from these trenches. Once a wall was defined, rooms and pit structures were excavated as units. All fill was removed in 6-inch (15-cm) levels and screened through one-fourth-inch hardware mesh. In practice, of course, each unit had its own particular excavation history, as described in the following sections. Soil was often either wet or frozen during the two January seasons, but I doubt that architectural components (walls, floors), major features, or modern intrusions (potholes and pits) were missed.

Fieldwork of the Upper Gila Project continued through 1973 at other sites. Most analyses of Saige-McFarland arti-facts were completed during the two years following the January 1972 session (the histories of these analyses and the names of the individuals who participated in them are given in later chapters). A final descriptive report of the architecture and stratigraphy of the site, however, was never prepared. With the passage of years, the various participants in the Upper Gila Project naturally pursued other projects and, in some cases, other careers.

Documentation

The surviving notes from Saige-McFarland occupy about two cubic feet and one small map tube, not a lot of paper from an excavation of this scale. That total includes photographs and bulky artifact analysis tally sheets. These notes, and the collections they document, had suffered through 15 years of storage, of repeated packing and shipping, and of intermittent use by literally dozens of people. However, enough remained to compile this report, and some of the earlier analyses aided greatly in this process. Most of the provenience difficulties had been resolved by Klinger years ago; his schematic renderings of proveniences within units made the process of description much easier. The reader should note that all graphics and descriptions herein are more-or-less idealized and simplified.

The site was excavated in units measured in feet, notes were taken using feet, and photoscales were marked in feet. Where appropriate or useful to others, metric measurements have been added. Scales on the architectural plans include meters, so comparisons may be made with architectural plans in other reports.

Segments of the primary documentation have been lost, specifically most of the Pit House 1 notes and the map of the pit house area. Room Blocks A, B, and C are well documented, as is Pit House 3. A preliminary report on Room Block A was published (Fitting and others 1971) and a draft of a similar report on Room Block B was prepared but never published (Brown 1971). Detailed manuscript reports were also prepared on Room 12 (Lekson 1972) and Pit House 3 (Draine 1971).

Constructing profiles of the room blocks was a challenge. Various vertical data were used throughout the excavations, and constructing a network of correspondences between and among these vertical data was possible only through a series of happy chances in the notes, including marginalia, one critical comment on the back of an envelope, and a casual aside in one letter that allowed comparison of January 1971 and Summer 1971 data in Room Block B. In the end, it was possible to cross-reference almost every vertical datum.

None of the figures (with the exception of Fig. 2.9, lower) are simply redrafted from plans or profiles in the notes; all have been reconstructed, to various degrees, from notes and sketch maps. It appears that maps were never prepared of the room blocks as units. The maps of the room blocks (Figs. 2.1 and 2.2) were constructed by piecing together individual room maps, supplemented by the occasional interroom measurement and photograph. The field maps of individual rooms and floors were of good quality and included a number of shared mapping points, so the plans of the room blocks are reasonably accurate. The style of field mapping differed between the 1971 January and Summer seasons, which accounts, to some extent, for the irregularity of the Room Block A plan and the right angle perfection of the Room Block B plan. However, these differences reflect reality, for Room Block A was, indeed, an irregular structure, whereas Room Block B was laid out much more carefully and regularly. Although these differences may be exaggerated in Figures 2.1 and 2.2 due to different styles of field recording, the exaggeration is probably slight.

The cobbles and stones shown in the walls of Room Blocks A and B (Figs. 2.1 and 2.2) represent the uppermost visible stones in those walls. Often, the top of the wall had deteriorated or eroded, and the number of wythes (horizontal rows of stones) shown on the maps is not necessarily representative of the wall's width at lower, better preserved levels. Wall construction data came from field notes and plans. Only the west wall of Room 2, the east wall of Room 5, the east wall of Room 11, and the south and east walls of Room 14 lacked scaled drawings of the visible wall stones. In all these cases, photographs existed that permitted the reconstruction of these plans with, in all likelihood, as much accuracy as a few of the more hastily made field drawings.

All the architectural profiles are reconstructions based on the stratigraphic notes, depths and elevations of features, and the level systems used in each room. No profiles were drawn in the field except of Pit House 1 (now lost) and of selected individual features. Thus all profiles should be considered simplified and to some degree schematic, but with that limitation they are reasonably accurate.

One of the biggest problems encountered was the site map. A manuscript plane-table map with the major features survives (but without, alas, the depressions and berms of the pit house area), but the map fails entirely to agree with the grid system used at the site. Excavations were initiated with a classic Midwestern grid system, with N500 E500 established about 80 feet (24 m) south of Pit House 1, and 5-foot (1.5-m) square units designated by the coordinate of their southwestern corners. Unfortunately, the use of the grid system was confused over the three seasons of excavation. During the summer of 1971, grid units in Room Block B were numbered with north reversed (that is, north became south), and the grid designations of Pit House 1 were apparently off by 40 feet (12 m) north and 10 feet (3 m) east.

Almost none of the grid designations (after the errors were caught and corrected) correspond to their locations as shown on the plane-table map. It was not possible to reconcile the plane-table map with the grid system; the error (whatever it was) was not consistent or systematic. Room Block A is 7 feet (2 m) too far west; Room Block B is 10 feet (3 m) too far east. Both Room Block B and Pit House 1 are 10 feet too far north, and Room Block A appears to be more-or-less correct with regard to the north coordinate. Considering the difficulties with the grid system documented in the field notes and the lack of grid coordinate data for Room Block C and Pit House 3, I decided to use the plane-table map in preference to the grid designations for various units. Thus the grid units shown on Figure 2 are not "correct" in terms of the grid origin (N500 E500) and scale of that map. The orientation of the grid units and the spatial relation of trenches to the room blocks and pit structures are quite accurate. The trenches themselves are in the correct locations, and it is their grid *designations* that are incorrect.

Some minor discrepancies in grid north exist between the orientation of Room Blocks A and C on field maps and their orientation on the plane table map. In both cases, I split the small difference between the two.

A numbering system for archaeological features was begun during the Summer 1971 season and continued through the January 1972 season. At least 53 numbers were sequentially assigned to features like burials, firepits, and postholes. The master list was lost, but almost all of it can be reconstructed from the notes. Only 6 of 53 feature numbers remain unknown. I have replaced the field feature number system with a new series of numbers in this report for two reasons. First, the January 1971 excavations did not use such a system, and a consistent descriptive format required feature designations for Room Block A. Second, the assignment of feature numbers in the field was rather whimsical, with an artifact in the fill receiving a feature number but eight postholes on the floor not receiving any feature numbers. To obtain a consistent system for the identification of architectural features and major artifacts with known locations, I have sequentially numbered any unit or artifact that could be mapped and identified on the plans and profiles (Table 2.1).

Despite the deficiencies discussed above, the plans and profiles are relatively accurate representations of the archaeology of the Saige-McFarland Site. The site documentation and collections remain the best and most extensive sample for Mimbres archaeology on the Upper Gila.

CHAPTER TWO

Architecture and Stratigraphy

The architecture and stratigraphy of the Saige-McFarland Site was reconstructed from student notes, manuscripts, photos, the odd map or plan, and, in the case of Room Block A, published accounts. Table 2.1 provides a listing of the renumbered features, as described in Chapter 1. Room blocks and rooms are described in alphabetic and numeric order, followed by discussions of the pit structures. Within each unit, information is provided on the sequence of excavation; walls and construction details; fill; roof remains (generally found as fragments in the fill); and floor, floor features and floor artifacts.

Where records are incomplete, descriptions are presented in the most appropriate format. Excavation units were originally measured in feet and tenths of feet. Metric measures have been substituted wherever possible. Despite the appearance of decimal place accuracy, all measurements should be considered approximate, rounded figures.

Occurrences of major artifacts like manos, metates, and ceramic vessels, are mentioned where possible. Items are identified by numbers (for example, Vessel 2, Ground Stone 101) that refer to artifact analyses in Chapter 3 and in Appendixes B and C.

ROOM BLOCK A

Room Block A (Fig. 2.1) was excavated in 1971 (January session) under the supervision of Fel Brunett, Jim Ross, Tom Gray, and Jim Fitting. In addition to using the original notes, parts of the following description paraphrase and occasionally quote without citation from the preliminary report of its excavation (Fitting and others 1971).

Block A was a mound rising about 2 feet (60 cm) above the terrace surface; its east edge was perched immediately above the steep road cut (Fig. 1.2), and some wall rubble had fallen over the edge. The room block was approached in a 5-foot by 10-foot trench (about 1.5 m by 3.0 m; N645 E670) that was abandoned as soon as a room (Room 1) was defined. At the beginning of excavations, the ground was solidly frozen, a condition evidently aiding in the definition of walls, because the frozen topsoil broke along wall lines. Some of the frozen uppermost fill of Rooms 1, 2, and 3 could not be screened. Large sherds were removed when observed, but otherwise the first 6 inches (15 cm) of the southern one-third of Room Block A was not systematically sampled for artifacts.

The standard tactics were to locate a wall, and then to outline the interior of the room with a shallow trench. The room fill was taken out in arbitrary 6-inch (15-cm) levels, down to the floor. All floors were removed to expose subfloor features, and any material below the floor was also removed in 6-inch levels. Fill was screened.

Room Block A was partially disturbed on its east edge by the highway road cut, and along its west margin by the bladed driveway between it and Room Block B (Fig. 1.2). Although earlier pothunting in Room Block A had been reported by the owners of the site, there was remarkably little damage done to the room block by previous excavation.

A possible wall was traced for a short distance north of Room 6, where it abruptly ended (no map of this feature survives); otherwise it appears that all of the original structure of Room Block A was cleared. No excavations were undertaken outside the walls (except a small portion of the N645 E670 trench). Exterior areas to the east were destroyed by the road cut and those to the west by the graded driveway. Just to the north of Room Block A, both aerial photography and the manuscript site map suggest the presence of a possible pit structure; it was not excavated. This pit structure may have been associated with Room Block A.

In general, prehistoric construction of the rooms of Block A began with the removal of existing soil to the reddish substrate level. The archaeologists believed that after stripping to this level, irregularities in the substrate were filled in and floors were constructed over the resulting level surface in Rooms 1, 3, and 5. In Rooms 2, 4, and 6, however, the walls begin at the substrate level and the floors (or probable floor levels) rest on up to 1 foot (30 cm) of fill spread over the substrate. The excavators suggested that in Rooms 2 and 4 the sequence of stripping and filling had been followed but that a thick subfloor base either had accumulated or had been placed in these rooms after wall construction. In Room 6, the construction sequence was interpreted differently. In this demonstrably later room, the excavators felt that the original soil was left in place and that walls were constructed in trenches through the original soil. The floor of Room 6 was then constructed on top of the old ground surface.

Rooms 2, 3, 4, and 5 clearly represent the core of Block A. With the exception of the wall separating Rooms 2 and 4, all corners in this group are bonded, and Rooms 1 and 6 abut onto this original unit. In general, the walls of the original unit are better built than those of the later rooms. In

Table 2.1. List of Features at the Saige-McFarland Site

Feature number	Provenience	Location	Feature
1	Room 1	Floor 1	Roof-support post
2	Room 1	Floor 1	Stone slab
3	Room 2 + 4	Wall	Door
4	Room 2A	Floor 1	Stone slab
5	Room 2A	Floor 1	Axes
6	Room 2B		Hearth on subsoil
7	Room 3	Floor 1	Bin
8	Room 3	Floor 1	Firepit
9	Room 3	Floor 1	Roof-support post
10	Room 3	Floor 1	Post along south wall
11	Room 3	Floor 1	Stone slab
12	Room 4A	Floor 1	Stone slab
13	Room 4A	Floor 1	Ash lens
14	Room 4A	Floor 1	Burial 2
15	Room 4A	Floor 1	Niche in Feature 14
16	Room 4B	Floor 1	Stone slab
17	Room 4B	Floor 1	Bin
18	Room 5	Floor 1	Firepit
19	Room 5	Floor 1	Posthole for roof support
20	Room 5	Floor 1	Stone slab
21	Room 6	Floor 1	Stone slab
22	Room 6	Floor 1	Firepit
23	Room 6	Floor 1	Roof-support post
24	Room 6	Floor 1	Mealing bin(?)
25	Room 6	Floor 1	Cobble pavement
26	Room 7		Burial 3
27	Room 8	Floor 1	Roof-support post
28	Room 10	Floor 1	Stone slab
29	Room 10	Floor 1	Plastered basin
30	Room 11	Floor 1	"Buttress" on west wall
31	Room 11	Floor 1	Stone slab
32	Room 11	Floor 1	Firepit
33	Room 11	Floor 1	Lithic concentration
34	Room 11	Subfloor	Firepit
35	Room 12	Fill	Wall section
36	Room 12	Floor 1	"Buttress" in southwest corner
37	Room 12	Floor 1	Stone slab
38	Room 12	Floor 1	Stone slab
39	Room 12	Floor 1	Posthole for roof support
40	Room 12	Floor 1	Firepit
41	Room 12	Floor 1	D-shaped pit
42	Room 12	Floor 1	Rectangular pit
43	Room 12	Floor 1	Artifact concentration
44	Room 12	Floor 1	Pit
45	Room 12	Floor 1	Burial 11
46	Room 12	Floor 1	Multiple burials
47	Room 12	Floor 1	Burial 4 in Feature 46
48	Room 12	Floor 1	Burial 5 in Feature 46
49	Room 12	Floor 1	Burial 6 in Feature 46
50	Room 12	Floor 1	Burial 8 in Feature 46
51	Room 12	Floor 2	South wall balk
52	Room 12	Floor 2	Firepit
53	Room 12	Floor 2	Posthole for roof support
54	Room 12	Floor 2	Posthole for roof support

Table 2.1. *Continued*

Feature number	Provenience	Location	Feature
55	Room 12	Floor 2	Posthole, north row
56	Room 12	Floor 2	Posthole, north row
57	Room 12	Floor 2	Posthole, north row
58	Room 12	Floor 2	Posthole, north row
59	Room 12	Floor 2	Posthole, south row
60	Room 12	Floor 2	Posthole, south row
61	Room 12	Floor 2	Posthole, south row
62	Room 12	Floor 2	Posthole, south row, in Feature 45
63	Room 12	Floor 2	Pit
64	Room 12	Floor 2	Burial 10
65	Room 12	Floor 2	Burial 7
66	Room 12	Floor 2	Burial 9
67	Room 13	Fill	Stone slab
68	Room 14	Floor 1	Stone slab
69	Room 14	Floor 1	Ceramic vessels
70	Room 14	Subfloor	Hearth
71	Room 15	Floor 1	Posthole for roof support
72	Room 15	Floor 2	Stone slab
73	Room 15	Floor 2	Plastered basin
74	Pit House 4	Floor	Ceramic concentration
75	12-NE	Floor	Jar with bead cache
76	12-NE	"Bench"	Ceramic vessel
77	12-NE	Floor	Posthole
78	12-SW	Floor	Ceramic vessel fragment
79	12-SW	Floor	Posthole
80	Pit House 1	Floor	Firepit
81	Pit House 1	Floor	Floor vault
82	Pit House 1	Floor	Floor vault
83	Pit House 1	Floor	Floor vault
84	Pit House 1	Floor	Floor vault
85	Pit House 1	Floor	Floor vault
86	Pit House 1	Floor	Posthole
87	Pit House 1	Floor	Posthole
88	Pit House 1	Floor	Posthole
89	Pit House 1	Floor	Posthole
90	Pit House 1	Floor	Posthole
91	Pit House 1	Floor	Posthole
92	Pit House 1	Floor	Posthole
93	Pit House 1	Floor	Posthole
94	Pit House 1	Floor	Posthole
95	Pit House 1	Floor	Posthole
96	Pit House 1	Floor	Posthole(?)
97	Pit House 1	Floor	Pit
98	Pit House 1	Floor	Pit
99	Pit House 1	North wall	Niche
100	Pit House 1	North wall	Niche
101	Pit House 1	Ramp	Reflooring(?)
102	Pit House 3		Upper vent opening
103	Pit House 3		Lower vent opening
104	Pit House 3	Floor	Stone slab
105	Pit House 3	Floor	Posthole
106	Pit House 3	Floor	Hearth
107	Pit House 3	Floor	Small pit
108	Pit House 3	Floor	Stone slab

particular, the main "spine" of the room block, the north-south wall between Rooms 2 and 4 and Rooms 3 and 5, was carefully built, with cobbles of relatively uniform size laid in an overlapping bond. The eastern and western walls of the original unit (Rooms 2, 3, 4, and 5) were less impressive, but because of road cuts and driveways they were in general less well preserved. Walls of Rooms 1 and 6, added onto this core, were much less well built and were constructed with considerably less stone and more mortar than the walls of the core unit.

Little evidence of roofing survived. Several charred beams were found, along with chunks of adobe with beam impressions (particularly in Room 1), but dense or massive roof fall was absent. Large slabs of adobe found in the upper

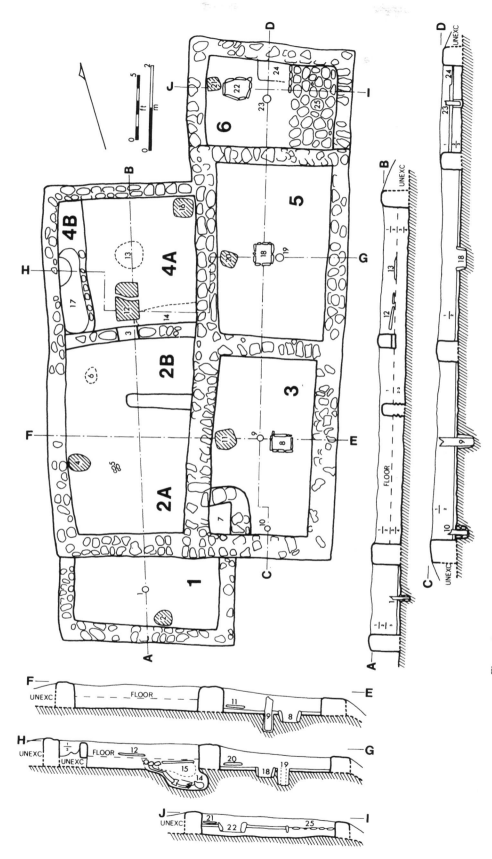

Figure 2.1. Room Block A. Hachure in plan indicates stone slabs and in profile indicates substrate. Dashed lines in plan indicate subfloor sealed features and in profiles indicate projections.

levels of Room 6, originally interpreted as roof material, probably represent adobe wall fragments (described under Room 6, below).

The possibility of earlier deposits below Block A is suggested by ill-defined depressions under the west wall of Room 2 and under the common wall of Rooms 3 and 5. The plan and depth of these depressions were not recorded, but they were apparently irregular. They were tested, at least in sections, to the sterile substrate and were found to be shallow. They clearly do *not* indicate pit structures, burials, or other subfloor features associated with Room Block A. These depressions were interpreted in the field as natural depressions in the substrate filled prior to construction of Room Block A.

Room 1

Room 1 was a late addition to Block A, its walls abutted the south walls of Rooms 2 and 3. It was about 5.5 feet (1.77 m) north-south by 11 feet (3.35 m) east-west (interior dimensions). The area of Room 1 was evidently cleared to the substrate. Walls and floor were constructed directly on that gravel surface, which sloped gently to the east.

Parts of several large corrugated jars (Vessels 3, 4, and 5) were found in the fill of Room 1. Two other corrugated jars (Vessels 1 and 2) and a large plain bowl (Vessel 72) also may have come from the upper fill of Room 1, but the provenience of these three vessels within Room Block A is less certain (Chapter 3).

The fill contained a great many cobbles from wall rubble, particularly in the western half of the room. Despite its collapse into the room, the north wall remained the highest standing wall in the room, 67 cm above the floor. The west wall was only slightly lower; the south and east walls sloped to the southeastern corner, which had been almost completely destroyed by the road cut. The west, south, and east walls appeared to be at least double wythe, although they were thinner than the earlier, double-wythe north wall to which Room 1 abutted.

Roofing was indicated by a layer of small adobe fragments, some with impressions of small beams, and portions of at least three burned beams lying directly on the floor. Roof material was found below the wall fall. A small charred fragment of matting was near the center of the room, and it was interpreted as part of the roof.

The mud plaster floor was thick, ranging from about 9 cm to 24 cm, and averaging about 15 cm. In the western end of the room, it lay directly on the substrate; in the eastern end of the room, the floor rested on a thin layer of cultural fill. The eastern half of the floor was extensively disturbed by rodent burrows. There was no indication that the floor's thickness represented replastering.

A single, center roof-support post (Feature 1), about 6 cm in diameter, was set in a pit some 10 cm to 15 cm in diameter and 30.5 cm deep (below the floor surface). Two levels of cobble shims completely surrounded the butt of the post, which was partially intact.

Two artifacts were found on the floor: a stone slab (Feature 2) and a complete mano (Ground Stone 30), located at the base of the southern wall near the middle of the wall. A small nodule of "turquoise" was evidently on or in the floor surface. (In the field notes, turquoise included malachite and chrysocolla.)

Room 2 (A and B)

Rooms 2A and 2B are two sections of a larger room (Room 2), which was divided by a partition wall. The partition ran only half-way across the larger, original Room 2. Room 2 (including both 2A and 2B) was 14.5 feet to 15 feet (4.4 m to 4.6 m) north-south (2A was 2.9 m and 2B was 1.2 m to 1.4 m, north-south), and 8 feet to 9.5 feet (2.4 m to 2.9 m) east-west (interior dimensions). No plastered floor was encountered; a probable dirt floor level is indicated on profiles in Figure 2.1.

Room 2 itself was originally part of a larger unit that included Room 4. The walls forming the eastern, southern and western sides of Room 2 were built directly on the substrate, whereas the north wall rose from the probable floor level, about 30.5 cm above the substrate level. The partition wall between Rooms 2A and 2B continued down to the substrate, but the lower portion below the floor level probably represents a foundation set into a trench excavated from the floor level.

Little information remains on the wall rubble found in the fill. There were evidently some indications that the east and south walls fell inward, but notes record that the south wall of Room 2A also supposedly fell into Room 1. The west wall, in particular, was difficult to define in its upper levels. It had been disturbed by the graded dirt driveway that ran between Room Blocks A and B. In addition, the wall had been built over the fill of a poorly defined shallow depression, which apparently caused the wall to bow out (west) in a marked arc. Substrate was found at the base of the south and east walls, and below other areas of the room. The east and south walls, as discussed above, either were built up from trenches placed through cultural fill to the underlying substrate or, more likely, were built up from a larger area cleared to the substrate. East, south, and west walls were thick, double- or triple-wythe constructions, bonded at their corners. The north wall was of single wythe, abutted at either end to the original continuous east and west walls of Rooms 2 and 4.

The partition wall was of unusual construction: it appears to have had an irregular cobble foundation below the probable floor level. From this stem or foundation rose a wall of puddled adobe "bricks," 30.5 cm by 15.2 cm by 15.2 cm, similar to the "turtle-backs" of the Anasazi area. The "bricks" were laid with their long axis across (perpendicular to) the length of the wall. The partition appears to have risen only 45.7 cm, at most, above the probable floor level, and was smoothly finished on top.

At the time of excavation, all walls (with the exception of the partition) stood to about 61 cm above the substrate and

24.4 cm to 30.5 cm above the probable floor level. The partition wall was about 15.2 cm shorter than the remaining wall stubs of the major walls and was not defined until the upper levels of the fill had been removed.

A blocked doorway (Feature 3) was located in the middle of the north wall of Room 2B, the abutted wall between Rooms 2 and 4. The door had been blocked with cobbles set in mud and plastered over from the Room 2B side. The door measured about 45.7 cm wide, with a sill about 6.1 cm above the probable floor level. A stone slab that almost certainly served to close this door temporarily was found in Room 4 and is discussed in the description of that room. Almost no remains of roofing were noted. A single beam fragment was found on the probable floor level of Room 2B. Some small adobe fragments were found in the fill below the probable floor level, but these could not represent the final roof of the room.

Notable in the upper fill was a concentration of bone (an "unknown hoofed animal") in the upper two levels of fill along the south wall of Room 2A. This concentration did not continue into the floor level or lower fill.

Although no finished floor was encountered, the location of several large artifacts, a distinct floor line on the face of the north wall and the partition wall, and the level of the evident foundation of the adobe partition all suggest a floor surface at the base of Level 2 (Fig. 2.1). A stone slab (Feature 4), two fragmentary manos in Room 2A and two more in Room 2B (possibly including Ground Stones 19, 20, and 50), and a pair of axes (Ground Stones 102 and 103, Feature 5) were all found lying horizontally at the base of this level. The axes (Feature 5) were near the center point of the room; they lay parallel to the long (north-south) axis of the room, less than 3 cm apart, with their bits pointing south. Confirmation of the probable floor level came from a similar probable floor level, at an identical depth, in Room 4 immediately to the north of Room 2.

The fill below the probable floor level consisted of trash and ash lenses in a sandy matrix. No surfaces were defined in this fill, which rested on the substrate level.

No floor features were found in either Room 2A or 2B. A shallow, irregular ash-filled hearth (Feature 6) was located on the substrate below Room 2B.

Room 3

Room 3 was directly above the road cut, and its east wall above floor level was largely gone (Fig. 2.1). Room 3 measured 13.5 feet (4.1 m) north-south and 7 feet (2.1 m) east-west (interior dimensions). The room was relatively shallow; the large quantities of cobble wall rubble in the fill made it difficult to maintain artificial excavation levels.

The area appeared to have been stripped to substrate, with walls and floor originating directly from this surface. At least part of the north wall was built over a shallow depression filled with ash and cultural material. This depression continued north under the floor of Room 5. A similar situation was noted on the eastern half of the south wall. The lateral

extent of this depression is unknown. Apparently, this section of the south wall slumped inward and was braced by a post (Feature 10).

A great deal of wall fall was encountered, but in no obvious pattern. There was some suggestion that the east wall fell inward (to the west). A stone slab (Feature 11) was in the rubble fill above the floor level, near the middle of the west wall. All walls were double wythe, bonded at all four corners. No evidence of roofing was noted, except for a roof-support post (Feature 9).

The floor was of plastered mud, for the most part directly on the substrate level. It ranged up to 12 cm thick. No evidence of replastering was noted.

Floor features included a masonry bin in the southwest corner (Feature 7), a firepit (Feature 8), a center roof-support post (Feature 9), a second post along the south wall (Feature 10), and a low platform along the north wall.

The bin (Feature 7) was a small masonry enclosure, about 76.2 cm by 45.7 cm interior dimensions, with a single-wythe wall. The walls of the bin rose no higher than about 45.7 cm above the floor level. It contained nothing unusual, either in the fill or on its floor, which evidently was identical to the floor in the rest of the room.

The firepit (Feature 8) was 45.7 cm by 30.1 cm and about 30.1 cm deep. Its walls were cobble-lined; the base was clay. It was filled with ash. The pit appears to have been built prior to or with the floor; floor plaster lipped up around the edges of the slab walls.

The center roof-support post (Feature 9) was in situ; it was over 18 cm in diameter and was set into a posthole 30.5 cm by 21.3 cm and 45.7 cm deep below the floor. No shims were noted.

The post along the south wall (Feature 10) was smaller, about 9 cm in diameter, but it was set into a more elaborate pit, about 36.6 cm in diameter with a number of cobble shims. This posthole was excavated into the fill below the south wall; the soft fill and the post's presumed function as a wall brace (with consequent lateral stress) may have required more elaborate shimming.

Another feature was a poorly defined "platform" along the north wall. Amid the dense rubble fill of the room, the excavators thought that they may have removed a cobble and adobe platform that ran along the base of the north wall. Although the reality of this feature is questionable, noteworthy is the possibility of a similar feature in Room 5 and the definite presence of a cobble surface in the eastern end of Room 6.

The notes mention only one artifact on the floor, a complete mano found between the firepit and the east wall. The mano is not listed in field inventories and subsequent analyses.

Room 4 (A and B)

Room 4 was a square room (about 10 feet by 10 feet, 3 m by 3 m, interior dimensions) with an elaborate bin-platform in its west end. This platform was termed Room 4B during excavation, and the main area of the room was labeled Room 4A.

Room 4 originally formed the northern end of a larger unit including both Rooms 2 and 4. As in Room 2, there was no plastered mud floor. A probable floor level was defined by floor lines on the south wall and on the base of the bin-platform (Room 4B), both of which originated in the fill about 30 cm above the substrate level, and by several artifacts and features located at the same depth as the floor line.

The west wall was badly disturbed by construction of the dirt road between Room Blocks A and B. The other walls were in reasonably good preservation, standing (at the time of excavation) no more than 30.5 cm above the probable floor level and 61 cm above the substrate. The east and west walls were double wythe and originated on the substrate level. The north wall was mostly single wythe but more substantial and much thicker than other single-wythe walls at the site (comparable to the single-wythe north wall of adjacent Room 5). The south wall originated at the probable floor level. Sequentially it appears that the area was first stripped to the substrate; the west, north, and east walls were constructed; the room was filled to the floor level; and then the south and lastly the bin-platform (Room 4B) walls were constructed. A blocked door in the south wall was described under Room 2.

The fill of Room 4 contained relatively less rubble than other units. Perhaps the masonry walls were low (presumably with adobe or jacal superstructures) or perhaps the walls fell outward. Excavations in Room 5 indicated that the east wall of Room 4 fell outward, into Room 5. Contradicting the general observation of little rubble was a specific notation that rubble was heavy along the south wall. The excavators at first suggested that a platform or other structure might have existed there, but that idea was subsequently dismissed.

No evidence of roofing was recorded. No plastered floor was identified, but a dirt floor, at the base of Level 2, was indicated by architectural evidence and by artifacts and features found on that level. These included a large stone slab (Feature 12), a smaller slab (Feature 16), an ash lens or informal hearth (Feature 13), a burial pit that originated at the same level (Feature 14), and the bin-platform (Room 4B). Moreover, two partial ceramic vessels (Vessels 6 and 10) were found on this level near the larger slab (Feature 12).

Feature 12 was the largest stone slab found at the site, measuring about 61 cm by 91 cm, and although it lay on the probable floor level, it was clearly associated with the door in the south wall. This slab may have been left leaning against the doorway on the Room 4 side and was later knocked out when cobbles were used to block the door from the Room 2 side. The slab was at least 15 cm larger than the door width.

A second, smaller slab (Feature 16) was found at floor level in the northeastern corner of the room. The slab measured about 45.7 cm square.

An ash lens or informal hearth (Feature 13) was found in the center of the room. This lens was not contained in a pit, but appeared to result from a fire built directly on the dirt floor surface.

Burial 2 (Appendix A) was found in Feature 14, a narrow but deep pit that ran along the south wall and slightly undercut both the south and east walls. The burial was of an extended adult. The head was to the east and in the deepest part of the pit, and the feet were to the west just below the probable floor level and over 30 cm higher than the head. A stone slab covered the upper part of the body, just below the floor level, and several cobbles covered the feet (shown in profile G-H, Fig. 2.1). From the depth of the slab and the cobbles, it is almost certain that the Feature 14 pit originated at or immediately below the probable floor level, although the pit outline was not defined at this level during excavation. The area was cleared to substrate prior to the construction of the west, north, and east walls, indicating that Burial 2 was associated with the room and was not an earlier feature fortuitously included within the Room 4 area. Further confirming this association was a cache of pottery (Vessels 11–32), clearly associated with Burial 2, deposited in a small niche (Feature 15) partially carved out of the base of the south wall of Room 4. Modification of the south wall for the nook clearly demonstrates an association of the cache and the burial with the final modification of the room. The pottery in this cache is described in Chapter 3. Other artifacts associated with the burial included a fragment of a burned slate palette (Ground Stone 98).

The final feature was the bin-platform that was called Room 4B. It was in fact a feature of Room 4A and it consisted of a masonry platform along the west wall of Room 4, about 61 cm wide and about 30 cm above the probable floor level. The northern third of the platform appears to have been a solid masonry surface. The southern portion was a long bin with plastered, rounded ends (Feature 17) with a carefully made, plastered half-basin at the base of the west wall in the northern end of the bin. The walls of the basin were lower than the walls of the bin itself. Neither bin nor basin appeared to have been fired. Beyond a fragment of a possible mano (Ground Stone 31), Feature 17 contained no materials remarkably different from the rest of the room fill.

Ash lenses or informal hearths were found on the substrate surface, at least partially underlying the north wall. No precise map or description of these features survive.

Room 5

Room 5 was a shallow room, 13.5 feet north-south by 8 feet east-west (about 4.11 m by 2.44 m, interior dimensions) built over an area cleared to substrate. The four walls and the floor were constructed from the substrate level.

All walls were double wythe except the north one, which was a substantial single-wythe wall similar to the north wall of Room 4. The four corners were evidently bonded. All four walls had sections standing up to 61 cm above the floor. Rubble was remarkably dense in the fill. The west wall appeared to have fallen eastward, but no other patterns in the rubble were defined.

A single charred beam fragment in the fill above the floor was the only evidence of roofing. The hole for a center roof-support post (Feature 19) is described below.

The floor was badly broken by rubble fall. It appeared to be slightly higher in the north than in the south, suggesting to the excavators that a possible platform may have existed in this area (no graphic record survives; Fig. 2.1 shows the floor as mapped in the notes). The plastered floor was thinner than other floors in Room Block A and was no more than 6.1 cm thick. It lay directly on the substrate, except in the southern third of the room where the cultural fill noted under the north wall of Room 3 apparently continued under the floor of Room 5.

Two floor features were defined: a firepit (Feature 18) and a posthole (Feature 19).

The firepit (Feature 18) was slab lined with a clay plaster floor. It measured 45.7 cm by 36.6 cm and 30 cm deep below floor. The firepit contained dense white consolidated ash, but almost no charcoal. The firepit had been built before the floor; floor plaster lipped up over the slabs.

The posthole (Feature 19) held a center roof-support post that probably was removed prehistorically. The posthole was 24.4 cm in diameter and 36.6 cm deep below the floor.

Only one artifact, a stone slab (Feature 20), was found on the floor. Two partial ceramic jars (Vessels 7 and 8) were in Level 2, immediately above the floor.

Room 6

Room 6 (7 feet north-south by 9 feet east-west, 2.13 m by 2.74 m, interior dimensions) was interpreted as a late addition to Room Block A. Its walls abutted the north wall of Room 5; its floor level was 15 cm to 21 cm higher than the floors of Rooms 3 and 5. The depth of the floor of Room 6 was comparable to the probable floor levels of Rooms 2 and 4. These facts suggested to the excavators that Room 6 was considerably later than Room 5. Although its walls actually originated on the same substrate level as the other walls of Block A, Room 6 was clearly younger than the rooms to the south.

The excavators' interpretation (Fitting and others 1971: 25–27) was that the walls of Room 6 were constructed in trenches through almost 30 cm of fill and soil, deposits that postdated the construction of Room 5. Although the walls of Room 6 originated on the substrate, the entire area of Room 6 was not stripped to that level prior to construction. The floor was plastered over the existing cultural fill.

The three walls are all single wythe; the south wall is the older north wall of Room 5. There was relatively less rubble in the fill of Room 6, but the room was considerably shallower and the walls much thinner than those of other rooms in Block A. The walls stood less than 30 cm above the floor, and no more than 61 cm above the substrate level at their base.

The lack of wall rubble and the low height of the wall stubs above the floor suggest that the walls of Room 6 may have been shorter or may have incorporated less rock than the other walls of Block A. These possibilities are supported by the discovery of massive "slabs" of adobe with beam and twig impressions in the upper levels of Room 6 fill. Adobe fragments of this size were absent in the other rooms of Block A. Although it is possible that roof material was better preserved in Room 6 than in other rooms, it is more likely that the adobe slabs do not represent roofing, but rather are fragments of adobe walls built above low masonry stem walls. Whether these walls would have been load bearing is unknown; Room 6 did have a center roof-support post (Feature 23), even though the room is smaller than Rooms 2 and 4 that lacked such supports.

The floor of Room 6, like Room 5, was much thinner than other plaster floors of Block A, particularly along the base of the walls. The floor appeared to have been about 6.1 cm thick at most. Floor features included a stone slab (Feature 21), a firepit (Feature 22), a roof-support post (Feature 23), a possible mealing bin (Feature 24), and a cobble paved surface (Feature 25).

The firepit (Feature 22) was lined with cobbles and metate fragments. It measured 45.7 cm square and about 24 cm deep below floor. The floor of the pit was plastered with clay. Unlike firepits in Rooms 3 and 5, the stone elements in the pit walls (which included metate fragments, Ground Stones 85, 87, and 88) protruded 3 cm to 6 cm above the floor surface. It is unclear whether the firepit was excavated into the floor, or if it was constructed as part of the floor. No record remains of the contents.

The roof-support post (Feature 23) was burned and partially intact. It was about 9 cm in diameter, set in a pit that was about 18 cm in diameter with a single cobble shim along the west side of the pit. The bottom of the pit reached but did not penetrate the substrate level; the base was about 30 cm below the floor. A tree-ring date of A.D. 1126vv was obtained from charred fragments of this post (Chapter 4).

A feature at the base of the north wall was called a mealing bin (Feature 24). The identification was based on size, form, and location; neither a metate nor any clear impression of a metate were observed. The feature consisted of a small adobe and rock platform sloping westward into an adobe lined pit. The eastern margin of the pit was formed by a row of upright cobbles, which also may have been associated with the paved area (Feature 25) to the east.

The eastern third of the floor was covered by a pavement of flat river cobbles (Feature 25). They appeared to have formed the floor surface. The cobbles were set into an adobe matrix but were not covered by mud plaster. The row of upright cobbles that formed the eastern margin of Feature 24 also formed the western margin of the pavement, and it is unclear if the uprights continued across the width of the room.

The subfloor fill, removed in Levels 2 and 3, contained multiple ash lenses and trash. The surface of the substrate appeared similar to the substrate below other rooms of Block A.

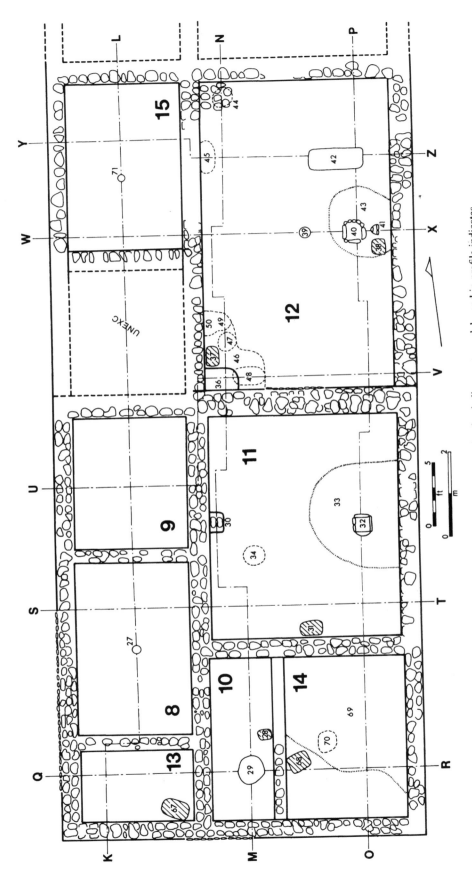

Figure 2.2. Room Block B, upper floors. Hachure in plan indicates stone slabs and in profile indicates substrate. Dashed lines in plan indicate subfloor sealed features and in profiles indicate projections.

ROOM BLOCK B

Rooms 8 and 9 of Room Block B (Figs. 2.2–2.6) were excavated during the 1971 January session under the direction of James Ross. The remainder of the room block was excavated during the summer of 1971 under the direction of Kenneth Brown, except the second floor and subfloor of Room 12 that were completed during January of 1972 under my direction. In addition to using the original notes, I paraphrase and occasionally quote without citation from the preliminary report on the January 1971 season (Fitting and others 1971), from an unpublished preliminary report on the 1971 summer season (Brown 1971), and from an unpublished manuscript on the excavation of Room 12 (Lekson 1972).

In January of 1971 the Room Block B mound was initially approached in a trench, consisting of a row of 5-foot by 10-foot (1.5-m by 3.1-m) units (N610 E540 through N650 E540) parallel and immediately adjacent to the west wall of the room block. The exterior wall surface of Rooms 8 and 13 (Fig. 2.2) was exposed in the northern end of this trench.

When it became evident that the trench was outside the room block, operations were moved into Room 8. Walls of this room and Room 9 to the north were outlined with shallow trenches and the fill was removed in 6-inch (15-cm) levels. Floors in both rooms were cleared and then removed to expose any subfloor features; there were none.

This same procedure was repeated during the 1971 summer season. The southern end of the mound was approached in a trench (N610 E555 through N640 E555), parallel to the first trench but 15 feet (4.6 m) farther east, until the south wall of Room 10 was defined. Operations then moved inside the room; walls were defined, and fill was removed in 6-inch (15-cm) levels. By defining Rooms 8, 9, and 10, the excavators then were able to follow other walls to define the remaining rooms in Room Block B.

All fill was screened. Counts were kept of the number of large cobbles (wall rubble) removed from the fill of several of the rooms. Floors were cleared and then removed to test for subfloor features, with the exception of Rooms 11 and 14 where subfloor testing was completed with a series of smaller pits and trenches.

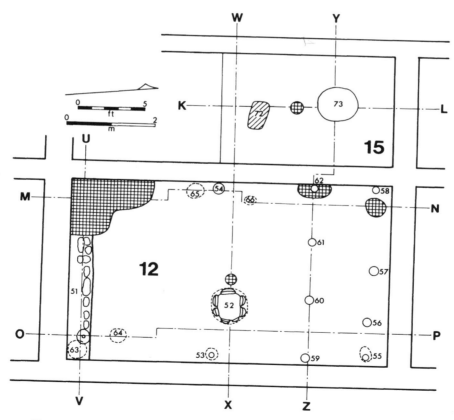

Figure 2.3. Room Block B, lower floors of Rooms 12 and 15. Hachure in plan indicates stone slabs and in profile indicates substrate. Dashed lines in plan indicate subfloor sealed features and in profiles indicate projections.

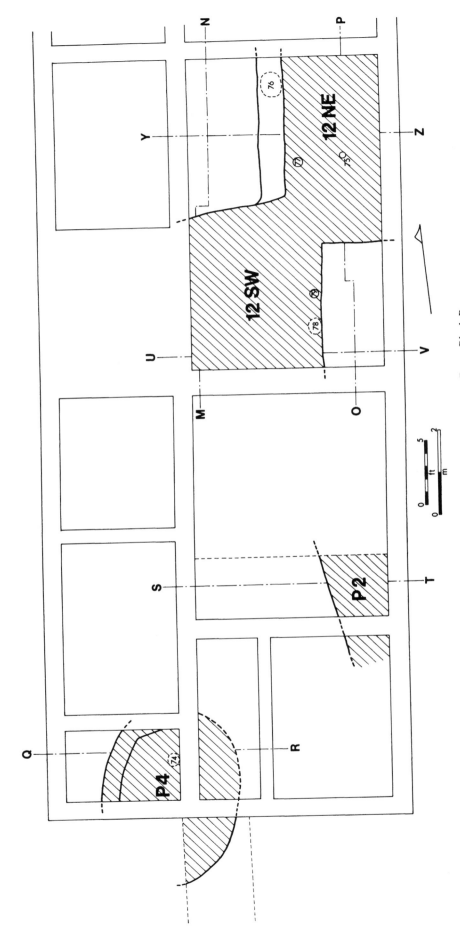

Figure 2.4. Pit structures (hachured) below masonry Room Block B.

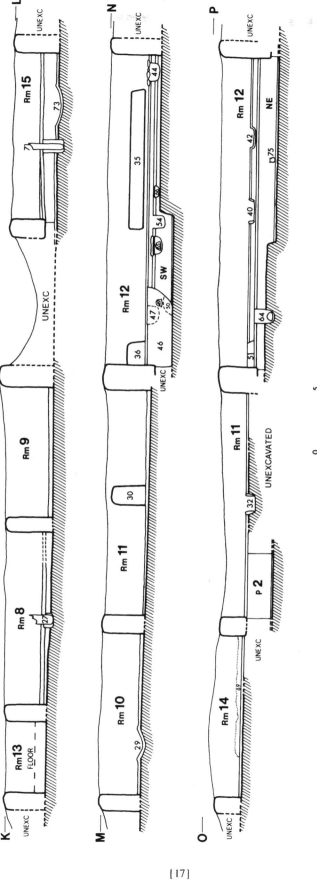

Figure 2.5. North-south profiles of Room Block B. Hachure indicates substrate; dashed lines indicate projections.

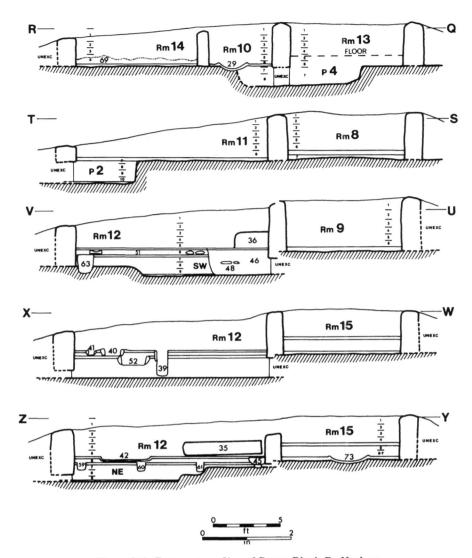

Figure 2.6. East-west profiles of Room Block B. Hachure
indicates substrate; dashed lines indicate projections.

In January of 1971 Room Block B was a mound rising
over 4 feet (1.2 m) above the surrounding area. A barbed
wire fence extended along the north-south crest of the
mound. The eastern half of the mound was covered with
piles of wire spools, lumber, line fittings, and other telephone company supplies. In general, however, the room
block was in good condition. The unnumbered room between Rooms 9 and 15 had been disturbed previously, and
there were smaller potholes in the northern half of Room 8
and, oddly, in the middle of the north wall of Room 12. This
disturbance failed to reach the floor of Room 12, although it
may have extended into the unnumbered room to the north.

Two or, more likely, three rooms at the northern end of
Room Block B had been destroyed or severely damaged by
the blading of a service road. These rooms appeared to re-
peat the pattern evident in the rest of the room block, with a

large room (comparable in size to Room 11) in the eastern
row and one or two smaller rooms in the western row. Thus,
out of a possible total of 12 rooms, 8 rooms were excavated
in Room Block B.

With the exception of the two trenches at the southern end
of the room block, no exterior excavations were attempted
around Room Block B. The area east of the room block had
been badly disturbed by a driveway bladed between Room
Blocks A and B. The area to the west, presumably to the rear
of the room block, was largely undisturbed. Excavations in
January of 1971 cleared an area 5 feet (1.5 m) wide along
the exterior walls of Rooms 13, 8, and part of 9, and failed
to expose any features associated with the room block.

Evidently, construction of rooms in Room Block B pro-
ceeded much as in Room Block A: the area was first stripped
to the reddish substrate, which in this area sloped slightly

down to the north, and irregularities were filled or leveled. Walls were constructed without foundations, directly on the substrate surface. Floors were built either directly on the substrate or, in Room 12, on fill over a complex of subfloor features. Only Room 13 had an unsurfaced dirt floor, apparently smoothed over a layer of fill above the substrate level. Rooms were subsequently modified and new floors were built, and these sequences are described below for each room.

Walls, in general, were more regularly and carefully constructed than those of Room Block A. All walls, with the exception of the one between Rooms 10 and 14, were at least double wythe. The major north-south walls and the south wall of the room block were compound walls up to four stones wide and were well coursed. The pattern of stones in Figure 2.2 shows the uppermost layer of each wall and is not an accurate reflection of the cross sections through the better preserved lower portions. Considering the rounded river cobbles being used, the major walls of Room Block B were especially well built. East-west walls between Rooms 13, 8, and 9 were double wythe only in parts, otherwise single wythe. They were thinner than the major north-south walls.

There is every indication that these walls were full height. The amount of rock taken from fill suggested a wall at least 6 feet (1.8 m) high in Room 9, and a section of the west wall of Room 12 that fell intact reached a standing height of at least 8.5 feet (2.6 m). The only possible exception might be the wall between Rooms 10 and 14, a single-wythe wall in its southern half with little or no stone present in its northern half. This may have been a full- or perhaps partial-height, non-load-bearing partition.

No direct evidence of doors or vents were observed in the walls. In most parts of Room Block B, walls stood sufficiently high that the sills of doors should have been visible, if present.

Roofing material, consisting of burned beam fragments and small chunks of adobe with beam impressions, was found in every room. Much larger slabs of adobe, similar to those in Room 6 of Room Block A, were found between the first and second floors of Room 15; they probably do not represent roofing material. Roof-support post patterns are intriguingly variable; when present, they are limited to a single post in the center of the room (Rooms 8, 12, and 15). Postholes are present in the largest room (Room 12) and in two medium-sized rooms (Rooms 8 and 15) of Block B, but curiously absent in two other large rooms (Rooms 11 and 14) and in all of the smallest rooms (Rooms 9, 10, and 13).

Room Block B was constructed over several earlier pit structures (Pit House 2, Pit House 4, and the complex of features under Room 12). They are described separately at the end of this section. The pit structures were filled with clayey sand containing trash and artifacts. From the excavations, there was no indication if this fill was deposited at the time of Room Block B construction or if these units had

filled previously. The temporal placement of the pit house fill is examined under ceramics in Chapter 3.

With two clear and two possible exceptions, all corners appeared to be bonded. The wall between Rooms 10 and 14 and the south wall of Room 15 clearly abutted the long walls they connected and were internal partitions of larger rooms. The possible abutments, which are by no means clear, run along the northern face of the common wall between Rooms 11 and 12.

It is possible, and I think likely, that the southern half of Room Block B predates the northern half, with the wall between Rooms 11 and 12 and its continuation as the north wall of Room 9 as the dividing line. The corners of this wall were obscured, for a number of reasons. The room to the north of Room 9 was not excavated, and neither the eastern nor western exterior faces of the room block were cleared at either end of this cross wall.

One construction feature of the north wall of Room 11 suggested that it was originally an exterior wall and that the east and west walls of Room 12 were later constructions abutted to it. This feature was a row of upright cobbles at the wall's base (Fig. 2.2). Similar rows of upright stones were observed in the only two exposures of exterior walls at Room Block B, in the trench outside Rooms 8 and 13 and in the second trench outside Room 10. This occurrence of upright cobbles at the base of both exposed exterior walls suggests that the upright cobbles along the north wall of Room 11 were also originally exterior features.

Upright cobbles along the bases of masonry walls are not uncommon at other Mimbres phase sites on the Gila River, in the Mimbres Valley, and along the Rio Grande. The specificity of their use on exterior (or originally exterior) walls has not yet been demonstrated, but appears to me to be likely. Interestingly, it is the base of an adobe or mud-mortared masonry wall that is often the most susceptible to rain erosion (through a ground splashing effect), and upright cobbles effectively protect the wall base from this type of erosion.

The lack of data from the unexcavated room between Rooms 9 and 15 is unfortunate, as is the ambiguity of data from the southern corners of Room 12. However, I suggest that the north wall of Room 11 was originally an exterior wall and that Room 12, and perhaps the entire northern half of Room Block B was added to the unit after construction of the southern half of the room block.

Room 8

Room 8 was a small room (13.5 feet north-south by 8.5 feet east-west, 4.1 m by 2.6 m, interior dimensions) in the western row of rooms. The northern half of the room had been disturbed by a pothole; no precise map of the extent of the disturbance survives.

As elsewhere in Room Block B, the area beneath Room 8 appeared to have been stripped to the substrate. The walls of the room were constructed on the substrate and stood about

1 m above it at the time of excavation. A mud plaster floor, about 15 cm thick, was constructed directly on the substrate on the southern end of the room and over a thin leveling fill in the northern half. No clear pattern of wall fall could be defined, but cobbles made up much of the fill.

Roof material (fragments of adobe with beam impressions) was encountered just above the floor.

Part of a Mimbres Black-on-white bowl (Vessel 36) was found in the levels immediately above the floor. At least one carbonized cob of corn was found in Level 6, the level just above the floor; the corn was probably on the floor itself, but the notes are not completely clear. A sample of this corn yielded a C-14 date, discussed in Chapter 4.

The only floor feature was a central roof-support post (Feature 27). The lower portion of the post (about 18 cm in diameter) was in place, set into a pit 24 cm in diameter and only 21 cm deep below the floor.

Room 9

Room 9 was a small, nearly square room (10 feet north-south by 8.5 feet east-west, 3 m by 2.6 m, interior dimensions) in the western row of rooms. Like Room 8, the area appears to have been cleared to substrate; walls and floor were built directly on this level. Walls stood to 4 feet (1.2 m) above the substrate. The excavators noted 607 large cobbles in the fill and estimated that this quantity of rock would raise the walls to well over 6 feet (1.8 m). There was some indication that the south wall fell inward (into Room 9) before the other walls collapsed. No evidence of roofing was noted.

The floor was about 15 cm thick; there was no evidence to indicate replastering, and no features were found.

Room 10

Room 10 was the western half of what was, structurally at least, a larger unit including both Rooms 10 and 14. It measured 12.5 feet (3.8 m) by 4.5 feet (1.4 m). The east wall of Room 10 was a single-wythe partition that may not have extended to full height. The building of this partitioning wall and the creation of two rooms followed closely the initial construction of the larger unit, because the cross wall seems to be associated with the floors of both Rooms 10 and 14.

The construction sequence in the area of Room 10 is not clear. The southwestern quadrant of the room overlay a large depression. The precise extent of this depression is not indicated in surviving notes (see Pit House 4, below). Presumably, the area was stripped to substrate and this depression was either filled or (if already filled) leveled. Construction of the south, west, and north walls began on this level. The depth of the base of the east (partition) wall is not recorded; it may rise from the surface of the floor and not from the substrate level. The floor of Room 10 closely resembled the floor of Room 14 on the other side of the partition.

Fewer than 40 large cobbles are recorded as coming from the fill of Room 10. The excavators concluded that the room filled prior to the collapse of the walls, and that the massive south wall fell outward. The east wall apparently slumped

into Room 10, but it contained relatively little rock.

Chunks of adobe with beam and reed impressions were found in levels immediately above the floor. Some of these fragments were burned.

The floor was poorly preserved in the western half of the room, particularly over the depression of Pit House 4, and in the northern half of the room. The remaining sections had a texture and composition different than the other floors of Room Block B (with the exception of contiguous Room 14). The floor was "composed of small pebbles set in a matrix of very powdery tan to 'dirty' soil." Part of a Mimbres Black-on-white bowl (Vessel 33), probably reused as a scoop, was in Level 5, above the floor. A stone slab (Feature 28) was found at floor level near the middle of the east wall. On the better preserved southern half of the floor was a clay-lined basin (Feature 29), 61 cm in diameter and about 7.6 cm deep.

Room 11

Room 11 was the second largest unit in Room Block B (17.5 feet north-south by 14 feet east-west, 5.3 m by 4.3 m, interior dimensions), located in the eastern row. Whereas the walls stood over 3 feet (91 cm) above the floor on the western side of the room, Room 11 was remarkably shallow to the east. Only about 30 cm of fill covered the floor along the east wall.

The southeastern corner of Room 11 was built over Pit House 2. In other areas of the room, existing fill was cleared to the substrate level, and walls and floor were constructed directly on that level. All walls were double wythe. Over a thousand large cobbles were removed from Room 11 fill; however, no orientation could be defined for any wall fall. The excavator suggested that the walls slowly deteriorated rather than collapsed as a unit. I suggest that the quantity of rock seems low for a room of this size, compared to the 600 cobbles taken from Room 9, a unit half the size of Room 11 with walls standing up to twice as tall at the time of excavation. Considering the low standing height of walls in the eastern half of Room 11, it seems possible that the east wall, at least, may have fallen outward.

Most of a large, indented corrugated jar (Vessel 38) was found in the upper fill levels. Other sherds from this jar were recovered in the uppermost level of Room 14. Part of a Boldface Black-on-white ladle (Vessel 34) was also in the fill.

A "buttress" (Feature 30) in the middle of the west wall consisted of a masonry pier, 45.7 cm long (north-south) and 76.2 cm tall (above the floor). It bonded the west wall and protruded perpendicularly from it about 30 cm into the room. The masonry in this odd stub was three courses tall and two wythes wide, capped by one course of stone with long axis north-south (that is, parallel to the west wall). The top of the feature was eroded and it was not possible to determine if it had been plastered. The function of Feature 30 is unclear. It was called a buttress in lieu of a better term, and this functional tag may possibly be correct.

Almost no indication of roofing remained. Intriguingly,

there was no evidence of roof-support posts in this large room (compare with Room 12).

A stone slab (Feature 31) was found at floor level midway along the south wall. The excavator believed that the slab was actually set into the floor rather than just resting upon it.

The floor of Room 11 was about 12 cm thick. It was better preserved in the western (deeper) half of the room. The fire-pit (Feature 32) measured 33.5 cm square, was 19.8 cm deep, and its walls were lined with flat cobbles. The dirt base of the firepit was ill-defined and probably unplastered. Firepit fill included small charcoal fragments and a large sherd from a Mimbres Black-on-white bowl (Vessel 37) probably reused as a scoop.

A concentration of lithic materials (Feature 33) surrounded the firepit. The excavator noted that a "very high percentage of the chipped stone and 75% of the points (a total of 30)" from Room 11 were found on or immediately above the floor in the area indicated on Figure 2.2.

A 5-foot (1.5-m) wide trench along the south wall exposed Pit House 2, described below. Elsewhere, the floor was tested for subfloor features with limited probes and spot soundings. The only other subfloor feature was a basin-shaped, unlined, ash-filled hearth (Feature 34) excavated 21 cm into the substrate. Seemingly associated with the hearth were a chunk of "turquoise" and a large sherd of a Mimbres Black-on-white shallow bowl (Vessel 35); a second sherd from this vessel was recovered from the upper fill of the room.

Room 12

Room 12 was the largest room in Room Block B. Its interior dimensions were 24 feet north-south and 14 feet east-west (7.3 m by 4.3 m). The construction sequence of Room 12 was somewhat more complex than the other rooms, with several subfloor features underlying the room. Only a short section of the west wall and perhaps parts of the south wall rose from the substrate level; all other walls were built over fill. Two plastered floors were defined; the earliest (Floor 2) was also built over fill, presumably leveling the surface of the subfloor features. This floor was almost 15 cm lower than the floor of adjacent Room 11. A thin layer of fill separated the lower floor (Floor 2) from the later, upper floor (Floor 1). Thus the sequence in the Room 12 area was: (1) construction of subfloor features; (2) filling and leveling of these features; (3) construction of walls (with the north and east walls beginning 24 cm lower than the south and west walls); (4) construction of the earlier Floor 2; (5) introduction of fill above that floor; and (6) construction of the later Floor 1.

The walls of Room 12 were all double or triple wythe, and the east and west walls may have abutted the north wall of Room 11. Over 1,250 large cobbles (including an unknown number of mano and metate fragments) were removed from the fill above Floor 1, including a large number that were incorporated in an intact section of the west wall (Feature 35) that fell into the west-central part of the room (Fig. 2.5,

profile M-N; Fig. 2.6, profile Z-Y). The wall section lay directly on the floor, or immediately above it. The combined height of the standing wall and this fragment totaled about 8.5 feet (2.6 m). The total number of rocks, which seems low, suggests that other walls may have fallen outward; in particular, the east wall may have fallen to the east. Wall debris was found directly on the floor in all sections of the room, and probable wall fall spilled into Features 40 and 42.

No roofing material of any kind appeared in the fill of Room 12. A single roof-support post (Feature 39) was removed prehistorically; it is possible that the entire roof was removed from this unit prior to the collapse of the walls.

A massive trough metate (Ground Stone 105) was in the upper fill (Level 2) near the west wall. Several complete manos (including Ground Stones K19, K21, 44, 84, 47, and 53) were also in the upper fill, mostly from this same area.

An adobe "buttress" or platform (Feature 36) was built on the surface of the upper floor in the southwestern corner of the room. This construction, of puddled adobe without rock, measured 51.8 cm north-south, 76.2 cm east-west, and rose 39.6 cm above the upper floor level. Its top surface was smooth and level. The function of this construction is unknown, but it may have served to stabilize the long west wall at its abutment with the north wall of Room 11.

One stone slab (Feature 37) was in the fill immediately above Floor 1, the uppermost floor. Another stone slab (Feature 38) appeared to be set into Floor 1 with the plaster lipped over its edges.

Floor 1

Floor 1, the upper and later floor, was a well-defined, plastered construction from 3 cm to 9 cm thick. It was built on sand fill over Floor 2. A number of thin ash lenses were discovered immediately below Floor 1 on top of the sandy fill; they were not mapped.

Features evident on the surface of Floor 1 included an open pit for a roof-support post (Feature 39); a firepit (Feature 40); a D-shaped pit (Feature 41) in close proximity to the firepit; and a large rectangular, clay-lined pit (Feature 42).

The roof-support post (Feature 39) had been removed prehistorically; the pit into which it was set was 30 cm in diameter and almost 61 cm deep below Floor 1.

The firepit (Feature 40) was a rectangular, slab-lined feature measuring 45.7 cm square and 15 cm deep. At least 6 of the slabs were fragments of broken metates (probably including Ground Stone 86). The floor of the pit was plastered with clay; the fill of the pit was similar to the room fill above it. Between the firepit and the east wall was a D-shaped pit (Feature 41), 24 cm north-south by 12 cm east-west, and 9 cm deep. The D-shaped pit was partially cobble lined and was otherwise plastered. In the center of the base of the pit was a small red "polishing stone," on top of which was a smaller lump of ashy clay.

A large, rectangular, unfired, plastered pit (Feature 42) was located north of the firepit complex. Feature 42 measured about 1.2 m east-west and 48.7 cm north-south, and was only 12 cm deep. This pit was partially filled with large cobbles, almost certainly from wall fall. The pit may have been part of a mealing bin; however, there were no impressions of metates to indicate such use. Feature 42 bears a superficial resemblance to the "floor vault" of a Chaco Anasazi kiva, but I can offer no definite idea of its function.

Immediately surrounding the firepit and the D-shaped pit was a concentration of ground stone (Feature 43), including three whole manos (one of which was Ground Stone K20) and a large, but battered, zoomorphic stone vessel (Ground Stone 104). These were resting directly on the floor, along with the large amount of wall fall in this area. The ground stone concentration may represent true floor artifacts, materials built into the wall, or some combination of depositions. Also associated with Feature 43 were parts of two vessels, a corrugated jar (Vessel 39) and a corrugated bowl (Vessel 40) with a smudged and polished interior.

Several sealed subfloor features on Floor 1 included a pit (Feature 44) in the northwestern corner that had been sealed with a cobble pavement, Burial 11 (Feature 45) along the west wall, and a large pit in the southwestern corner (Feature 46) that included several interments (Appendix A): Burial 4 (Feature 47), Burial 5 combined with Burial 8 (Feature 48 and Feature 50), and Burial 6 (Feature 49).

The cobble pavement over Feature 44 was discovered while clearing the floor. The nine cobbles were lying flat, directly on the floor, in contrast to the wall fall in this area, which stood either on edge or at random in the fill just above the floor. Beneath the cobbles was an unlined pit, 61 cm north-south by 46 cm east-west and about 30 cm deep below Floor 1. It contained fine brown sand and a few sherds. It appears that Feature 44 was intentionally filled and the cobbles placed over it prior to the abandonment of the room.

Burial 11 (in Feature 45) was discovered in a sealed pit along the base of the west wall. The pit was 61 cm north-south, 46 cm east-west, and reached a depth of 18 cm below Floor 1. The pit was not lined, but the floor surface had been replastered over it. Burial 11 was a child with associated Vessels 44 and 45. The burial was extended, on its back, with the head to the north and the feet to the south. Just above the head was a corrugated jar (Vessel 45); just above the hip was a plain ware everted-rim bowl with smudged and polished interior (Vessel 44); on the left arm was a shell bracelet. Also associated with the burial were nine beads and a small fragment of worked turquoise.

In the southwestern corner of the room, and partially covered by the adobe "buttress" (Feature 36), was a large pit (or more probably a series of two or three pits) that had been sealed over with floor plaster. This entire L-shaped complex was defined as a single feature (Feature 46), but portions of the outlines of several distinct pits within it were noted; all contents of Feature 46 were associated with Floor 1. Although Feature 46 was unlined, its outline was evident through the definition of even lower features (Floor 2, Feature 47) in section in the Feature 46 pit wall. The Feature 46

pit extended to the floor of the pit structure designated 12-SW about 61 cm below Floor 1. Feature 46 contained a fine sandy fill, with several flat cobbles on a level about 30 cm below Floor 1. These cobbles appeared to be placed intentionally over Burial 5 (Feature 48).

The southeastern extension of Feature 46 was probably a pit for Burial 5 + 8 (Features 48 and 50), and may have been the earliest part of Feature 46. Burial 5 + 8, a fragmentary collection of bits and pieces, was removed as two separate burials. Subsequent analysis suggested that the bits of Burial 5 might in fact belong with the pieces of Burial 8. The burial was in rodent disturbed fill below the layer of flat cobbles. The burial was a youth or young adult; the bone was badly decayed, but stains indicated orientation. The head was in a niche undercutting the west wall of Room 12, and the body lay on its right side, extending to the east. The legs were flexed to the south. No artifacts were associated with the burial.

Burials 4 and 6 may have been introduced into the Feature 46 pit (and specifically, into the pit for Burial 5 + 8) some time later. The excavators thought that Burial 6 preceded Burial 4.

Burial 6 (Feature 49) was a cremation in a Mimbres Classic Black-on-white seed jar (Vessel 52), covered by an inverted Mimbres Classic Black-on-white bowl (Vessel 51). It was placed in the northwestern extension of Feature 46, almost directly above Burial 8 but only 37 cm below Floor 1 (to the base of the vessels). A large sherd of a Mimbres Black-on-white bowl (Vessel 43), three shell bracelet fragments, six beads, six concretions, several worked red shale-slate fragments, and one chunk of "turquoise" were also associated with Burial 6.

Burial 4 (Feature 47) was higher still, only 24 cm below the floor; it may have been the last burial placed in the Feature 46 pit. The Burial 4 pit was 61 cm in diameter and extended to 30 cm deep below Floor 1. It was unlined, but well defined in the fill of the surrounding Feature 46. Burial 4 was an infant inhumation located slightly above the base of the pit, presumably on a thin layer of earth fill. The infant, extended with the head west and the feet east, was placed in a partial Mimbres Black-on-white bowl (Vessel 49) and had a small corrugated jar (Vessel 46) near the head. A large cobble, placed over the burial in the pit, crushed both vessels.

The fill between Floors 1 and 2 (Level 6) consisted of fine sand. Thin ash lenses, mentioned above, were found directly below Floor 1 but did not continue into the fill between the two floors. Many sherds and flakes were recovered from this fill; whether they represent trash used as fill or primary trash associated with lower Floor 2 is unknown.

Floor 2

Floor 2 (Fig. 2.3) was a smooth, well-finished, mud-plastered surface (well preserved by the sand fill and overlying Floor 1). It was nearly identical to Floor 1 in texture and construction and was 3 cm to 9 cm thick.

A curious balk or platform (Feature 51) extended along the base of the south wall, about 15.2 cm high and 45.7 cm wide, truncated at its west end by Feature 46 from Floor 1 (Fig. 2.3). This platform was constructed by laying a row of cobbles on Floor 2, about 30 cm away from and parallel to the south wall. The cobbles were mortared together with adobe, and the area between this "retaining wall" and the south wall of Room 12 was then filled with adobe (Figs. 2.3, 2.5 profile O-P, 2.6 profile V-U). The easternmost element of the stone wall was a large mortar (Ground Stone 105).

The upper surface of Feature 51 was flat, and it was difficult to distinguish it from the plaster of Floor 1, which immediately covered it. Floor 1 plaster appeared to be extremely thin over Feature 51. At the time of excavation the ground was frozen along the base of the south wall of Room 12, and fine distinctions were extremely difficult to make. I do not know if Feature 51 was originally taller and was truncated to Floor 1 level prior to Floor 1 construction, or if it remained at its original height. If so, it may represent a low platform used with Floor 2. If it was originally higher, Feature 51 may have been a structural buttress for the south wall of Room 12 or, more likely, for the southern ends of the east and west walls of Room 12. Because it was constructed on the Floor 2 surface, Feature 51 definitely postdated initial construction of Room 12.

Evident on Floor 2 were a firepit (Feature 52) and a number of postholes from which the posts had been removed prior to construction of Floor 1. Two large postholes were found near the middles of the east (Feature 53) and west (Feature 54) walls, and a series of smaller postholes appeared to form a framework for a shelf or platform in the northern half of the room (Features 55 through 62).

The firepit (Feature 52) was in nearly the same position as the firepit (Feature 40) on Floor 1, but slightly farther west. The slab-lined pit was about 55 cm square and 24 cm deep. The base of the pit was unlined. It had been constructed by digging the pit through the Floor 2 surface; Floor 2 plaster did not lip up to the stone slabs. Feature 52 may be a remodeling of an earlier pit, but there was no direct evidence to confirm this suggestion. The stone lining, which was set at or slightly below floor level, included three fragments of a single metate (not present in the 1987 collections). A fragment of a mano (Ground Stone 48) was probably also incorporated into the firepit wall. The fill of Feature 52 consisted of six alternating layers (each less than 3 cm thick) of ashy sand and less ashy gravels. A complete mano (Ground Stone 46) was evidently on Floor 2 immediately northeast of the firepit.

Two large postholes (Features 53 and 54), one along the east (Feature 53) and one along the west (Feature 54) walls, appear to be aligned just south of the midline of Room 12. Both were 30 cm in diameter and 24 cm deep below Floor 2. The posts had been removed from both; fill consisted of a fine sand, similar to the fill between Floors 1 and 2. No shims were present. Feature 53 had a possible post mold in

the sandy fill of the pit, indicating a post about 9 cm or less in diameter. These posts may have been roof supports for a beam crossing the room just south of the firepit (Feature 52). Their placement would suggest a possible opening, or at least an absence of primary beams, over the firepit itself. After these posts were removed, a center roof-support post (Feature 39) was used on Floor 1, suggesting that either (1) the roof beam arrangement was altered or replaced at the time of Floor 1 construction, or (2) Features 53 and 54 do not, in fact, represent roof-support posts.

Two rows of postholes formed the base of a possible platform along the north wall. The northern row (Features 55 to 58) was located along the base of the north wall of Room 12; the southern row (Features 59 to 62) was 1.4 m south and parallel to the northern row. Most of the pits were about 15 cm in diameter and only 15 cm to 18 cm deep below Floor 1. Feature 55 was 45.7 cm in diameter at the floor level, but narrowed to 15 cm just below the floor. Feature 57 was larger, 30 cm in diameter at the top and base and 24 cm deep. All these pits, except Feature 62, were filled with a fine sand identical to the fill between Floors 1 and 2. Feature 62 survived as a remnant in the base of Floor 1 Feature 45 and was nearly filled with a large cobble, perhaps placed there during construction of Feature 45.

I suggest these were not roof-support posts because of their small size and depth, and because the northern row (Features 55 to 58) was located only 30 cm from the north wall of Room 12, an unlikely location for a primary beam. The posts would not have supported beams running north-south because of the lack of alignment between postholes of the north and south rows. They may represent an understructure for a broad platform, similar to the "bed platforms" of Casas Grandes (Di Peso and others 1974: 238), for shelves, or for storage racks; however, there is no direct evidence of the nature of the superstructure they supported.

Floor artifacts were limited to one mano (Ground Stone 46). Some of the sherds and lithics in the fill between Floors 1 and 2 may have been associated with Floor 2, but that question is now moot.

Four subfloor pits were sealed under Floor 2: a pit in the southeastern corner of the room (Feature 63), Burial 10 (Feature 64), Burial 7 (Feature 65), and Burial 9 (Feature 66; burials are discussed in Appendix A).

Feature 63 was an unlined pit discovered under the eastern end of the low adobe platform along the south wall (Feature 51). The pit measured 61 cm north-south and 76 cm east-west. It was filled with sandy soil, which contained a few sherds, a few animal bones, and nothing else.

Burial 10 (in Feature 64) was a cremation contained in a red-slipped seed jar (Vessel 71) with a worked sherd disk cover. The jar was inverted and then put into a large Mimbres Black-on-white bowl (Vessel 50). Both vessels were then placed in the bottom of the pit (Feature 64) near the southeastern corner of the room. The pit was 30 cm in diameter and 45.7 cm deep below Floor 2. The fill in the pit was a reddish clayey sand with small pockets or lenses of fine brown soil, perhaps the remnants of organic materials included with the burial. The pit had been sealed with mud plaster on the Floor 2 level. A quartz crystal, 4 fragments of shell bracelets, and 10 beads were found with the cremation.

Burial 7, in Feature 65, was another cremation, placed in an inverted Mimbres Black-on-white seed jar (Vessel 48). One fragment of a shell bracelet and five beads were associated with the cremation. The jar had been "killed" with a small hole in its bottom. A smudged plain ware bowl (Vessel 41) was inverted over the seed jar as a nonfunctional cover. (Presumably the seed jar had been closed with a perishable cover prior to placement in the pit.) The Feature 65 pit, which was located at the base of the west wall, measured 30 cm north-south by 49 cm east-west, and was 15 cm deep below Floor 2. A large flat cobble had been pressed into the Floor 2 surface to seal the Feature 65 pit.

Burial 9 was a flexed infant, head to the south and feet to the north, placed in a shallow pit (Feature 66). The body lay on its left side, with the knees pulled up to the chest; the arms were extended to the north on either side of the head. The pit measured about 27 cm north-south by 21 cm east-west, and was only 9 cm deep below Floor 2. The pit was carefully resealed with floor plaster. There were no artifacts associated with the burial.

Two possible pit structures were located beneath Room 12. They are described at the end of this section.

Room 13

Room 13 (Fig. 2.2) was a small unit (5 feet north-south by 8.5 feet east-west, 1.5 m by 2.6 m, interior dimensions) in the southwestern corner of Room Block B. No plastered floor was found, but there was evidence of a dirt floor or surface located at the base of Level 3 (Fig. 2.5, profile K-L; Fig. 2.6, profile R-Q). The eastern half of Room 13 was over Pit House 4. In this area, the walls were built over the fill of the pit structure; elsewhere in the room the walls originated on the substrate layer. It appears that the Room 13 area was stripped to the highest substrate, leveled off at that depth, and the walls built on that level.

All four walls were at least double wythe, and exterior walls to the west and south were compound walls three or four stones wide. Only 50 large cobbles were recovered from the fill of Room 13; evidently none of the walls fell into the room. The walls stood 1.06 m above their bases, and about 0.76 m above the probable floor level.

A large stone slab (Feature 67) was found almost at the surface (Level 1) in the southeastern corner of the room. The height of this slab in the fill was unlike similar slabs in other rooms of Blocks A and B; it may have been redeposited, perhaps recently. The fill of the room was sand with scattered ash lenses, sparse artifacts, and small adobe fragments. One thick slab of adobe, measuring 76 cm square by about 9 cm thick, was lying relatively horizontal in Level 3, just above the probable floor level. The slab was perfectly flat on its upper surface; the lower surface was covered with reed and small beam or pole impressions. Similar sections of probable roofing material are discussed under Room 15.

The orientation of the adobe slab indicates that at the time it was deposited a level surface existed at the base of Level 3. This surface was probably the floor, or at least the last floor, of Room 13.

Room 14

Room 14 was a medium sized room (12.5 feet to 13 feet north-south, 9 feet east-west, 3.8–4.0 m by 2.7 m, interior dimensions). The west wall of Room 14 was a single-wythe partition between it and Room 10 to the west. The other three walls were at least double wythe. The walls were reduced to 61 cm or less above the floor level, which rested directly on the substrate except in the extreme northeastern corner.

As with other rooms in Block B, the area below Room 14 appears to have been stripped to substrate, and the north, east, and south walls erected from that level. The floor was constructed directly on the substrate, and unlike the smooth clay plastered floors of other rooms in Block B, the floor here consisted of tightly packed pebbles or very small gravels set in a powdery tan soil, identical to the floor of Room 10 to the west. It is likely that the narrow west partition wall was constructed after the floor was laid.

Only 200 large cobbles were recovered from the fill of this room, mainly in the upper levels. Compared with 1,000 cobbles from Room 11, north of Room 14, the low height of the remaining walls and the relatively few cobbles in the fill suggest either that the walls of Room 11 fell outward or that all the walls were not of full-height masonry.

A complete or nearly complete metate of unknown type was found high in the fill, in Level 1, just north of the center-point of the room. This metate could not be identified in the 1987 collections.

The excavators noted an unusually dense layer of adobe fragments over the floor and over the artifacts on the floor. It was described as a "sheet" of adobe fragments, some with reed impressions. They may be evidence of roof fall prior to wall collapse or may, in part, represent adobe from the upper, nonmasonry portions of the walls themselves. The material was identified in the field as roof debris.

A stone slab (Feature 68) was on the floor at the base of the west wall.

The most spectacular materials from Room 14 were several crushed utility vessels (Vessels 53–64) that formed a dense layer of sherds over the northern two-thirds of the floor (Feature 69). Several manos (including Ground Stones 52 and K13) and other ground stone artifacts were reported in the layer (Chapter 3).

The subfloor of Room 14 was tested less thoroughly than other subfloors in Room Block B due to time constraints at the end of the Summer 1971 season. All tests exposed the reddish substrate immediately under the floor except in the northeastern corner, where Pit House 2, better defined under Room 11, evidently continued under Room 14. Testing also revealed an irregularly shaped ash-filled hearth (Feature 70), measuring 48.7 cm north-south and about 42.7 cm east-west. The depth is unknown, but Feature 70 was evidently rather shallow. Two small cobbles formed its northwest wall.

Room 15

Room 15 was a small room to the west in the northern end of Room Block B. It had a complex architectural history. In its final configuration, Room 15 measured 12.7 feet north-south and 8.5 feet east-west (3.9 m by 2.6 m), interior dimensions.

As elsewhere in Room Block B, the area appears to have been cleared to substrate. The west, north, east (and presumably a fourth wall south of the present south wall) were raised from this level. The original floor, Floor 2, was constructed directly on substrate, and it continued south under the present south wall of Room 15, indicating that the room was originally longer. Approximately 30 cm of fill was introduced into the room, and a new south wall was built on fill above Floor 2. There is some confusion in the notes and inventories about the thickness of the fill between Floors 1 and 2. Apparently materials labelled Level 7 were later combined with those of Level 6. I assume that this means the Level 7 designation was mistaken; however, a seventh 15-cm level would do much to explain the disconformity in depth of substrate between Rooms 12 and 15 (Fig. 2.6, Profile Z-Y). Floor 1 was constructed within the resulting smaller room, at a level 6 cm above the base of the new south wall.

All walls were double wythe, although the north wall appeared to be of somewhat thinner construction than other major walls in Room Block B. The south wall, built on fill over Floor 2, may have been a non-load-bearing partition, although it appeared to be of wide, double-wythe construction identical to the west and east walls. That the south wall may have been load-bearing is also suggested (1) by the fact that the roof of Room 15 was apparently removed and replaced with the construction of the upper floor, and (2) by the evident settling of the south wall into the fill on which it was built.

No count survives of cobbles removed from fill, but the notes indicate that relatively few were found. The upper floor (Floor 1) was high in the room, so there was relatively less fill compared to other rooms of Room Block B. The excavators felt that the north and west walls fell outward, and we know from Room 12 that a section of the east wall fell into Room 12. Thus there probably was relatively little wall rubble in the fill of Room 15. With the exception of the collapsed east wall, the walls stood to about 1 m above the lower floor (Floor 2) and about 0.6 m above the upper floor (Floor 1). Part of a bowl with a smudged and polished interior (Vessel 65) was in the fill above Floor 1.

Floor 1 was the highest plastered floor in Room Block B,

over 30 cm above the floor level in Rooms 11 and 12. However, it was not much higher than the probable floor level in Room 13, at the south end of the west row of rooms. The Room 15 floor showed clear evidence of replastering. The original Floor 1 surface sloped slightly to the south, particularly in the southern half of the room, perhaps reflecting the settling of the south wall into the fill between Floors 1 and 2. The southern third of Floor 1 was subsequently resurfaced, with the second application of plaster reaching a thickness of up to 6 cm along the south wall.

A single floor feature, an adobe-lined(?) posthole (Feature 71), was located in the middle of Floor 1. The roof-support post had been removed, but a possible mold in the pit fill suggested a post of about 12 cm in diameter. The pit itself was about 30 cm in diameter and was quite deep, continuing into the substrate to 52 cm below Floor 1. The adobe lining of the pit was unusual and may have served to hold back the relatively loose fill between Floors 1 and 2 while the post was being emplaced.

The fill between Floors 1 and 2 contained a layer of closely packed, large, adobe slabs. These slabs continued under the south wall of Room 15 and were perfectly flat on one side. Their smoothness suggested a plastered interior surface rather than exterior surfaces exposed to the elements. The reverse of the slabs bore reed and small beam impressions consistent with roofing. These slabs were interpreted as roof debris and they probably represent the removal of the original roof over Floor 2, followed by replacement with a roof structure incorporating a center roof support post (and a new load-bearing south wall) on Floor 1. A similar large adobe slab was on the floor level of Room 13.

The remarkable smoothness of the fragments puzzled the excavators, and it is worth considering alternate explanations. It is possible the adobe slabs were remnants from upper jacal portions of the walls of Room 15 that had been smoothed on the interior. The jacal walls could have been replaced with masonry during Floor 1 construction. However, there is little other direct evidence to indicate that these fragments were from walls, rather than from the roof. The load-bearing south wall and the introduction of a center roof support post suggest a change in roofing with the construction of Floor 1, making it more probable these fragments, found in the fill between Floors 1 and 2, were the remains of a replaced or remodeled roof. If so, the roof had a carefully smoothed and maintained upper surface that may have been used as a floor.

Several very fragmentary manos (Ground Stones 18, 27, and 28) and part of a bowl (Vessel 66) with a smudged and polished interior were also in the fill between floors. Their relationship to the adobe slabs is unknown. I suspect they were found below the slabs, perhaps in the fill immediately above Floor 2.

The lower floor (Floor 2) of the room was badly disturbed by rodents. Floor 2 represented only the northern portion of the original floor, because it continued under the south wall of Room 15. The floor was plastered adobe, much like the floors of Room 12 to the east. It was built directly on substrate, which was slightly higher under Room 15 than the corresponding levels recorded under Room 12 (a discrepancy discussed above and also below in the section on pit structures below Room Block B). A stone slab (Feature 72) lay on the floor south of the Floor 1 posthole (Feature 71). In the center of the northern end of the room, the floor plaster formed a large but shallow basin (Feature 73), about 91 cm north-south by 76 cm east-west. Depth was not recorded, but Feature 73 was shallow, probably less than 15 cm deep at most. It was remarkably similar to the clay-lined basin (Feature 29) on the floor of Room 10.

Pit Structures Beneath Room Block B
(Sub-B)

Two and perhaps as many as four pit structures were found beneath Room Block B (Figs. 2.4–2.6). Only one, Pit House 2, was recognized as a pit structure at the time. Pit House 4 was reconstructed from the notes in 1987, and the features referred to here as 12-SW and 12-NE are still problematic. These last two units represent artificial features excavated into the substrate but structurally they are unrelated to the walls of Room 12 above them and may not be pit structures.

Pit House 2, beneath Rooms 11 and 14, was recognized as a pit structure at the time of excavation. Unfortunately, time allowed only limited testing of this feature. Pit House 2 was discovered in a 5-foot-wide (1.5-m) subfloor trench, along the south wall of Room 11. Reddish substrate was encountered immediately below the Room 11 floor in the western two-thirds of this trench, but in the eastern third the substrate sloped off sharply. The excavators removed the fill in this restricted area until a well-smoothed clay floor was encountered about 49 cm below the floor of Room 11. This floor, in turn, was laid on substrate. During the excavation of Pit House 2, a higher surface was detected about 27 cm above the plastered floor, but it could not be confirmed as a floor in the exposed profiles.

Subfloor testing in Room 14, immediately to the south, revealed deep fill below the northeastern corner of the floor. This fill was determined to be a continuation of Pit House 2, but the extent and depth of the pit structure below Room 14 was not resolved. In summary, Pit House 2 was exposed with a small test (about 1.5 m square) along its west wall. Beyond the presence of a plastered floor, no features or architectural details were discovered.

Pit House 4 was not recognized during the original excavations. The feature shown as Pit House 4 on Figure 2.4 combines data from subfloor excavations in Rooms 10 and 13 and from excavations in units N620 E555 and N630 E555 of the Summer 1971 approach trench. No plastered floor was defined in Room 13, and the fill was removed throughout the room (in 30 cm levels) to the reddish substrate. Sub-

strate was reached about 90 cm below the surface in the western half of the room, but dipped sharply in the eastern half to a flat, unplastered surface 1.3 m below ground surface with the configuration shown in Figure 2.4. Less systematic testing below the floor level in Room 10, to the east, disclosed that in the southwestern quadrant of the room the substrate was at a depth identical to its depth in Room 13. Elsewhere in the room, substrate was found immediately below floor level. Unfortunately, the plan of the depression thus indicated below Room 10 has not survived. The outline suggested by the dashed line in Figure 2.4 is simply a projection, supported by some cryptic comments in the field notes. Intriguingly, the floor of Room 10 was preserved in a broken arc outside the projected line, but had completely deteriorated within it. Another portion of Pit House 4 was excavated in the approach trench (Fig. 2.4); at the time it was termed a hearth. Its base reached precisely the same depth as the substrate in the eastern end of Room 13. Study of the notes and photographs of the "hearth" suggested that it was instead part of a pit structure, with other segments of the pit structure exposed under Rooms 10 and 13. Pit House 4 definitely did not extend under Room 8.

Pit House 4 appears to have been an oval structure, approximately 13 feet north-south and 10 feet east-west (3.9 m by 3.0 m), and 2.75 feet to 3.00 feet deep (84 cm to 91 cm) below the substrate level (which, of course. was not the old ground surface). No plaster was found either on the walls or floor. A ceramic concentration (Feature 74) was found on the "floor" of the structure.

The possible pit structures below Room 12 are difficult to understand. I excavated these structures and their interpretation is not hampered by incomplete notes. They are fairly well documented in the existing maps and photographs. Their nature was not clear at the time, and it is not clear now.

Two rectangular areas below Room 12 (shown on Figure 2.4 as 12-SW and 12-NE) had been excavated into the substrate and then floored with a smooth mud plaster. The floors (together called Floor 3 of Room 12 at the time of excavation) are at precisely the same level and appear to be continuous across the small area of overlap between 12-SW and 12-NE. When the area below Room 12 was excavated to substrate, 12-SW and 12-NE appeared to be a single floor. Above it rose two platforms, cut in the substrate at a higher level than the floor in the northwestern and southeastern quadrants of the room. Although "Floor 3" and the substrate continued under all four walls of Room 12 and were clearly not associated with those walls, the quartering of the room by these features seemed too precise to be coincidental.

At the time, I speculated that the depressions and rises below Room 12 represented foundations of walls planned and never built or of walls built and subsequently removed, on the Room 12 level. The plaster floor remained unexplained (Lekson 1972).

At a remove of 15 years, that scenario seems strained. None of the other walls of Room Block B have foundations or foundation trenches. I now believe that rather than being construction associated with Room 12, units 12-SW and 12-NE are probably rectangular pit structures, one of which postdates and cuts into the corner of the other. Which was the older and which the younger we may never know. The fill in this area was badly disturbed by superimposed firepits and postholes and no outline of walls was found in the area of 12-SW and 12-NE overlap.

The continuous "Floor 3" between the two quadrants and other aspects of the deposits below Room 12 make my current pit structure explanation less certain than I would like. First, there is no evidence of the proposed pit structures continuing under Rooms 11 and 15. Considering the projected lines of the 12-SW and 12-NE walls, the lack of pit structures under Room 15 may be no reason for concern; however, it does appear that 12-SW would continue under Room 11.

The only intensive subfloor testing in Room 11 was the trench along the south wall (Figure 2.4). Although spot tests were conducted elsewhere in the room, it is possible that they missed the continuation of 12-SW. From the notes and my recollections of the extent of subfloor testing, however, I believe that subfloor tests in Room 11 would have revealed a subfloor feature of this size had it been present, just as tests in Room 14 picked up Pit House 2.

Second, although it is possible that the walls of 12-SW were almost exactly aligned with those of Room Block B (thus negating the problem of no 12-SW under Room 11), this seems an unlikely coincidence. The apparently precise alignment of 12-SW and 12-NE with the axis and the walls of Room Block B is puzzling, compared with the total lack of alignment of the room block over Pit Houses 2 and 4.

It is possible that 12-SW and even 12-NE were open pit structures occupied along with Room Block B. This interpretation means that Room 12 was constructed later than the southern half of Room Block B (as argued above) and that a rectangular pit structure (similar in size and shape to Pit House 3) was built in alignment with and as part of the earlier (southern half) Room Block B. The architectural pattern of a room block with a square pit structure immediately adjacent, at one end, is known from other excavated Mimbres phase sites in the Cliff Valley (Hammack and others 1966); this explanation best fits the evidence, at least for 12-SW.

Pit Structure 12-NE

Pit structure 12-NE may date earlier than pit structure 12-SW. The south wall of the unit was nearly perpendicular; the west wall appeared to have been a step or bench, about 61 cm wide and 24 cm above the floor. No plaster was noted on either the bench or the wall below it. The floor was a well-smoothed mud plaster, 3 cm to 6 cm thick, applied directly over the substrate. It appeared to have been burned over most of its southern half, but no large masses of charred material were found in contact with it.

A small brown ware jar with pinched decoration around the neck (Vessel 47) sat upright in the middle of the floor (Feature 75); the jar contained 325 shell beads and pendants. A crushed bowl (Vessel 42) was on the "bench" surface, shown as Feature 76 in Figure 2.4.

The one floor feature was a possible posthole (Feature 77) at the base of the west wall of 12-NE. It was 30 cm in diameter and about 34 cm deep below the floor. Fill was identical to the sandy fill of Levels 7, 8, and 9.

Pit Structure 12-SW

The north wall of 12-SW was nearly perpendicular; the east wall, as excavated, sloped. I believe the slope was caused by excavation while the soil was frozen. The floor was a carefully smoothed clay surface, 3 cm to 9 cm thick over the substrate. A posthole (Feature 79) was located at the base of the east wall. It was 15 cm in diameter and only 18 cm deep below floor. Fill was the same as that of Levels 7, 8, and 9. A large fragment of a utility vessel (Feature 78) was on the floor of 12-SW at the base of the east wall (this may be Vessel 73, but identification is uncertain).

ROOM BLOCK C

Room Block C (Fig. 2.7) had been almost completely destroyed by road construction. Room 7 was excavated during the January 1971 season and a burial was removed from this area during the Summer 1971 season. The preliminary report from the January season (Fitting and others 1971) summarizes almost all the data available; this will be quoted here with a few additions from the notes.

Room Cluster C was located between the highway and the telephone company road near the point where the latter divided from the former. It had been partially destroyed by both, and one room was sectioned by the highway while the footings of another was visible in the telephone company road.

It was clear that only one room, Room 7, could be excavated in this group. It had been subjected to much depredation. . . .

It was a very long room with north to south [interior] length of 17 feet [5.2 m]. Eight feet of the north and south walls remain. In depth, it was similar to the rooms of Cluster [Room Block] A with a total wall height of approximately 2.5 feet [76.2 cm], or a height of 2.0 feet [61 cm] above the adobe floor. An adobe divider, similar to that found in Room 2, was found to run 6 feet [1.8 m] into the center of the room. This divider was 0.75 feet [22.9 cm] in width, 1.5 feet [45.7 cm] in height and had a smooth finished adobe top, although no trace of separate bricks could be seen.

This divider separated the room into Room 7A on the north, which was 7.2 feet long and 8.0 feet wide [2.2 m by 2.4 m], and a southern room, 7B, which measured 7.0 feet by 8.0 feet [2.1 m by 2.4 m]. The floor was a relatively loosely packed adobe with no trace of either center post or hearth.

We would interpret Room 7A and 7B as two sections of a very long, low storage room, similar to Room 2 in Cluster [Room Block] A. It is a very large room not to have any internal support but I doubt that it was ever

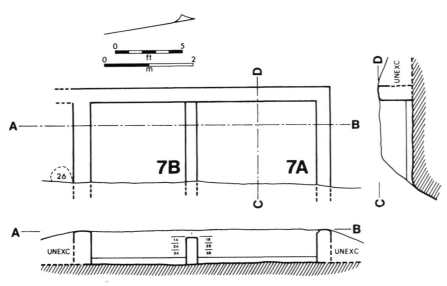

Figure 2.7. Room Block C. Hachure in plan indicates stone slabs and in profile indicates substrate. Dashed lines in plan indicate subfloor sealed features and in profiles indicate projections.

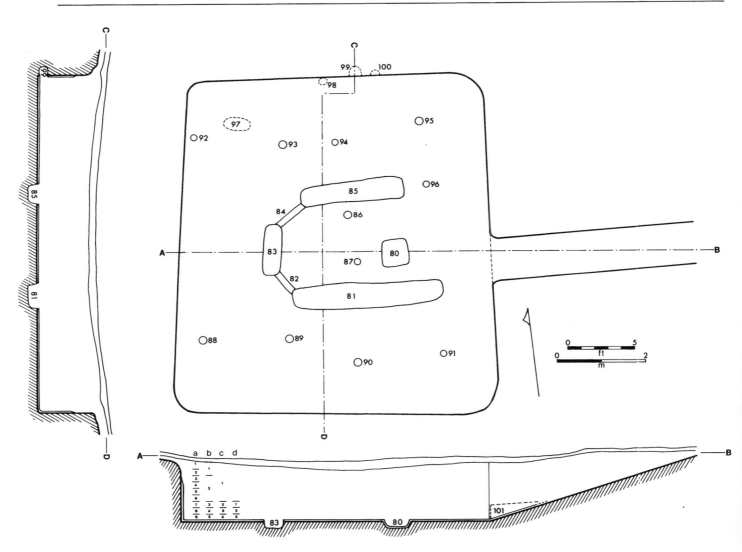

Figure 2.8. Pit House 1. Hachure in profile indicates substrate. Dashed lines in plan indicate possible features and in profiles indicate projections.

much wider than it is today. Like the major construction in both other clusters [room blocks], the top soil was stripped to hardpan [substrate] before construction began (Fitting and others 1971: 36).

One mano was found on the floor of Room 7A and a second mano was found on the floor of Room 7B. Neither mano remains in the 1987 collections.

During the Summer 1971 season, part of a burial (Feature 26, Appendix A) was noted eroding out of the road cut immediately south of Room 7. This burial, presumably a subfloor feature from the room south of Room 7, consisted of the lower leg of an adult (the rest of the burial was probably removed by the road cut). A single projectile point was found in possible association with the burial.

PIT HOUSE 1

A number of pit house depressions were evident west of Room Block B. At least two of those depressions were conspicuously larger than the others. One of these was excavated and was designated Pit House 1 (P1). It was recognized at the time as a "Great Kiva" or communal structure.

Pit House 1 (Fig. 2.8) was a square pit structure about 26 feet north-south by 24 feet east-west (7.9 m by 7.3 m). The floor was 5.5 feet (1.7 m) deep below present ground surface. An east ramp entry, about 3.5 feet (about 1.1 m) wide, extended 15.5 feet (4.7 m) from the center of the east wall. The walls were of mud plaster on soil. The floor was carefully plastered and had a firepit surrounded by a U-shaped series of long, narrow pits (or "foot vaults"). Ten holes in the floor represented the posts of a post-and-beam roof framework. The roof apparently had burned; carbonized beams were found in the fill and the wall plaster was reddened.

Excavations began in the Summer 1971 season under the supervision of B. Thomas Gray. The depression was approached with a line of 5-foot by 10-foot (1.5-m by 3.0-m) units (N600 E510, N610 E510, N620 E510, and N630 E510). This trench line was expanded to the west (N604 E505) and east (N604 E515) when the south wall of Pit House 1 was discovered. The south wall, after it was exposed in these units, was then followed in two irregular trenches, about 3 feet (91 cm) wide and at least 3 feet (91 cm) deep, termed "P1 East" and "P1 West" (Fig. 2.9, *top*).

Following the definition of the south wall, the remainder of the pit house was cleared to a depth of 42 inches (1.07 m) below datum (or 1.5 feet, 45.7 cm, above the floor level exposed in the trench).

When the general outline of Pit House 1 had been defined to a depth of 42 inches (1.07 m) below datum, the remainder of the fill was divided into 5-foot (1.5-m) square units, designated by the letters A through Z. Letters E and W were omitted, as they had been used to designate materials from the "P1 East" and "P1 West" trenches. The 5-foot by 10-foot trench units, and the 5-foot square units A through Z were

used for horizontal provenience for both fill (below a depth of 42 inches below Pit House 1 datum) and floor (Fig. 2.9, *bottom*).

The arbitrary level system varied from trench units to lettered units, as did the screening policy. These differences are complicated, and reference should be made to Figure 2.8, profile A-B. The southern trench units (N600 and N610) were excavated entirely in 6-inch (15-cm) arbitrary levels; all fill was screened (Fig. 2.8, profile A-B, *a*). Northern trench units (N620, N630, and both N604 extensions) were excavated in two much thicker levels. Level 1 equaled 0–18 inches (0–46 cm); Level 2 equaled 18–42 inches (46–107 cm) below Pit House 1 datum to 1.5 feet (46 cm) above floor; all material from these trenches was screened (Fig. 2.8, profile A-B, *b*). Following the initial trench, all fill outside the trench units (in the lettered 5-foot square units) was removed to 1.5 feet (46 cm) above the floor without screening. In units N and S, this first unscreened level was designated Level 1 (Fig. 2.8, profile A-B, *c*), and in the remainder of the structure this first unscreened level was not numbered (Fig. 2.8, profile A-B, *d*). For convenience, a single system of lettered levels is used to allow comparison of the various level numbering systems in Appendixes B and C.

The final 1.5 feet (46 cm) above the floor was excavated in two different ways. To simplify, imagine a line drawn diagonally from the southwestern to the northeastern corner of Pit House 1, dividing the structure into northwestern and southeastern halves. The fill above floor in the southeastern half was excavated in three 6-inch (15-cm) screened levels (Levels 1, 2, and 3). Due to the short time limits of the January 1972 season, the upper 12 inches (30 cm, Levels 1 and 2) of the 18 inches (45 cm) of fill above floor in the northwestern half was removed without screening; the 6 inches (15 cm) directly above the floor (Level 3) was screened. Thus the final 6 inches (15 cm) of fill above floor was screened in both the northwestern and southeastern halves.

Pit House 1 is the most frustrating unit at the site for me to describe. It was carefully excavated, and detailed maps, plans, and profiles were drawn for every feature in the fill and on the floor (over 25 feature numbers were assigned). All of these primary notes have vanished. The description that follows comes from the daily journals of the excavators (with reference after tantalizing reference to plan and profile drawings), a sketch map compiled by Tim Klinger (out of the field), and a number of photos. The sketch map and the photos, together, constitute a usable record of floor feature locations, but precise measurements and descriptions of these features are lost. The outline of the pit structure itself is probably accurate (measurements and angles for the various corners survive in the notes). The width and length of the entry ramp are also accurate, but the orientation of the ramp is only approximate. The locations, forms, and dimensions of all floor features must be considered approximate, although I am fairly confident that their locations *relative to each other* are accurate.

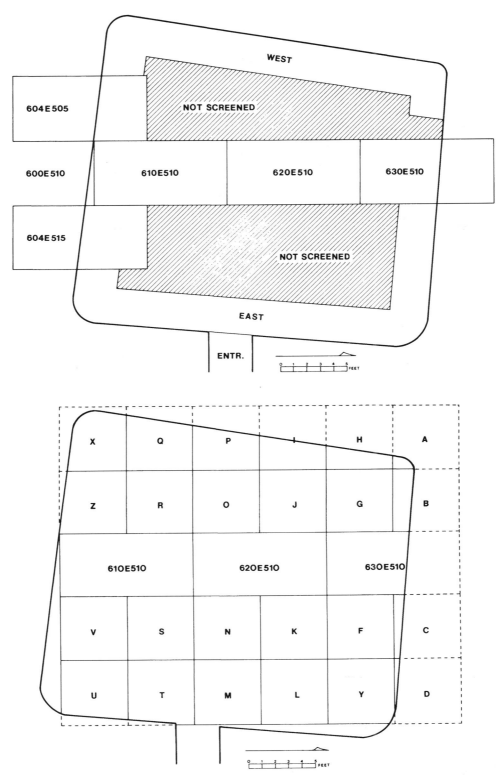

Figure 2.9. Excavation units of Pit House 1: *top*, upper
fill units; *bottom*, floor fill and floor units.

The saving grace of Pit House 1 is that it was a simple structure. There was, apparently, no clear internal stratigraphy of fill. Although the floor in places was re-plastered at least twice, there were no separate floor levels with varying arrangements of features. And, fortunately, there were no complications of superimposition at other structures, earlier or later.

Fill

By conservative estimates, Pit House 1 contained about 100 cubic yards of fill, not including the approach trench and the ramp. About 40 percent of this fill was screened; the remainder was simply removed with only selective recovery of artifacts (see Table 3.2).

Fill was described as very rocky, and much of the excavation required picks to lever out tightly packed cobble fill. This density of cobbles in fill appears to have been heaviest around the edges of Pit House 1. There is no natural reason for large cobbles to have accumulated in the pit, and this quantity of rock is curious. Clearly, the cobbles did not originate from masonry walls lining the pit itself, because the walls of Pit House 1 consisted of plaster on substrate. It is possible that cobble walls originally rose over the plaster-on-soil walls around the perimeter. Figure 2.8, profile C-D (based on field data) indicates that masonry walls rising directly above the pit structure walls would have been completely lost with the erosion of the upper edge of the pit. Although there is no positive evidence, the quantity of cobbles in Pit House 1 fill suggests possible masonry walls of unknown height rising above the pit itself. Less likely, the rocks in the fill may represent an unknown element of roofing, or they may have been intentionally placed in the pit after the roof was removed or destroyed.

That Pit House 1 was roofed was evident from the quantities of burned roof debris found in levels immediately above the floor. Although the burned roofing cannot be quantified, nor can its orientation be described, the notes repeatedly mention burned beam fragments and other burned roofing near the level of the floor.

Large quantities of trash or, possibly, roof artifacts were found in the final three levels (45 cm) above the floor, including one partial Boldface Black-on-white (Style I) bowl (Vessel 67).

Compared to the room fill in Room Blocks A and B, the fill of Pit House 1 was relatively free of rodent disturbance.

Walls

At the time of excavation, the walls of Pit House 1 were defined by the exposed substrate into which the structure had been dug. Small patches of clay plaster survived on at least three walls. The walls were originally fully plastered, as shown on Figure 2.8, profiles A-B and C-D. Possible vertical extension of the below-grade plaster-on-soil walls with above-grade masonry walls, suggested by cobbles in the fill of Pit House 1, is discussed above under *Fill*.

Two niches (Features 99 and 100) had been excavated into the substrate just above floor level near the center of the north wall. They were filled with the "normal stony fill," that is, there was nothing to distinguish their fill from the general fill in this area. Neither niche was lined or floored. No measurements survive; the sizes of these two features on Figure 2.8 are approximate, but the locations are reliable.

Ramp-Entrance

A ramp-entrance was located in the middle of the east wall. The size of this feature, as shown on Figure 2.8, is correct; its orientation is only approximate.

The ramp-entrance was 4.7 m long and 1.1 m wide. The side walls were soil with no evidence of plastering. The floor of the ramp was plastered, with three distinct layers of plastering evidently corresponding to the three layers of plaster noted on the floor of the main chamber.

A possible remodeling (Feature 101) of the lower end of the ramp is shown on Figure 2.8, profile A-B. It appears from the notes and photographs that the lowest 3 to 4 feet (0.9–1.2 m) of the ramp were leveled with puddled adobe or plastered fill (Feature 101) added over the original ramp floor. This addition made the ramp enter the room about 24 cm to 30 cm above the floor level.

Judging from the presence of floor plaster, the ramp-entrance was probably roofed, but no postholes were noted along its length. The two large center posts (Features 86 and 87) may have been structurally involved with the ramp roofing.

There was evidently some discussion in the field concerning possible puddled adobe steps in the ramp. The final assessment appears to have been negative; none are evident in photographs of the cleared ramp-entrance.

Roof

An unknown quantity of burned roof material was in the fill above the floor. No notes or plans remain to allow reconstruction of the roof from the burned material. The posthole pattern (Features 86 through 95, and perhaps Feature 96) suggests something of the roof's structure.

Postholes were large and deep; in two cases, caches evidently had been placed in the pits prior to emplacement of the posts. Specifically, Feature 87 contained fragments of mica, a quartz crystal, and two shell bracelet fragments. The cache in Feature 88 was far more spectacular; it consisted of a concentration of calcite pendants found 51.8 cm below the floor in the fill of the pit. The cache was probably a necklace of over 70 large pendants at or near the base of the Feature 88 post. It is described in more detail in Chapter 3.

The posts themselves either had been removed from the postholes or, as was likely true of Features 86 and 87, had rotted away. No data remain on post mold diameters. The exact locations of floor features on Figure 2.8 are approximate, but the relative locations of postholes are reasonably well documented in surviving photographs.

The two center posts (Features 86 and 87), about 1.2 m apart north-south, were represented by deep pits. Feature 86 was at least 91 cm deep, and probably more. Feature 86 was defined in the north margin of a larger, shallow, irregular pit (not mapped on Fig. 2.8), implying that a mold of the rotted post was indeed present in this posthole. Feature 87 was of comparable size. The posthole as excavated was at least 45.7 cm in diameter. A post mold of "dark clayey material in a matrix of fine light gray sand" in the center of Feature 87 was mentioned in the notes. At least five feature numbers were assigned in the field for elements of Feature 88; these numbers may refer to the post mold and its matrix, but also may indicate a complex internal structure, perhaps niches, associated with the necklace cache.

Photographs show the other postholes (with the possible exception of Feature 88) as smaller than Features 86 and 87. Two east-west rows of postholes were defined in the northern (Features 92–95) and southern (Features 88–91) halves of the pit structure. This pattern is seen in other Mogollon Great Kivas (Anyon 1984). As shown on Figure 2.8, however, these rows are not very linear; a straight line will not pass through all four posts of either row. Instead, the postholes appear to form two (east and west) quadrangular sets of posts: an eastern quadrangle, Features 90, 91, 94, and 95, and a western quadrangle, Features 88, 89, 92 and 93.

Photographs also substantiate the location of Feature 96 (Fig. 2.8), apparently a posthole aligned with posthole Features 91 and 95. The spacing suggests a fourth post might have been located in the eastern end of Feature 81, the larger of two parallel floor vaults, similar to the placement of posts at either end of floor vaults in Anasazi Great Kivas.

The two central postholes (Features 86 and 87) are approximately aligned with posthole Features 90 and 94 of the eastern quadrangle, and these four posts, although slightly east of the north-south center line of the structure, were probably intended to run along or very close to that center line. It is possible that a complementary pair of central posts, forming a central square framework, was set in Feature 83, the smallest floor vault. If so, these posts were set shallower and were smaller in diameter than the large posts indicated for Features 86 and 87. Again, there was no positive evidence from notes or photographs of post molds in Feature 83.

In any event, it appears that the roof support framework was not simply two large center posts flanked by parallel lines of smaller posts. Instead, it seems likely that the roofing structure consisted of two, largely independent post-and-beam frameworks (the east and west post quadrangles), with "leaner" beams running from these sets to the ground surface (or perhaps to masonry walls) at the edge of the pit structure. The area between the two frameworks was probably also spanned with flat beams.

The function of the two large center posts (Features 86 and 87), which seem to be part of the eastern post quadrangle, is unclear. It is possible that a central ridge, adding further complexity to the roof profile, was supported on these two posts. Or, if my suggestions about Feature 83 are correct, four posts may have supported a central peak.

If the center posts (Features 86 and 87) were not part of a more elaborate roofing framework in the center of Pit House 1, the east-west section of this roof may have had as few as three and as many as five angles (with the center of the five angles being flat); whereas the north-south section would have had only three, with a flat roof in the middle and pitched roofing on the "leaners" at either end. Obviously, if a more elaborate structure existed in the center of the roof, the roof line or profile could have been much more complex.

No evidence was found of roofing over the ramp; it is possible that the two center posts (Features 86 and 87) were structurally involved with the ramp roofing. The alignment of ramp and posts (as shown on Fig. 2.8) is not particularly straight, but the orientation of the ramp itself (on Fig. 2.8) is only approximate.

Floor

In several areas, two and perhaps three levels of floor plaster were reported. The uppermost, a thin (0.3 cm) wash of clay, rested directly on an intermediate layer (0.6 cm to 3.0 cm thick) of fine silty sand, which rested on a much thicker (3.0 cm to 6.1 cm thick) clay plaster floor. This lower floor was either directly on substrate or was laid on a thin sand fill over irregularities in the substrate. In a few cases, there appeared to be a second thin clay layer above the first. The superimposed floors were observed almost entirely in units along the base of the pit structure walls; this floor stratigraphy could not be defined in the center of Pit House 1. Gray speculated that the upper, thin layer of clay might be plaster washed off the walls, and that Pit House 1 only had one floor. His observation seems reasonable; however, in subsequent notes, the "three floor" interpretation was accepted (as noted for the ramp-entrance).

In addition to the posthole features described under *Roof*, above, the outstanding floor features of Pit House 1 were the firepit (Feature 80) and the series of floor vaults (Features 81 through 85) that surrounded the firepit on three sides. The firepit was roughly 61 cm square and at least 15 cm deep. It was plastered; only one rock is mentioned, located in the east wall.

The series of floor vaults consisted of three large troughs (Features 81, 83, and 85) on the southern, western, and northern sides of the firepit (respectively); these were joined at the corners by narrow trenches (Features 82 and 84). The floor vault complex, as shown on Figure 2.8, is drawn from the sketch maps and photographs. Almost no measurements survive, and the size and location of these units on Figure 2.8 are only approximate.

None of the floor vaults and trenches appeared to have been plastered or lined; all were simply excavated into the substrate. The average depth of Features 81, 83, and 85 was about 21 cm to 24 cm, and the depths of Features 82 and 84 were probably similar. The fill of all the floor vault units contained relatively few artifacts, with the exception of a small piece of worked turquoise in the fill of Feature 85.

Large rocks and some fragmentary stone artifacts were found in these features; whether or not they served some structural function remains unknown. Parts of at least five fragmentary metates (Ground Stones 2, 3, 9, 89, and 90) were recovered from the fill of Feature 81. Similarly, the fill of Feature 83 contained several (presumably) unmodified rocks, evidently on similar levels in the fill, 7.6 cm to 15.2 cm below the floor and about 9.1 cm to 12.2 cm above the base of the pit.

Feature 81 was about 91 cm longer than comparable Feature 85. The eastern extension of Feature 81 may have contained a posthole aligned with Features 91, 95, and 96. Photographs show Feature 81 to be more complicated than the other floor vaults, with at least two smaller pits in its southern margin (the eastern end is not visible). Other than their presence, no further description is possible.

Of unknown function were an oval pit in the northwestern corner (Feature 97) and a posthole-sized pit (Feature 98) at the base of the north wall. These features are indicated on sketch maps, but there are no notes or photos to suggest what they might have been. A single quartz crystal was recovered from Feature 97.

PIT HOUSE 3

Pit House 3 was excavated by Patrick Draine during the January 1972 season. This description is taken almost entirely from Draine's manuscript report (Draine 1971).

Pit House 3 (Fig. 2.10) was a small (9 feet north-south by 7 feet east-west, 2.7 m by 2.1 m, interior dimensions), masonry walled pit structure, with a floor about 1.8 m below present ground surface. The floor had a center posthole (Feature 105), a firepit (Feature 106), and a ventilator system (Features 102 and 103) in the east wall.

The unit was initially discovered in the eastern end of a 3-foot by 20-foot trench (0.9 m by 6.1 m; the Trailer Test Trench, "TTT," named for a nearby mobile home). The trench cut through a low mound at the northern end of the site (Fig. 1.2). The mound appeared to be artificial, and the trench was excavated to determine if it was a room block or a midden. The results were inconclusive, but I believe the mound was a room block. The trench was segmented into four 5-foot (1.5-m) sections, lettered A through D. A 10-foot extension to the eastern end of the trench was designated E, and it cut across the southern half of Pit House 3.

Segment E was excavated in 6-inch (15-cm) arbitrary, screened levels, except Level 1 was 12 inches (30 cm) thick. Levels 1 through 5 (to a depth of 91 cm below Pit House 3 datum) were excavated in segment E before the east and west walls of Pit House 3 were well defined. When the walls

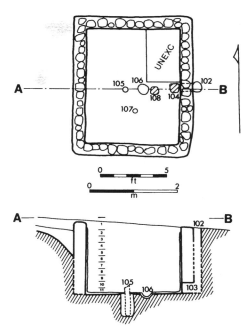

Figure 2.10. Pit House 3. Hachure in plan indicates stone slabs and in profile indicates substrate. Dashed lines in plan indicate sub-floor sealed features and in profiles indicate projections.

were outlined, the fill in the remaining area of Pit House 3 was then removed, without screening, to this level (91 cm below Pit House 3 datum). A telephone pole in the northeastern corner of Pit House 3 precluded removal of fill, and in that area excavations were limited to definition of the upper part of the walls.

When the fill had been removed to 3 feet (91 cm) below Pit House 3 datum, the remainder of the fill above floor was excavated in six 6-inch (15-cm) levels, with the last level (Level 11) being only 6 cm thick.

Fill

The excavated portion of the room produced 790 large cobbles, mostly from Levels 1 through 4. Cobbles were still encountered below Level 5, but the matrix of dry gray sand contained increasing amounts of adobe fragments, with the highest density in Level 7. "At the bottom of Level 7 a much denser layer of adobe chunks was encountered, upon which was a large metate [Ground Stone 106] leaning against the south wall, a tuff slab, and a concentration of sherds of a plain ware interior-smudged bowl [Vessel 68] and two corrugated ollas [Vessels 69 and 70]. Apparently this was the collapsed roof and these artifacts were on the roof at the time of its collapse" (Draine 1971: 2). Large fragments of roof fall continued into Level 10, just above the floor. Scattered pockets of ash and charcoal were also found in the fill directly above the floor. Five mano fragments (Ground

Stones 29, 38, 69, 78, and 79) were catalogued as "Pit House 3-F" which almost certainly means "fill."

Walls

The walls of Pit House 3 consisted of single-wythe, well-coursed cobble lining of an excavated pit. The masonry construction evidently was begun directly against the exposed substrate, but in their upper reaches the walls were probably free standing and the pit excavated for Pit House 3 was filled in behind them (Figure 2.10, profile A-B). From the number of large cobbles recovered from fill, Draine calculated an additional 4 feet (1.2 m) of wall above the standing wall, for a total height of about 8 feet (2.4 m).

The wall interiors were carefully plastered with a continuation of the floor plaster. The maximum thickness of plaster on the walls was 3.6 cm.

A ventilator shaft (Features 102 and 103) was constructed behind the middle of the east wall. The upper opening of the shaft (Feature 102) was immediately adjacent to the wall; the lower opening, through the east wall, was at floor level. The lower opening (Feature 103) was square, about 15 cm wide and 21 cm tall, and was plastered to an unknown distance into the shaft. The lower opening was equipped with a small stone slab (Feature 104), probably for closure. Only the upper and lower openings were excavated; it is unknown if the shaft was fully lined with masonry. (No notes survive that describe the upper opening.)

Roof

Roof fall was encountered in the lower half of the fill of Pit House 3. From the position of the tuff slab, or hatch cover, Draine concluded that an entrance or opening in the roof was located along the east wall.

A single roof-support post was located slightly west of the center of the room (posthole Feature 105). The average span between this post and the walls was about 4.4 feet (1.3 m).

Floor

The floor consisted of a thick (6 cm) white clay plaster applied directly to the substrate. Major artifacts found directly upon the floor included two stone slabs (Features 104 and 108), a mano ("complementary to the metate from the roof," Draine 1971: 3), and an unspecified "grinding stone." The first slab (Feature 104) was clearly associated with the lower opening of the ventilator (Feature 103); its size and placement indicate that it was used to close or damp the vent opening. The second slab (Feature 108) lay on the floor between the ventilator opening and the firepit. There is no indication in the notes that it originally stood upright as a deflector, a possibility of which the excavator was clearly aware.

No evidence of the post remained in the posthole (Feature 105), which was filled with gravelly soil and cobble shims. The pit reached a depth of 54.9 cm below floor level.

A firepit (Feature 106) was located 76.2 cm directly west of the lower ventilator opening (Feature 103). The firepit was about 18 cm to 21 cm in diameter. "It was a circular, earth-lined [plastered] pit, filled with ash interspersed with thin lenses of brown soil. At its deepest point, it is 5.5 inches [14 cm] below the floor surface" (Draine 1971: 3). The rim of the firepit was elevated very slightly above the floor level in a low lip.

A small unlined pit (Feature 107) about 7.6 cm by 9.1 cm and 9.1 cm deep below floor was located in the southern half of the floor; its function is unknown.

TRENCHES N775 AND N790

Two small trenches were excavated in the northwestern part of the site. Both trenches were abandoned before the precise nature of the deposits being excavated could be determined, and in neither case did useful notes survive. Items recovered from them are not included in the artifact analyses that follow, although material from these units remains in the collections.

At the beginning of the Summer 1971 season, a series of three 5-foot by 10-foot (1.5-m by 3.1-m) units along the N775 line at E425, E435 and E445 were begun in what appeared to be a large pit structure depression. Four 6-inch (15-cm) levels were excavated; work then shifted to Pit House 1. The trench exposed an ill-defined, shallow surface, much higher than expected for a pit structure of the magnitude indicated by the depression. Klinger's ceramic counts indicate an assemblage remarkable for the paucity of identifiable decorated ceramics. Out of 880 sherds, 1 was Mogollon Red-on-brown, 2 were Mimbres Classic Black-on-white and 52 were undifferentiated Mimbres series black-on-white.

Trench N790, a 5-foot by 10-foot (1.5-m by 3.1-m) unit at N790 E405 was opened in January 1971, but work ceased after three 6-inch (15-cm) levels were excavated because the ground was frozen. The unit had been placed over what was believed to be the ramp-entry of a pit structure; however, no architectural features were defined in this limited excavation. Ceramics (in Fitting and others 1971) indicate a Bold-face Black-on-white assemblage similar to Pit House 1.

The precise location of Trench N790 is not clear. The grid designation may not be reliable, and the notes and maps of the site are ambiguous. The N790 unit was probably in the northwestern quadrant of the same depression tested by Trench N775, but I have not shown this unit on the site map (Fig. 1.2).

CHAPTER THREE

Artifacts

Many of the artifacts from the Saige-McFarland Site were analyzed in the early and mid-1970s. I have consolidated those data with my own analyses and interpretation.

Repeatedly in their notes, the excavators remarked that no clear stratigraphic distinctions were seen in above-floor fills of rooms and pit structures. The only possible exception was Pit House 3 (Chapter 2). In the absence of evident natural stratigraphy, room fills were excavated in arbitrary 6-inch (15-cm) levels. Arbitrary stratigraphy is used in several analytical arguments, but how reliable is it?

Both room blocks at Saige-McFarland were riddled with rodent burrows. Notes frequently mention rodent disturbance, including the destruction of sizable areas of flooring. Stratigraphic difficulties are best illustrated by matching sherds of single vessels that were scattered from top to bottom of rooms. (The partial and reconstructible vessels were numbered in an arbitrary series, 1–75, Table 3.8).

Sherds of Vessel 22, from the subfloor burial in Room 4A (Feature 14), were found in the uppermost levels of that room.

Several sherds of Vessel 38, a large indented corrugated jar from the above-floor fill of Room 11, were found in the upper levels of Room 14.

Sherds of Vessel 40, a partial vessel found on Floor 1 of Room 12 (Feature 43), were found throughout the above-floor fill of this room (Levels 1–5).

Sherds of Vessel 42, a partial vessel found in Room 12 (Levels 8 and 9), were found as high as Level 1 in that room.

Sherds of a miniature jar (Vessel 63) from the concentration of vessels on the floor of Room 14 (Feature 69) were found in Levels 1 and 6 of Room 11, and Level 3 of Room 10.

Despite the obvious movement of sherds, rodents did not turn the whole world upside down. Disturbance at Saige-McFarland was probably no more severe than at other Mimbres sites in southwestern New Mexico. Stratigraphy in pit structures (Pit House 1 and Pit House 3) seems to have been far less disturbed by rodent activity. Indeed, I believe that most materials were more or less in situ; but the reader should be aware that things were moved around a bit, particularly within the fill of Room Blocks A and B.

Because stratigraphy within individual room fills was evidently absent, horizontal separation of the different architectural units offers the best possibility for exploring site chronology. There are five separate architectural units: Room Blocks A, B, and C, and Pit Houses 1 and 3. Stratigraphic divisions are possible within two of these units, Room Block B and Pit House 1. Specifically, Room Block B is divided into the room block proper and a subfloor unit ("Sub-B") that includes the pit structures under Room Block B. The very deep fill of Pit House 1 is separated into an upper fill unit and a lower fill-and-floor unit, which correspond to the two main excavation strategies employed there. Thus there are seven analytic units, hereafter referred to as "grouped proveniences." They are arranged in approximate chronological order in Table 3.1 and in subsequent tables dealing with chronology throughout this and the following chapters.

Table 3.1. Contexts and Dating of Grouped Proveniences Used in Artifact Analysis

Grouped proveniences	Location	Approximate date (A.D.)
Room Block C	Fill and floors	1050–1150
Room Block B	Fill and floors	1050–1150
Room Block A	Fill and floors	950–1150
Sub-B	Pit Houses 2 and 4, 12-SW and 12-NE	950–1000
Pit House 1 Upper	Levels A–F (0–107 cm below datum)	950–1000
Pit House 3	Fill and floor	900–950(?)
Pit House 1 Lower	Levels G–I (107–152 cm below datum)	900(?)

Although finer arbitrary stratigraphic units are used for particular arguments, these seven grouped proveniences form the analytical framework for descriptive analyses. Table 3.2 summarizes the volume of excavated and screened fill in the grouped proveniences.

CERAMICS

Over 90,000 sherds and 75 whole or partial vessels were recovered at the Saige-McFarland Site. They were analyzed between 1971 and 1973 by Timothy C. Klinger. Klinger

**Table 3.2. Volumes in Cubic Feet
of Excavated and Screened Fill**

Grouped proveniences	Location	Total fill (cubic feet)	Screened fill (cubic feet)	Percent of screened fill of total site
	Room 1	115	115	
	Room 2A	160	160	
	Room 2B	70	70	
	Room 3	142	142	
	Room 4A	160	160	
	Room 4B	8	8	
	Room 5	174	174	
	Room 6	95	95	
ROOM BLOCK A TOTAL		924	924	14.7
	Room 8*	399	399	
	Room 9*	326	326	
	Room 10	177	177	
	Room 11	584	584	
	Room 12	962	962	
	Room 13	142	142	
	Room 14	256	256	
	Room 15	355	355	
ROOM BLOCK B TOTAL		3201	3201	51.1
	Pit House 2	41	41	
	Pit House 4	64	64	
	Sub-Room 12	314	314	
SUB-B TOTAL		419	419	6.7
	Room 7A	185	185	
	Room 7B	135	135	
ROOM BLOCK C TOTAL		320	320	5.1
PIT HOUSE 1 UPPER		1916	521	8.3
PIT HOUSE 1 LOWER		876	671	10.7
PIT HOUSE 3		333	216	3.4
	Total	7990	6272	100.0

*Volumes for Rooms 8 and 9 recalculated at about 5% less than the values shown in Fitting and others 1971, Table 37.

sorted the sherds into then-defined ceramic types; in the process, he separated the worked sherds, trade sherds, and handles and selected other sherds for further study. These pieces were stored in individual numbered envelopes; they are referred to in this report as "special sherds." Klinger also completed a computer analysis of design motifs (unpublished) and initiated the reassembly of many of the reconstructible vessels.

My analysis consists of three parts: first, re-sorting decorated sherds according to type descriptions developed since 1972; second, an analysis of vessel form assemblages based on rim sherds of both decorated and utility wares; and third, an analysis of whole and partial vessels.

By 1987, most of the reconstructed vessels were broken, or rather re-broken. Not fancying puzzles much, I did not attempt to reassemble these vessels (for the second time); instead, I reconstructed as little of each as possible to obtain vessel form data. Several bags of sherds and a few of the vessels from the site (as indicated in Table 3.8) are now lost. In most proveniences, the 1987 counts of decorated sherds averaged about 10 percent higher than the 1973 tallies. Breakage of sherds in storage and transit, different percep-

tions of undecorated white wares, and (perhaps) more careful screening of bulk sherd bags for decorated sherds in 1987 generally resulted in slightly higher total counts.

Ceramic Densities

In several of the following analyses, densities and distributions of artifacts are compared among various units at Saige-McFarland. Before we can discuss patterns of artifact distribution, we must establish that the evident patterns do not simply result from the varying intensity of excavations or recovery methods. Room Block A may have had five golden frogs whereas Room Block B may have had only one; but if five times as much fill was excavated from Room Block A as from Room Block B, the disparity in golden frogs is not disproportionate. Various measures are used to normalize artifact counts (90,000 sherds require a different approach than 10 manos) and the different excavation strategies employed at Saige-McFarland. For sherds, counts are best normalized by using *densities* of sherds per cubic foot of fill. Ceramic vessels may be more reasonably compared by using numbers of vessels per unit of architectural space.

Densities of sherds within individual rooms and units varies from 2.26 sherds per cubic foot of fill in Room 7A to 27.01 in Room 10 (see Table 4.1). Despite the wide range of values between individual rooms, the sherd densities for some grouped proveniences show surprising consistency. Room Block C has the lowest sherd density, at about 3 sherds per cubic foot; this value may reflect the fact that excavations in Room Block C were limited to what were probably rear (storage?) rooms of a larger room block, mostly destroyed by the modern highway. Both Room Blocks A and B (and the pit structures of Sub-B) are similar with an average of about 11 to 12 sherds per cubic foot. Pit House 1 Upper and Lower both have the highest values at about 16 to 17 sherds per cubic foot. No data are available from Pit House 3. The highest of the average values is for Pit House 1 Upper, one of a long series of unusual aspects of this unit's artifact distributions.

Densities of sherds (see Table 4.1) are also a way of initially examining ratios of decorated to nondecorated utility sherds. The ratios are notably consistent between grouped provenience units, in all but one case ranging from one decorated sherd to about five or six utility sherds. The exception is Pit House 1 Upper, with a ratio of 1:9.

Whole vessels are discussed in detail later in this chapter. To set the parameters of ceramic vessel densities, only the floors and fills of Room Blocks A and B are considered here. The floor assemblage of Room Block A included three corrugated jars, one bowl smudged and polished on the interior, and a partial white ware tecomate (a closed jar form). The floor assemblage of Room Block B was much more extensive, with seven to nine corrugated jars, three bowls smudged and polished on their interiors, and one white ware jar (this list excludes miniature vessels and partial vessels reused as tools). The floor assemblage of Room Block B contained a similar array of vessels but about two to three times more vessels than in Room Block A. The total floor area and the total number of rooms (including unexcavated rooms) of Room Block B was similarly over twice as large as Room Block A. Thus the two ceramic vessel assemblages seem proportional to room block architectural area.

Such is not the case for vessels found in room fill. Room Block A had five large corrugated jars and one bowl with a smudged and polished interior, whereas Room Block B had only one partial corrugated jar and a single bowl smudged and polished on the interior. Room Block B was over twice as large as Room Block A, but had a much smaller collection of vessels from room fill. This disparity may reflect differences in abandonment mode.

Typology

The nomenclature of Mimbres decorated pottery has an involved history, and certain aspects of that history clarify both the descriptive types used here and the purposes they were intended to serve.

The early, Pit House period red-on-brown and red-on-white types were named and defined by Haury (1936). His type names and definitions continue to be used today with the single exception of San Lorenzo Red-on-brown. This type, an early variety of Mogollon Red-on-brown, is no longer used (LeBlanc 1982; Anyon 1980).

The typology of the Mimbres black-on-white series began with the Cosgroves' report on Swarts Ruin (Cosgrove and Cosgrove 1932), in which they defined two varieties of Mimbres Black-on-white: Mimbres Bold Face Black-on-white and Mimbres Classic Black-on-white. The use of "Bold Face" and "Classic," both descriptive tags for specific decorative styles, was at odds with the binomial system that was then being developed by Colton, Hargrave, and others. The binomial system, which became standard Southwestern usage, required a geographic first term followed by a descriptive second term. Gladwin and Gladwin (1934) attempted to bring "Bold Face" and "Classic" varieties of Mimbres Black-on-white into line with binomial usage by substituting the names Mangas Black-on-white and Mimbres Black-on-white for the Cosgroves' Bold Face and Classic varieties, respectively. However, Gila Pueblo's more complete treatment of Mogollon pottery (Haury 1936), published two years later, returned to the Cosgroves' original terms.

Over the next two decades, the literature vacillated between Mangas (or Mangus) and Bold Face (eventually that name shrank from two words to one, "Boldface") and between Mimbres and Classic. The Cosgroves' original formulation was generally favored, but for Boldface the first term, "Mimbres," was usually dropped, producing Boldface Black-on-white, which sounded like a binomial name, but was not. Mimbres remained Mimbres Classic Black-on-white.

In his study of Mimbres decorated ceramics, Jerry Brody (1977) preferred the Mangas Black-on-white and Mimbres

Black-on-white type names. Brody's use of Mangas Black-on-white in the definitive work on Mimbres pottery did not sit well with some ceramicists. The Mimbres Foundation, in their analyses during the middle and late 1970s, eschewed Mangas and instead argued that Boldface, although not a binomial term, had chronological priority. (It did, by two years.) Mangas Black-on-white was dismissed not so much for reasons of scholarly protocol as for its association with the similarly named Mangas phase, anathematized by the Mimbres Foundation. They purged the phase and all its appurtenances: "Mangus Black-on-white, often used synonymously for Boldface, does not have temporal precedence and has been equated with a Mangus Phase which does not exist" (LeBlanc 1982: 113). As a sometime partisan of the Mangas phase (Lekson 1988a), I do not share this aversion; but "Boldface" has currency so I will not insist on Mangas Black-on-white.

And in fact, more recent analyses have reformulated the typology in such a way that makes the argument moot. The Mimbres Foundation introduced a third variety of Mimbres Black-on-white wares, transitional between Boldface and Classic. The transitional style was defined by designs that, for the most part, previously would have been called Boldface Black-on-white (Scott 1983; Anyon and LeBlanc 1984: 152). LeBlanc (1983) suggested the term "Oak Creek" for this transitional style, based on that usage by Richard Ellison, an archaeologist from Silver City, New Mexico. Thus a strictly correct sequential binomial series would run: Mangas Black-on-white, Oak Creek Black-on-white, and Mimbres Black-on-white. Things had reached such a confusing pass, however, that the Mimbres Foundation wisely substituted instead a series of numbered styles for these binomial types: I, II and III (Scott 1983; Anyon and LeBlanc 1984). The numbered styles are used here, and their characteristics are described in Appendix B.

It has long been recognized that Boldface and Classic form a stylistic continuum, in which Boldface temporally precedes Classic. The I-II-III sequence is an attempt to subdivide this continuum more finely. The Mimbres Foundation established that the three styles were sequent, with Style II "replacing" Style I (Scott 1983: 45), and itself subsequently being eclipsed by Style III. "Style II really did occur temporally between Styles I and III. It is not a spatial or stylistically contemporaneous variant of the two previously recognized types" (Anyon and LeBlanc 1984: 159; see also LeBlanc 1983: 114). This sequence has been independently demonstrated at the NAN Ranch Ruin, where deposits of Style II have been found stratigraphically between Style I and III deposits (Shafer 1987, 1988; Shafer and Taylor 1986). Thus, ideally, decorated ceramic assemblages should change through time from Style I, to Style II, to Style III.

Analysis of Decorated Sherds

The Upper Gila Project followed the traditional Mimbres ceramic typology (Haury 1936, Cosgrove and Cosgrove

1932). Fitting (and others 1971) and Timothy Klinger divided the Mimbres series decorated wares into five types: Mogollon Red-on-brown, Three Circle Red-on-white, Boldface Black-on-white, Mimbres Classic Black-on-white, and Mimbres Polychrome. The last named type is often, and probably correctly, considered a variety of Mimbres Classic Black-on-white. The importance of the distinction is moot since only one sherd of Mimbres Polychrome was found at Saige-McFarland.

To translate Saige-McFarland ceramics into the typology of the 1980s, it was necessary to re-sort the Mimbres series black-on-white wares according to the Style I-II-III typology. This was accomplished, with certain reservations. The sorting categories used here are described in detail in Appendix B; the thinking underlying those distinctions is discussed briefly here.

Almost all deposits excavated at Saige-McFarland were screened through one-fourth-inch mesh. Although this admirable practice ensures full and unbiased recovery, screening produces huge numbers of tiny sherds, too small and too fragmentary for classification into the Mimbres series types, even with the intermediate Styles I-II and II-III categories provided by the Mimbres Foundation typologists. Several sorting categories (Table 3.3) were established to allow the tabulation of "untypable" sherds.

Most analyses of Mimbres ceramics do not allow the luxury of uncertainty. Every sherd, except the smallest ceramic crumb, finds its place in the typological cosmos. It may be

possible to pigeonhole every sherd in the system used here, by combining the "untypable" sorting categories with the named types as in Table 3.3. However, there is no way to assign, unambiguously, sherds from the nonspecific sorting categories to named types, and throughout this report, typological discussion is limited to sherds actually assigned to unambiguous "type" categories (21, 22, 31–36).

A series of tests was made using sherd collections from several levels in each room block and pit structure to see if the inclusion of sorting categories that are not type-specific with the appropriate type categories (as suggested in Table 3.3) made a significant difference in assemblage proportions. In every case, combination of nonspecific sorting categories with named types made little or no difference in the relative proportion of those types to each other. The addition of the "untypable" categories did not affect the proportional outcome; but since these categories exist precisely because they carry ambiguous designs, I feel reasonably confident in using counts and proportions of the "named" types (Styles I, I-II, II, II-III, and III) and excluding their nonspecific little brethren (or sistren).

Further refinements and subdivisions of Style III, arising from recent research at the NAN Ranch Ruin (Shafer and Taylor 1986) require larger portions of designs than those usually seen on sherds and therefore were not incorporated into the bulk sherd sorting categories discussed below. Relevant aspects of the NAN Ranch ceramic framework were recorded during the rim sherd study and are used to expand the discussion of the decorated sherds.

Typological Stratigraphy

Proportions of the principal decorated types in each grouped provenience are given in Table 3.4. "Intermediate" sorting categories (Styles I-II and II-III) are combined with the later type; thus Style I-II has been combined with Style II, and Style II-III with Style III. The sorting categories are combined chronologically "up" rather than "down," because arguments in the literature (discussed below) question the unusually high proportions of early types reported for Saige-

Table 3.3. Ceramic Sorting Categories

Sorting category	Description*
20	Plain white wares, Mimbres series
21	Mogollon Red-on-brown
22	Three Circle Red-on-white
30	Undifferentiated Mimbres series black-on-white
31	Style I Black-on-white
32	Indeterminate Style I-II
33	Style II Black-on-white
34	Indeterminate Style II-III
35	Style III Black-on-white
36	Mimbres Polychrome
37	Thick parallel lines, black-on-white fragment (Style I or II?)
38	Thin parallel lines, black-on-white fragment (Style II or III?)
39	Thick-line spiral, black-on-white fragment (Style I or II?)
40	Thin-line spiral, black-on-white fragment (Style II or III?)
41	Zigzag and scalloped black-on-white fragment (Style I or II?)
42	Negative design black-on-white fragment (Style III?)
OT	Other non-Mimbres decorated types
PLAIN	Alma plain and related types
SCORED	Alma scored, Alma punctate, and related types
CLAP	Clapboard corrugated
INDENT	Indented corrugated
RED	Slipped red wares, including San Francisco Red

*Additional description in Appendix B.

Table 3.4. Percentages of Typable Decorated Pottery by Grouped Provenience

Grouped provenience	Mogollon Red-on-brown	Three Circle Red-on-white	Black-on-white Style I	Styles I-II, II	Styles II-III, III	Total number of sherds
Room Block C	7.6	3.1	20.0	10.8	58.5	65
Room Block B	12.3	4.9	23.2	15.8	43.9	2007
Room Block A	6.1	3.5	33.4	18.1	38.9	509
Sub-B	12.8	4.7	37.2	19.8	25.5	358
Pit House 1 Upper	7.8	4.4	58.7	20.3	8.7	344
Pit House 3	20.9	7.9	48.7	19.9	2.6	191
Pit House 1 Lower	13.5	9.8	63.7	12.3	0.7	758

Note: Totals and percentages do not include sorting categories 20, 30, 37–42 (Table 3.3).

McFarland. The data in Table 3.4, if they are biased at all, inflate the proportions of later types and diminish the proportion of the earlier types.

Red-on-brown and Red-on-white Types

Mogollon Red-on-brown and Three Circle Red-on-white are two Late Pit House period types found at the Saige-McFarland Site. The dating and development of these types are not as well understood as we might like (Withers 1985a, 1985b; Lekson 1989). Although the total amount of red-on-brown at Saige-McFarland is miniscule (about 0.5% of the total sherds), Mogollon Red-on-brown makes up a remarkably high proportion of the later, Mimbres phase assemblages at the site, compared to other Mimbres sites.

The sherd sample from Galaz Ruin (in the Mimbres Valley) is about half the size of the Saige-McFarland collection, roughly comparable in temporal span, and contains almost the same proportion of red-on-brown (0.4%). However, at Galaz, almost all (85%) of the Mogollon Red-on-brown recovered came from San Francisco phase trash in the fill of just two pit structures (Anyon and LeBlanc 1984: 158). Mogollon Red-on-brown was almost nonexistent in other units at Galaz.

Although in general both Three Circle Red-on-white and Mogollon Red-on-brown decrease through time at Saige-McFarland (compare Pit House 1 Lower and Pit House 3 to later units in Table 3.4), they do not behave as one would expect from the traditional framework, or as they apparently behave in the Mimbres Valley. Indeed, Mogollon Red-on-brown forms a sizable portion of the later assemblages (12.3% of the decorated ceramics from Mimbres phase Room Block B). Red-on-brown types form a consistent element of all Mimbres assemblages at Saige-McFarland. Since analysts working in the Mimbres Valley seem certain that Mogollon Red-on-brown fades into virtual obscurity by Classic Mimbres times, the situation at Saige-McFlarland is perplexing.

Two explanations of the anomalous occurrence of red-on-brown pottery immediately come to mind: the stratigraphy of the site could be at fault, or the typology could be suspect.

First, the stratigraphy at the site could be so badly mixed that the distribution of early and late types is effectively "homogenized." Three Circle Red-on-white, another Late Pit House period type, co-occurs in all grouped proveniences. However, the Style I-II-III continuum behaves in proper and predictable stratigraphic fashion at the site, so although the stratigraphy at the site is not exactly pristine, neither has it been blended into extinction.

Regarding typology, if red-on-brown types did indeed make up a sizable portion of later (Mimbres phase) ceramic assemblages, the question becomes: is the pottery in fact Mogollon Red-on-brown? To the west of the Cliff Valley red-on-brown types of the San Simon and San Carlos series continued to be made long after the accepted demise of Mogollon Red-on-brown. Red-on-terracotta pottery was made and used to the east of the Mimbres area long after the

last Style III pot came out of the kiln. These red-on-brown types were a part of late Mogollon assemblages outside the Mimbres Valley. Could late Mogollon red-on-browns, or a local red-on-brown type, be represented in the Mimbres phase assemblages at Saige-McFarland? Or, could the Mogollon Red-on-brown sherds be misidentified examples of late western red-on-browns?

In my opinion, the red-on-brown sherds (other than those specifically identified as non-Mimbres types) conform more closely to the published descriptions of Mogollon Red-on-brown than to any other described red-on-brown type (see Appendix B). If my assessment is correct, then in the Gila Valley, red-on-brown pottery typologically similar to Mogollon Red-on-brown continued to be made after this style ceased to be made in the Mimbres Valley and in the Reserve area. This conclusion would be better substantiated if we had whole-vessel assemblages including red-on-brown vessels, but we do not.

As the data now stand, it seems more likely that high proportions of red-on-brown types in late contexts are the result of stratigraphic mixing, but what perverse little rodents they were to muddy red-on-brown waters while leaving the black-on-white stratigraphy recognizably intact. I can only suggest that the possibility of late red-on-brown types be considered in future work on the Upper Gila.

Mimbres Series Black-on-white Types

The main stratigraphic trend at Saige-McFarland tracks the sequence of Mimbres series black-on-white Styles I, II and III. The grouped proveniences in Table 3.4 are arranged by increasing frequencies of Style III and the corresponding decreasing frequencies of Style I (except Pit House 3, a small sample). Because Styles I, II, and III are by far the most abundant decorated types at the site and because they are chronologically sequent, the graphic device of a tripolar graph is an appropriate way to examine their stratigraphic relationships. In a tripolar graph, an ideal seriation of Style I, II, and III assemblages would form a sharp arc, beginning at the Style I vertex, curving sharply toward the Style II vertex, and ending at the Style III vertex.

Figure 3.1 shows a tripolar graph of the proportions of Style I, Style II, and Style III in each of the seven grouped provenience units. A linear pattern is formed from Pit House 1 Lower Fill (earliest) to Room Block C (latest), confirming the ordering of units in Table 3.4 but departing from the theoretically ideal arc. This linear pattern formed by the seven grouped proveniences suggests that either the Style II period is poorly represented at the site, or, more likely, stratigraphic recognition of Style II assemblages may be difficult at multicomponent sites like Saige-McFarland.

A Style II component is definitely present, but is masked in sherd assemblages at the resolution of grouped proveniences. Burial 2 vessels in Room Block A, in fact, form a temporally discrete Style II deposit. If Style II is a short-lived transition between more abundant Styles I and III, it may indeed be difficult to stratigraphically isolate Style II

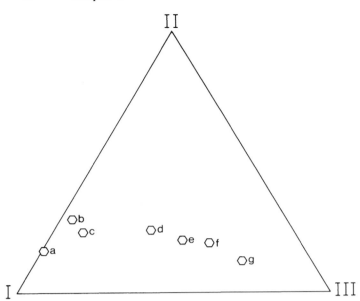

Figure 3.1. Tripolar graph of proportions of Mimbres Style I-II-III series, grouped proveniences. Each vertex equals 100 percent of the indicated style. *a*, Pit House 1 Lower; *b*, Pit House 3; *c*, Pit House 1 Upper; *d*, Sub-B; *e*, Room Block A; *f*, Room Block B; *g*, Room Block C.

assemblages. This is evidently the case in the Mimbres Valley, where there are no predominately Style II deposits in the Galaz Ruin sections (Anyon and LeBlanc 1984, Table 10.1). At Galaz, Style II makes up at most only 46 percent of the Style I-II-III continuum in any unit (and this 46% is in a stratigraphic unit with only 48 sherds). In units with over 100 sherds, Style II makes up at most only about 20 percent (Anyon and LeBlanc 1984, Tables 9.3, 9.6). A few "pure" stratigraphic assemblages of Style II have been defined at the NAN Ranch Ruin (Shafer 1987, 1988; Shafer and Taylor 1986), with its happy combination of good preservation and superb, long-term excavation.

Style II makes up at most about 28 percent of the decorated sherds from grouped proveniences at Saige-McFarland. Stratigraphy at a finer level than the grouped proveniences shows the Style II assemblage with greater clarity. The most useful vertical stratigraphy at the site comes from Room 12 of Room Block B. This large unit, with two floors, was constructed over earlier pit structures. The large size of the unit ensures relatively high numbers of sherds from all levels. Room 12 is the only stratigraphic situation at Saige-McFarland that appears to span the entire Style I-II-III sequence with sufficient numbers of sherds to make proportional comparison possible. Figure 3.2 demonstrates that within this unit, a series of three distinct proportional assemblages do indeed form an arc-like and less linear pattern: upper fill and floor levels of Room 12, along with Level 7 (immediately below the lower floor of Room 12) cluster in a Style III group; Level 8, just below Room 12, has relatively

more Style II; and Level 9, immediately above the floors of the pit structures, is strongly Style I.

The calculation of a "center point" (average value) for the Style III cluster, and the addition of a similar "center point" for the Pit House 1 and Pit House 3 grouped proveniences and the Room Block C values create an arc that approaches the expected curve, with the apex of this arc (Room 12, Level 8) approaching 45 percent on the Style II vertex. The 45 percent is not a "pure" Style II assemblage (as at the NAN Ranch Ruin), but it approximates Style II proportions at Galaz. Along with the Mimbres Valley archaeologists (Anyon and LeBlanc 1984), I suggest that an absence of "pure" Style II sherd assemblages at Saige-McFarland need not indicate an absence of a Style II temporal component, an important point dating construction and intial use of Room Block A.

Mimbres Classic Black-on-white

Mimbres Classic Black-on-white (Style III) was the single most common decorated type at Saige-McFarland, making up almost 30 percent of the decorated sherds at the site. Shafer and Taylor have defined a temporal series of rim attributes in Style III decoration. From early to late, these are: (1) "unbordered" designs, (2) "framed" designs, and (3) "extended rim lines" (Shafer and Taylor 1986: 60).

These attributes were not considered in the general typological anlysis at Saige-McFarland, but were recorded in the rim study. "Unbordered" designs continued to the rim, or to

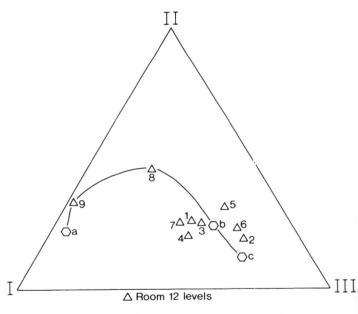

Figure 3.2. Tripolar graph of proportions of Mimbres Style I-II-III series, Room 12 and selected proveniences. Each vertex equals 100 percent of the indicated style. *a*, Mean center point of Pit Houses 1 and 3; *b*, mean center point of Room 12, Levels 1 through 7; *c*, Room Block C. Triangles indicate Room 12 levels.

a single line just below the rim (evidently continuing the layout of Style II). "Framed" designs had multiple parallel lines separating the design from the rim, typical of most Mimbres Classic Black-on-white. "Extended rim lines" were defined as "a lip band that carried over onto the interior and formed a thick rim band" (Shafer and Taylor 1986: 60), in effect replacing the multiple framing lines of earlier Style III bowls with a solid, very wide band.

Table 3.5. Style III Vessel Rim Attibutes by Grouped Provenience (Rim categories after Shafer and Taylor 1986)

Grouped provenience	Number of sherds			
	Unbordered	Framed	Extended rim line	Other
Room Block C	8	7		
Room Block B	134	304	8	6
Room Block A	37	43		3
Sub-B	17	31		
Pit House 1 Upper	10	24		
Pit House 3	5	1		

Note: Style III includes Styles II-III and III.
　　 Pit House 1 Lower had no Style III sherds.

Table 3.5 shows the occurrence of these attributes on Style II-III and III rim sherds for each grouped provenience. As would be expected, pit house proveniences (Pit House 1 Upper, Pit House 3, Sub-B) have few Style III rims (Pit House 1 Lower has none). Of greater typological interest are the proportions of earliest "unbordered" designs to the later "framed" designs in Room Blocks A and B, the two units with relatively large samples. The ratio of "unbordered" to "framed" rims in Room Block A is about 1:1, in Room Block B about 1:2. That is, there are proportionately more early, "unbordered" Style III rims in Room Block A than in Room Block B. The 1:2 ratio also characterizes the Style III of Sub-B and Pit House 1 Upper, and suggests that Style III sherds from those units are temporally closer to Room Block B than Room Block A.

The latest variation of Style III is marked by "extended rim lines," which were noted on only eight rim sherds, all from Room Block B. Four came from upper fill levels of Rooms 8, 11, and 12; four others came from levels immediately above the floor of Room 8 and from floor associations in Room 12 (Floors 1 and 2).

One further subdivision of Style III black-on-white has been proposed by LeBlanc and Khalil. They defined a subtype of Style III termed "flare rim bowls." They noted that "at present, the flare-rimmed shape is not known to have antecedents in Mimbres Bold Face" (LeBlanc and Khalil 1976: 296). Variations of this distinctive rim form were observed on 37 Mimbres white ware sherds or vessels at Saige-McFarland. Although the sample is small, the distribution of rim forms and the association of rim forms with decorative styles are of interest.

The "flare rim" as defined by LeBlanc and Khalil (1976, Fig. 1) explicitly included a range of rim forms. I divided this range into two classes: A, rims on which the junction of flare rim and the vessel body formed a visible line or crease on the bowl's exterior (LeBlanc and Khalil 1976, Fig. 1, examples C, D, E, H, I, and J); and B, rims on which this juncture was not visible (LeBlanc and Khalil 1976, Fig. 1, examples A and F). In form B the "flare" was shaped by a thickening of the interior wall just below the rim. Thickening frequently occurs on form A as well, and it is the visibility of the crease that is diagnostic. In addition to rim forms A and B, I also noted decorated white ware bowls with everted rims, an incurvate-excurvate ogee curve similar to the everted rims of many nondecorated jars. Thus, three rim forms on Mimbres white ware bowls from the site deviated from the much more common direct or slightly closed rims: A, flare rims with visible exterior creases (26 in Room Block B); B, flare rims with interior thickening (3 in Room Block A, 1 in Sub-B); and C, everted ogee rims (1 each in Room Blocks A and B; 2 in Sub-B; 3 in Pit House 1 Upper).

LeBlanc and Khalil note that the flare rim in the Mimbres Valley is found only on Style III vessels. This observation is confirmed at Saige-McFarland for rim form A, which is found only on Style III sherds and bowls and only in Room Block B. Rim form A sherds were found in upper fill, floor, and floor feature associations in this unit. Rim forms B and C were not found on Style III rims, but rather on Style I, II, and I-II sherds (and three indeterminate Mimbres white ware fragments). As indicated above, these sherds are found almost exclusively in the fill of pit house units (Pit House 1 Upper, Sub-B) or in floor contexts in Room Block A.

Although the sample is small, the associations of styles and rim forms and their distribution among the grouped proveniences are intriguing. In the Gila Valley, at least, the B (interior thickened) form of "flare rims" begins with Style I, and appears to be associated with an everted C form. As in the Mimbres Valley, the most exaggerated "flare rim" form A is clearly associated with Style III. Thus the present analysis largely confirms the earlier work of LeBlanc and Khalil, and perhaps refines the rim-form chronology for the Upper Gila.

The A form rim represented only about 7 percent of the Style III bowl rim sherds of Room Block B. Similarly, B and C forms represented 7 percent of the Style I and II bowl rim sherds from Room Block A. The number of Mimbres white ware rim sherds in Pit House 1 Upper and Sub-B are very small and the proportions may be meaningless; however, B and C forms represent 2 percent and 5 percent of Style I and II rim sherds in those units, respectively. In total, "flare" and everted rims of all three forms represent only about 2.5 percent of all Mimbres white ware bowl rims. Rim form A makes up precisely the same proportion of the total Style III rims at the site. These figures are much lower than the 13.6 percent frequency of flare rims in collections of Style III vessels and sherds from the Mimbres Valley (LeBlanc and Khalil 1976: 291).

Rim Sherds and Vessel Forms

The analysis of rim sherds was undertaken to estimate vessel form assemblages. Rim sherd counts do not translate directly into numbers of vessels and vessel assemblages. Initially, I hoped to use a "minimum number of individuals" (MNI) analytic framework that would combine rim sherds of each ware for vessels with the same diameter; however, few rim sherds in the collection were of sufficiently large arc for accurate estimation of diameter. Only 64 rim sherds were over 30° arc (and these 64 rims were significantly biased toward small and miniature vessels). Even combined with the measurable whole or partial vessels, the total rim sample of sufficient size to determine vessel MNI is less than 5 percent of the total number of rim sherds.

Although the total number of vessels represented by rim sherds could not be accurately estimated, varying proportions of vessel forms represented by rim sherds could be used to reflect gross differences in vessel form assemblages between grouped provenience units. The proportions of vessel forms and wares for the entire site are given in Table 3.6.

Table 3.6. Vessel Form-Ware Assemblage Composition Expressed as a Percentage of All Rims in the Matrix*

Ware	Bowls	Undifferentiated jars	Large jars	Small jars	Tecomates
Plain	6.1	11.9	3.2	2.0	1.5
Corrugated		2.3	5.9	1.3	
Red	10.7	0.1		0.5	0.8
Smudged-polished	5.5				
White	46.7		0.6	0.4	0.5

*Total number of rims = 3213. The sum of all values in the table equals 100 percent.

Of 25 possible combinations of wares and vessel forms, white ware bowls are by far the most frequent class (46.7% of all rims), followed by undifferentiated plain jars (11.9%) and red ware bowls (10.7%). These three classes alone equal over two-thirds of the rims. Several of the observed form-ware categories are too rare to be of much use in assemblage composition studies. Therefore, several categories were combined or eliminated to produce a more manageable "trimmed" array of data.

1. All plain and corrugated jar forms were combined. Sherds that could be assigned to vessel size classes (large and small) were fewer than sherds that could not. Because there were more undifferentiated jar rims than sized jar rims, the significance of the size differences was largely compromised by the number of undifferentiated sherds.

The large category of "plain undifferentiated jars" included many sherds from corrugated jars, since rims of corrugated jars were almost always smoothed. Thus, within the broad category of jars, the distinction between corrugated and plain rims was not useful in defining functional assemblages. Consequently, the plain and corrugated jar categories were combined to produce a larger and more useful group of "plain and corrugated jars" without reference to size.

2. Several rare vessel forms were eliminated for analysis of ware-form assemblages, including all categories in Table 3.6 with one percent or less of the total rims. Significantly, white ware jars (combining both large and small forms) totaled only one percent, a very low proportion for vessels commonly thought of as water jars, but not exceptional when compared to other Mimbres sites. At Galaz, white ware jar sherds (not limited to rims) made up only about 5 percent to 15 percent of decorated ceramics (Anyon and LeBlanc 1984: 160). Since jar rims, on the whole, represent orifices of smaller diameter than bowl rims, the Galaz percentage of rim to body sherds is probably consistent with the Saige-McFarland figures for rim sherds alone. The relatively rare but easily identified tecomate (seed jar) form was retained for summary tables, with rims of all wares combined. Table 3.7 summarizes this "trimmed" data.

Bowls

Bowls of all wares equal about two-thirds of the total rim sherd count (Table 3.7); within each of the seven grouped proveniences, bowls average about 67.4 percent (sd = 5.6). The variation in the proportion of bowls in each assemblage is relatively small, and does not indicate significant differences in proportions of bowls and jars among the grouped proveniences.

Bowls form a relatively constant proportion of the total vessel assemblage, but frequencies of different wares within the bowl form vary. White wares are by far the most common bowls, averaging 45 percent; the proportion of other wares in the bowl form varies. Two trends suggest that some of this variation is in part chronological. First, bowls with smudged and polished interiors are much more frequent in Room Blocks A, B, and C than in Pit House 1, Pit House 3, and Sub-B. This ware-form is a major component of later assemblages at the site. During comparable time periods, bowls with smudged and polished interiors are rare in the Mimbres Valley, but relatively common in the San Francisco Valley. Second, plain and red ware bowls are more frequent in the earlier pit structure units (Pit House 1 Lower and Pit House 3) than in later units. These two observations suggest that the difference in bowl wares may be temporal, with smudged-polished bowls replacing plain and red ware bowls through time.

Jars

Jars co-vary mechanically with bowls. The relative frequency of bowl to jar rim sherds at Saige-McFarland is almost precisely the opposite of the relative frequency of these vessel forms in all sherds (both body and rim sherds) at Galaz (Anyon and LeBlanc 1984, Table 9.3). If vessel form

Table 3.7. Vessel Form-Ware Assemblages Expressed as Percentages of Rims Within each Grouped Provenience

Grouped provenience	Plain %	Red %	Smudged-polished %	White %	Plain and corrugated jars %	Tecomates %	Total number of rims
Room Block C	3.7	1.9	5.5	48.1	38.9	1.9	54
Room Block B	5.5	7.9	7.3	51.3	25.3	2.7	1646
Room Block A	7.7	9.1	12.3	35.1	34.5	1.3	316
Sub-B	7.4	11.4	3.0	49.5	21.8	6.9	202
Pit House 1 Upper	1.6	7.8	0.2	53.8	33.8	2.8	320
Pit House 3	13.3	18.5	2.0	33.3	30.8	2.1	195
Pit House 1 Lower	7.4	21.7	0.6	45.1	22.3	2.9	448

Note: Some trenches not included.

assemblages differ dramatically between the Mimbres and the Upper Gila, this difference would be important indeed; however, I suspect (but cannot demonstrate) that the difference reflects the differing measures: all sherds versus rim sherds.

Tecomates

Tecomates (seed jars) make up a small but consistent proportion of all vessel form assemblages, ranging from about 2 percent to 3 percent. The only exception is provenience Sub-B, where tecomate rims make up almost 7 percent of the vessel assemblage. Sub-B also has the lowest proportion of jars of any grouped provenience, suggesting that tecomates replaced jar forms in this provenience or that the Sub-B vessel assemblage differed functionally from other assemblages at Saige-McFarland.

Vessel Assemblages

Whereas the rim sherds offer information on vessel form assemblages within grouped proveniences, whole or partial vessels are much more specific temporal and functional indicators. Vessel assemblages are discussed by grouped provenience, ordered by subfloor features, floor and fill divisions, as appropriate. Table 3.8 lists the provenience, classification, and diameter for the whole and partial vessels.

ROOM BLOCK A
(Figs. 3.3–3.8, 3.15, 3.16)
Features

About two-thirds of the Block A whole and partial vessels came from a single burial, Feature 14, below the floor of Room 4A. This cache consisted of 22 vessels. The 18 decorated vessels, almost all of Style II Black-on-white, represented a diverse series of unusual forms, including two large bowls, six small bowls, five small shallow bowls or plates, two small closed bowls, one straight-walled ("flowerpot") bowl, two small narrow-necked jars, and one small effigy jar (Figs. 3.5–3.8).

The black-on-white decorations on the two narrow-necked jars (Vessels 11 and 22) and the effigy jar (Vessel 21) are problematic, but are certainly not Style III; two vessels are Style I (Vessels 12 and 14); all others are clearly Style II. The decorative treatment on the vessels is not conspicuously uniform, and there is no compelling reason to think that they were all decorated by the same hand, although it is certainly possible.

The forms of the "utility" vessels in the cache are no less unusual. They include parts of two small corrugated jars with identical, friable pastes (Vessels 29 and 32). Both have similar surface texturing. The third "utility" vessel is the base of a jar (Vessel 30), with a paste much like that of Vessels 29 and 32, decorated with a pattern of fingernail punctations. The last vessel from Feature 14 is one-third of a small red ware bowl (Vessel 31) of unusual, composite shape.

Not one of these vessels was found intact, and only one (Vessel 28) was completely reconstructible. It is unlikely that more were originally complete or nearly complete. One sherd of Vessel 22 was found high in the fill of Room 4A, but no additional sherds of these distinctive vessels were found in the nearly complete (and almost entirely screened) excavation of Room Block A. Interestingly, the fragmentary vessels do not appear to be worn or heavily used and the breaks all appear remarkably "fresh." It is only the two large bowls (Vessels 27 and 28), which are also the two most complete vessels, that show any signs of use and wear. I believe that at least 12 and perhaps as many as 20 of these vessels were deposited with the burial as half vessels, which raises two obvious questions: why halves of vessels, and where are the other halves? I cannot answer either question, but I suspect that the answers probably involve burial ritual rather than postoccupational processes.

The chronological significance of the vessels in the Feature 14 cache lies in their stylistic homogeneity, clearly a Style II assemblage, and in their positive and unambiguous association with the use of Room Block A. Feature 14 originated from the floor level of Room 4A, and Feature 14 clearly postdates construction of the west wall of that room, since the ceramic cache was placed in a niche partially carved into the base of the wall.

Table 3.8. Provenience, Classification, and Rim Diameters of Whole and Partial Vessels

Vessel number	Figure number	Provenience		Type and Form	Rim diameter (in cm)	Arc (degrees)
1	3.3, 3.4	Room Block A	Fill	Clapboard Corrugated jar	22	120
2	3.3, 3.4	Room Block A	Fill	Clapboard Corrugated jar	9	130
3	3.3, 3.4	Room 1	Fill	Clapboard Corrugated jar	23	100
4	3.3, 3.4	Room 1	Fill	Clapboard Corrugated jar	20	120
5	3.3, 3.4	Room 1	Levels 1–3	Clapboard Corrugated jar	19	190
6	3.3, 3.4	Room 4A	Floor	Clapboard Corrugated jar	21	130
7	3.3, 3.4	Room 5	Level 2	Clapboard Corrugated jar	?	15
8	3.3, 3.4	Room 5	Level 2	Indented Corrugated jar	?	15
9	3.3, 3.4	Room 4A	Floor	Plain bowl, smudged and polished interior	24	90
10	3.3, 3.4	Room 4A	Floor	Style III black-on-white tecomate	10	180
11	3.5, 3.6	Room 4A	Feature 14	Style II(?) black-on-white jar	?	?
12	3.5, 3.6	Room 4A	Feature 14	Style I black-on-white bowl	17	140
13	3.5, 3.6	Room 4A	Feature 14	Style II-III black-on-white bowl	7	130
14	3.5, 3.6	Room 4A	Feature 14	Style I black-on-white bowl	10	260
15	3.5, 3.6	Room 4A	Feature 14	Style II black-on-white bowl	12	190
16	3.5, 3.6	Room 4A	Feature 14	Style I-II black-on-white bowl	13	?
17	3.5, 3.6	Room 4A	Feature 14	Style I-II black-on-white bowl	10	240
18	3.5, 3.6	Room 4A	Feature 14	Style II black-on-white bowl	16	110
19	3.5, 3.6	Room 4A	Feature 14	Style II black-on-white bowl	15	170
20	3.5, 3.6	Room 4A	Feature 14	Style II black-on-white bowl	18	90
21	3.5, 3.6	Room 4A	Feature 14	Style II black-on-white effigy jar	?	?
22	3.5, 3.6	Room 4A	Feature 14	Style II(?) black-on-white pitcher	5	330
23	3.7, 3.8	Room 4A	Feature 14	Style II black-on-white bowl	12	310
24	3.7, 3.8	Room 4A	Feature 14	Style II black-on-white bowl	17	200
25	3.7, 3.8	Room 4A	Feature 14	Style II black-on-white bowl	17	35
26	3.7, 3.8	Room 4A	Feature 14	Style II black-on-white bowl	26	45
27	3.7, 3.8	Room 4A	Feature 14	Style II black-on-white bowl	28	200
28	3.7, 3.8	Room 4A	Feature 14	Style II black-on-white bowl	27	360
29	3.7, 3.8	Room 4A	Feature 14	Clapboard Corrugated jar	8	60
30	3.7, 3.8	Room 4A	Feature 14	Punctated jar	?	?
31	3.7, 3.8	Room 4A	Feature 14	Unknown red ware bowl	13	100
32	3.7, 3.8	Room 4A	Feature 14	Clapboard Corrugated and punctated jar	8	270
33	3.11, 3.12	Room 10	Level 5	Style III black-on-white bowl	18	60
34	3.11, 3.12	Room 11	Level 4	Style I-II black-on-white scoop	--	--
35	3.11, 3.12	Room 11	Feature 34	Style III black-on-white bowl	26	80
36	3.11, 3.12	Room 8	Levels 5–6	Style III black-on-white bowl	22	40
37	3.11, 3.12	Room 11	Feature 32	Style III black-on-white bowl	29	45
38	3.11, 3.12	Rooms 11, 14	Fill	Indented Corrugated jar	17	280

Table 3.8. Provenience, Classification, and Rim Diameters of Whole and Partial Vessels

Vessel number	Figure number	Provenience		Type and Form	Rim diameter (in cm)	Arc (degrees)
39	3.11, 3.12	Room 12	Feature 43	Clapboard Corrugated jar	18	45
40	3.11, 3.12	Room 12	Feature 43	Corrugated bowl, smudged and polished interior	37	60
41	3.9, 3.10	Room 12	Feature 65	Plain bowl, smudged and polished interior	25	360
42	3.15, 3.16	Room 12	Feature 76	Style II black-on-white bowl	30	165
43	3.9, 3.10	Room 12	Feature 49	Style III black-on-white bowl	19	60
44	3.9, 3.10	Room 12	Feature 45	Plain bowl, smudged and polished interior	13	360
45*	3.9, 3.10	Room 12	Feature 45	Clapboard Corrugated jar	8	360
46*	3.9, 3.10	Room 12	Feature 47	Clapboard Corrugated jar	?	?
47*	3.15, 3.16	Room 12	Feature 75	Punctated jar	3	360
48*	3.9, 3.10	Room 12	Feature 65	Style III black-on-white tecomate	20	360
49*	3.9, 3.10	Room 12	Feature 47	Style III black-on-white bowl	22	360
50*	3.9, 3.10	Room 12	Feature 64	Style III black-on-white bowl	29	360
51*	3.9, 3.10	Room 12	Feature 49	Style III black-on-white tecomate	15	360
52*	3.9, 3.10	Room 12	Feature 49	Style III black-on-white tecomate	16	360
53*	3.13, 3.14	Room 14	Feature 69	Clapboard Corrugated jar	17	185
54*	3.13, 3.14	Room 14	Feature 69	Clapboard Corrugated jar	17	360
55*	3.13, 3.14	Room 14	Feature 69	Clapboard Corrugated jar	22	360
56	3.13, 3.14	Room 14	Feature 69	Clapboard Corrugated jar	23	205
57*	3.13, 3.14	Room 14	Feature 69	Clapboard Corrugated jar	20	360
58	3.13, 3.14	Room 14	Feature 69	Corrugated bowl, smudged and polished interior	20	220
59	3.13, 3.14	Room 14	Feature 69	Clapboard Corrugated jar	6	360
60	3.13, 3.14	Room 14	Feature 69	Clapboard Corrugated jar	7	180
61	3.13, 3.14	Room 14	Feature 69	Corrugated bowl, smudged and polished interior	11	310
62	3.13, 3.14	Room 14	Feature 69	Clapboard Corrugated jar	25	250
63	3.13, 3.14	Room 14	Feature 69	Clapboard Corrugated jar	4	140
64*	3.15	Room 14	Feature 69	White ware jar base (scoop)	?	?
65	3.11 3.12	Room 15	Level 4	Plain bowl, smudged and polished interior	29	65
66	3.11 3.12	Room 15	Level 6	Corrugated bowl, smudged and polished interior	22	160
67	3.15, 3.16	N620 E510	Level 5	Style I black-on-white bowl	27	160
68	3.15, 3.16	Pit House 3	Level 7	Plain bowl, smudged and polished interior	26	140
69	3.15, 3.16	Pit House 3	Levels 8–10	Clapboard Corrugated jar	?	?
70	3.15, 3.16	Pit House 3	Levels 8–10	Clapboard Corrugated jar	24	120
71*	3.9, 3.10	Room 12	Feature 64	Unknown red ware tecomate	16	360
72	3.3, 3.4	Room Block A	Fill	Plain bowl, smudged and polished interior	23	65
73*	3.15, 3.16	Room 12	Feature 78(?)	Corrugated bowl, smudged and polished interior	15	360
74	3.15, 3.16	Room 4A	Feature 14(?)	Three Circle Red-on-white bowl	14	165
75	3.15, 3.16	Unknown		Corrugated bowl, smudged and polished interior	18	85

*Vessels not in the 1987 collections; dimensions taken from photographs.

Figure 3.3. Vessels from Room Block A, fill and floor proveniences. Vessels are not to scale; see Figure 3.4 for size and type classification.

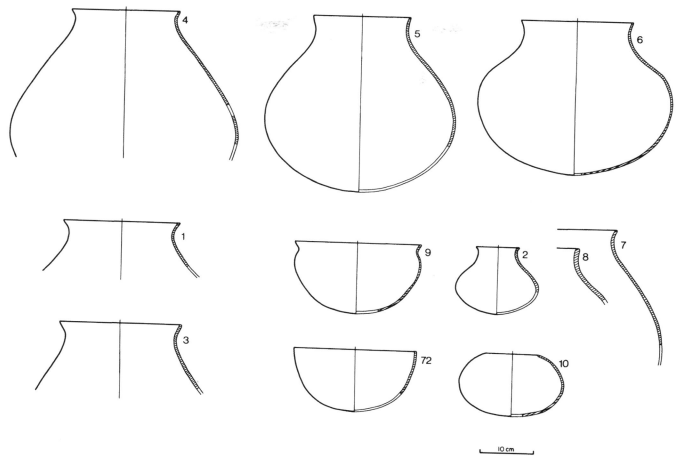

Figure 3.4. Profiles of vessels from Room Block A, fill and floor proveniences. Hachure in section indicates portion of vessel present; vessels without center-lines are drawn from photographs. Clapboard Corrugated jars (Vessels 1–7), Indented Corrugated jar (Vessel 8), Plain bowls with smudged and polished interiors (Vessels 9 and 72), Style III black-on-white tecomate (Vessel 10).

Floors

On the floor level of Room 4A (from which Feature 14 originated) were three partial vessels (Figs. 3.3, 3.4): a nearly complete corrugated jar (Vessel 6); about one-third of a flare-rim bowl with smudged-polished interior (Vessel 9); and half of a Style III tecomate (Vessel 10). This assemblage appears to date later than the Feature 14 cache. If the Style III floor assemblage dates Room Block A, it would be necessary to argue that the Feature 14 vessels represent heirlooms or stylistic anachronisms specific to mortuary ceremony. The alternative, which I prefer, dates Room Block A construction and initial use to the period of Style II Black-on-white, with the rooms continuing in use into the Style III period.

Two partial corrugated jars (Vessels 7 and 8, Figs. 3.3, 3.4) were recovered from Room 5, probably from the floor. These both appear to be big sherds rather than complete vessels. The overall corrugation indicates a relatively late ceramic period (probably Mimbres phase) for the final use or abandonment of Room Block A.

Fill

Postabandonment use of Room Block A may have been either as a storage area or dump for the occupants of later Mimbres room blocks (perhaps Room Block B). There are portions of five corrugated jars (Vessels 1–5) and part of a bowl with a smudged and polished interior (Vessel 72, Figs. 3.3, 3.4) in the upper fill of Room 1 (or other nearby rooms). Considering the unsystematic nature of recovery in these upper levels, it is possible that more of these vessels were originally present. If whole vessels when deposited, they must have been placed on the fill of a room already collapsed or on the roof of a nearby room. They were not on the floor of Room 1 because burned remains of the roof were observed stratigraphically below these vessels.

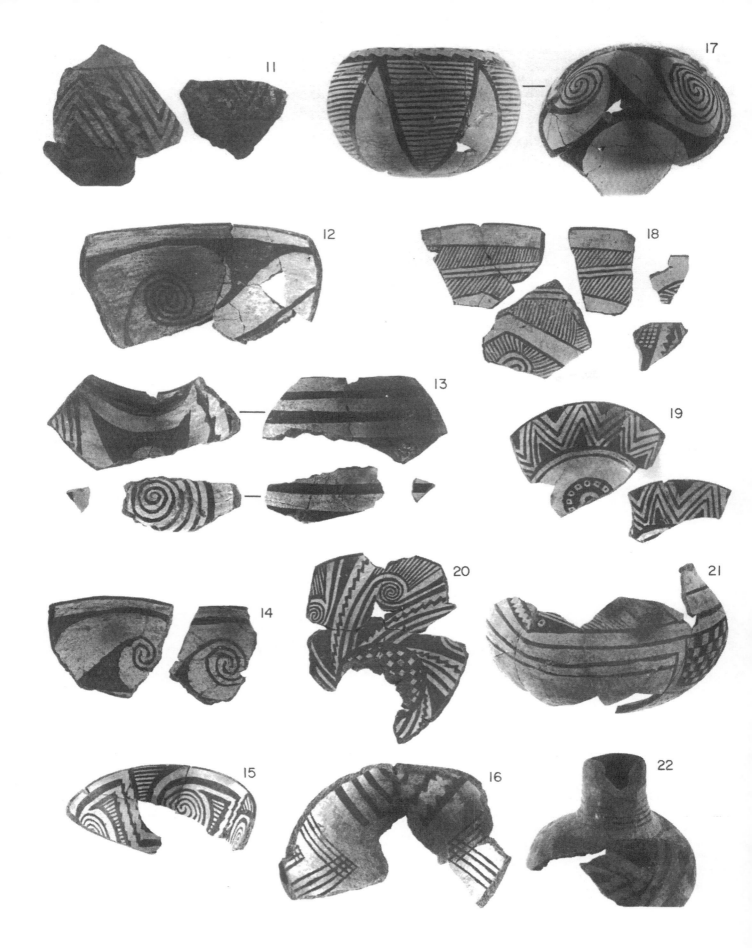

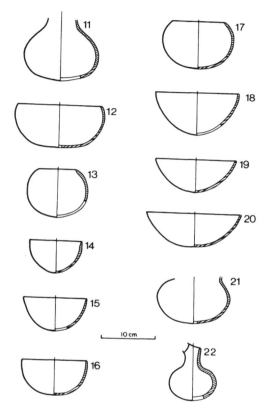

Figure 3.6. Profiles of vessels from Room Block A, Room 4A, Feature 14, Burial 2. Hachure in section indicates portion of vessel present; vessels without centerlines are drawn from photographs. Style I black-on-white bowls (Vessels 12 and 14), Style I-II black-on-white bowls (Vessels 16 and 17), Style II black-on-white bowls (Vessels 15, 18–20, 21), Style II(?) black-on-white jar (Vessel 11) and pitcher (Vessel 22), Style II-III black-on-white bowl (Vessel 13).

Figure 3.5. Vessels from Room Block A, Room 4A, Feature 14, Burial 2. Vessels are not to scale; see Figure 3.6 for size and type classification.

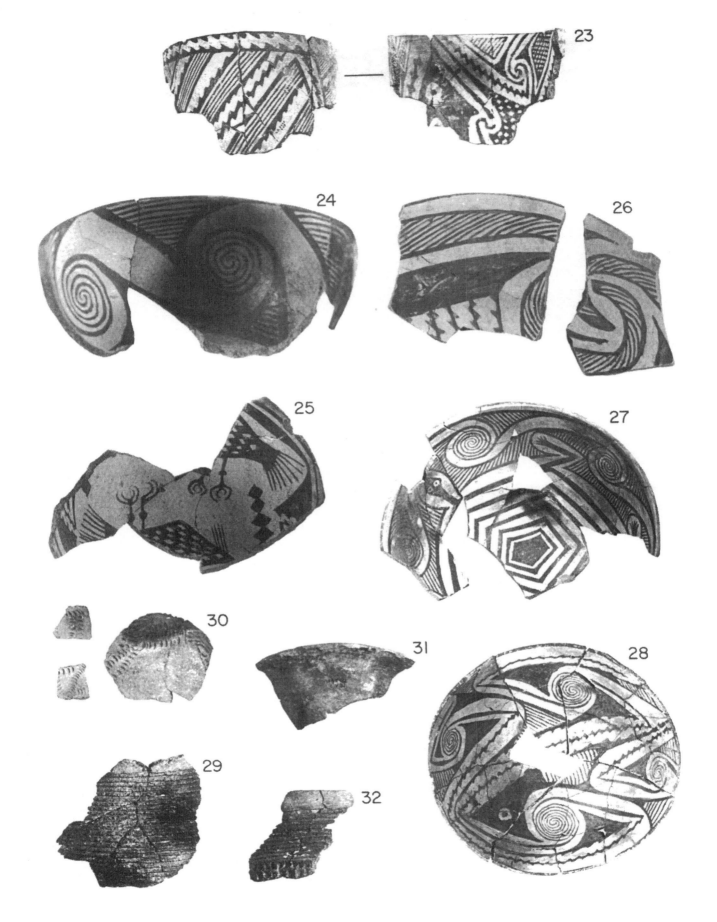

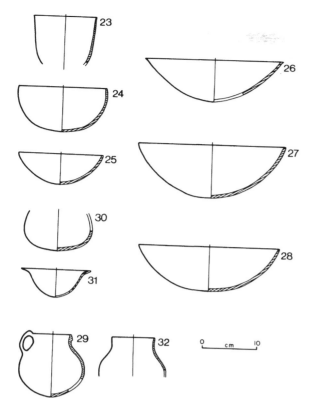

Figure 3.8. Profiles of vessels from Room Block A, Room 4A, Feature 14, Burial 2. Hachure in section indicates portion of vessel present. Style II black-on-white bowls (Vessels 23–28), Clapboard Corrugated jar (Vessel 29), Punctated jar base (Vessel 30), unknown red ware bowl (Vessel 31), Clapboard Corrugated and Punctated jar (Vessel 32).

Figure 3.7. Vessels from Room Block A, Room 4A, Feature 14, Burial 2. Vessels are not to scale; see Figure 3.8 for size and type classification.

ROOM BLOCK B
(Figs. 3.9–3.14)

Features

Burials, all in Room 12, definitely associate the use of that room with a Style III Black-on-white assemblage (Figs. 3.9, 3.10). Since some of the Style III vessels came from burials associated with earlier Floor 2, we can be reasonably certain that construction of later Floor 1 was associated with Style III. These vessels include five Style III bowls and jars, two smudged-polished interior bowls, one red ware tecomate, and two small corrugated jars.

Floors

A number of vessels were found on floors or just above floors in the rooms of Room Block B. Presumably, these vessels (Figs. 3.11, 3.12) represent a last-use assemblage for the room block. They include four Style III bowls (Vessels 33, 35, 36, 37). In all four cases, the bowls were not complete; rather, the vessels are represented by large sherds that may have been used as tools. Vessel 33 was clearly a large sherd reused as a scoop; Vessels 35 and 37 probably had similar functions. Two of these vessels (Vessels 33 and 36) were from flare-rim bowls.

Two other partial utility vessels from floors are a corrugated jar (Vessel 39) and about one-third of a huge corrugated bowl with smudged-polished interior (Vessel 40). Both were found on the upper floor of Room 12, scattered around the firepit (Feature 43).

The most dramatic floor assemblage from Room Block B included the 12 vessels on the floor of Room 14 (Feature 69). At least nine were complete; three are represented in the collection by large portions of vessels, and these, too, could have been whole (Figs. 3.13–3.14). These included six whole or partial large corrugated jars, two small corrugated jars, two small bowls with smudged-polished interiors, one miniature corrugated jar, and the base of one white ware jar (Fig. 3.15). The style of surface texture on these utility vessels (all-over corrugation) suggests a late (Mimbres phase) association.

Fill

Three partial vessels came from the upper fill of rooms in Room Block B. These included a fragment of a very worn Style I scoop (Vessel 34), most of a large indented corrugated jar (Vessel 38), and about one-third of a corrugated bowl with smudged-polished interior (Vessel 66; Figs. 3.11, 3.12). The indented pattern on the corrugated bowl is consistent with a Mimbres phase association for the materials from the upper fill of Room Block B.

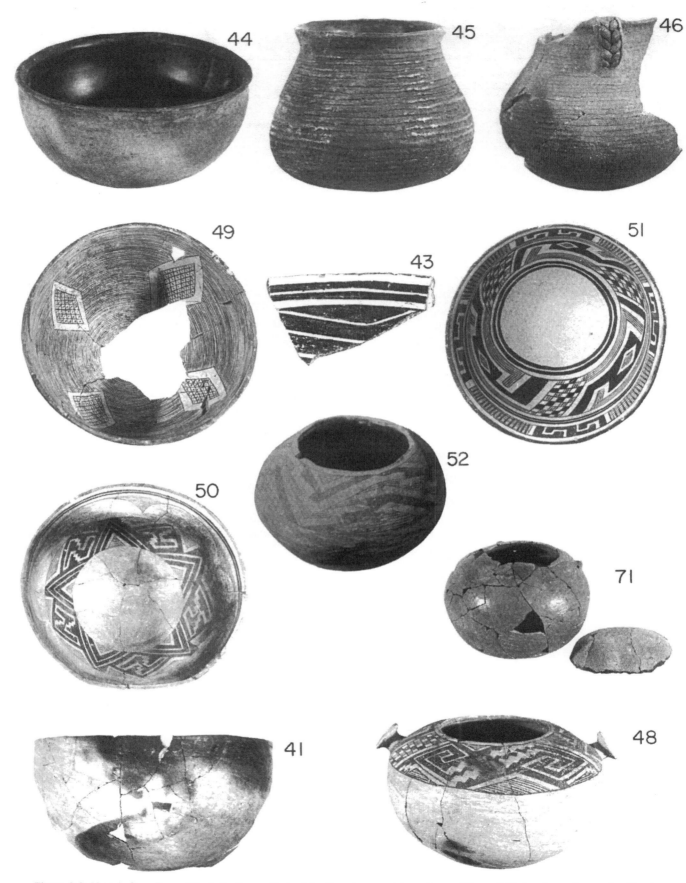

Figure 3.9. Vessels from Room Block B, Room 12, burials. Vessels are not to scale; see Figure 3.10 for size and type classification.

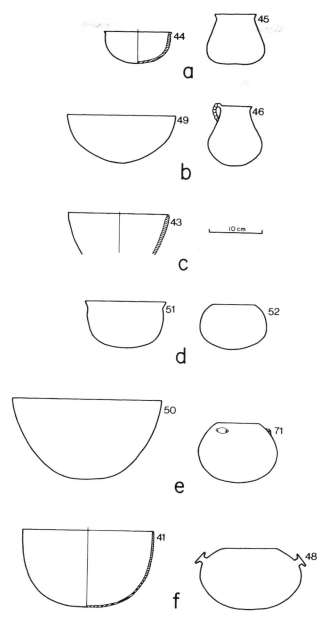

Figure 3.10. Profiles of vessels from Room Block B, Room 12: *a*, Burial 11; *b*, Burial 4; *c*, Burial 6(?); *d*, Burial 6; *e*, Burial 10; *f*, Burial 7. Hachure in section indicates portion of vessel present; vessels without centerlines are drawn from photographs. Plain bowls with smudged and polished interiors (Vessels 41 and 44), Clapboard Corrugated jars (Vessels 45 and 46), Style II-III black-on-white bowl (Vessel 49), Style III black-on-white bowls (Vessels 43, 50, 51) and tecomates (Vessels 48 and 52), unknown red ware tecomate (Vessel 71).

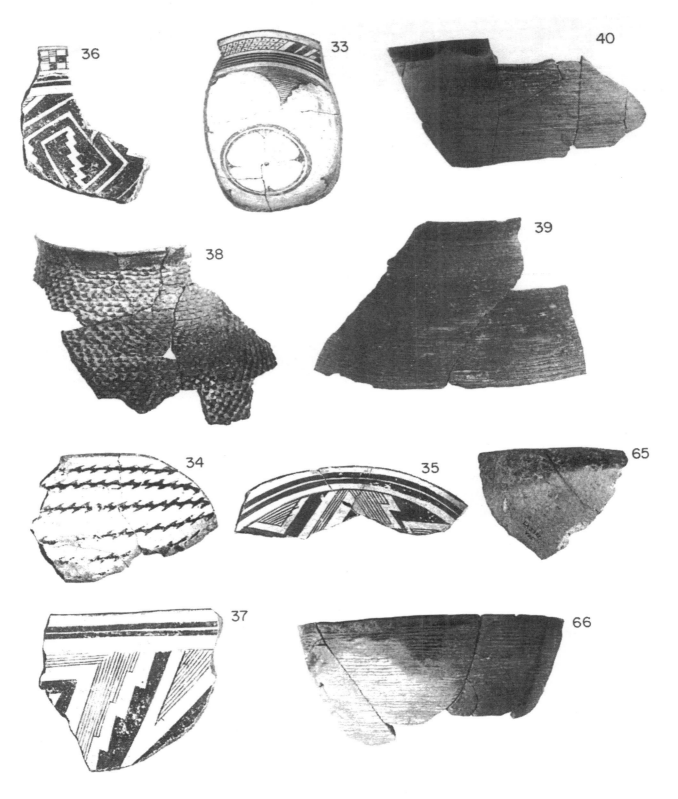

Figure 3.11. Vessels from Room Block B, fill and floor proveniences. Vessels are not to scale; see Figure 3.12 for size and type classification.

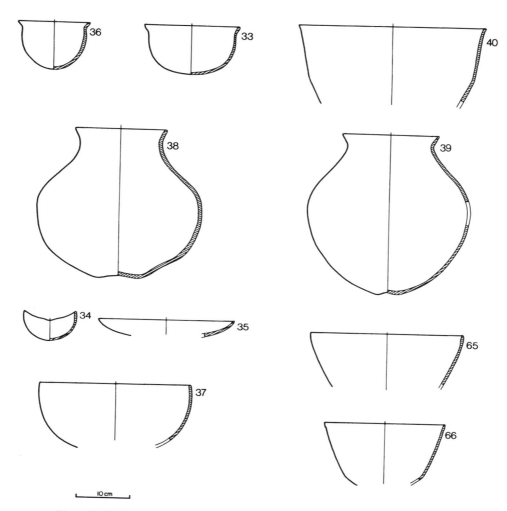

Figure 3.12. Profiles of vessels from Room Block B, fill and floor proveniences. Hachure in section indicates portion of vessel present. Clapboard Corrugated jar (Vessel 39), Indented Corrugated jar (Vessel 38), Corrugated bowls with smudged and polished interiors (Vessels 40 and 66), plain bowl with smudged and polished interior (Vessel 65), Style I-II black-on-white scoop (Vessel 34), Style III black-on-white bowls (Vessels 33, 35–37).

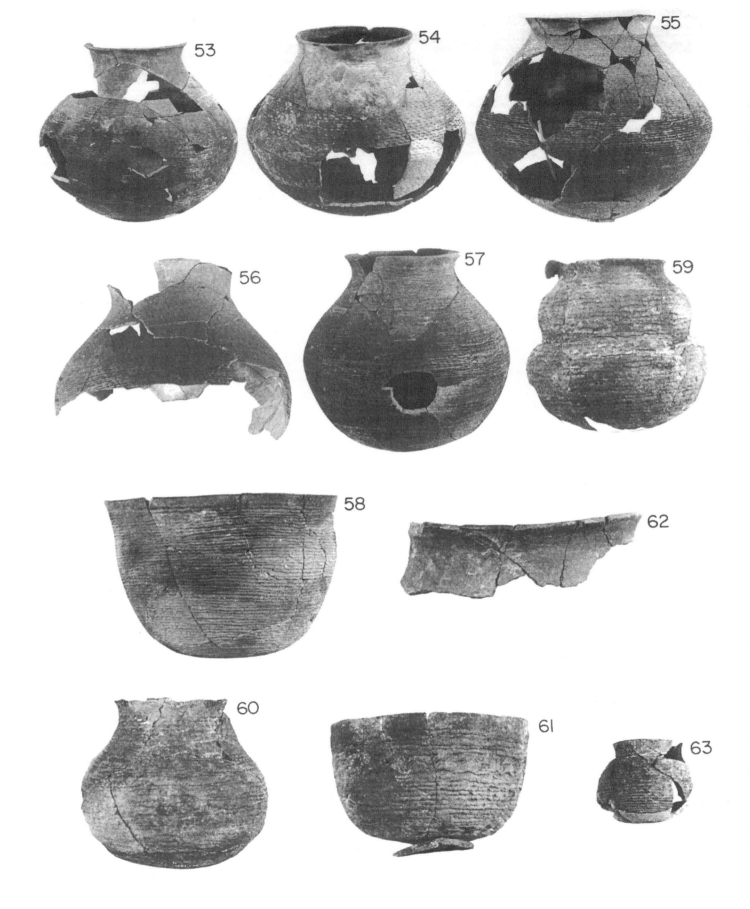

10 cm

Figure 3.14. Profiles of vessels from Room Block B, Room 14, Feature 69 floor assemblage. Hachure in section indicates portion of vessel present; vessels without centerlines are drawn from photographs. Clapboard Corrugated jars (Vessels 53–57, 59, 60, 62, 63), Corrugated bowls with smudged and polished interiors (Vessels 58 and 61).

Figure 3.13. Vessels from Room Block B, Room 14, Feature 69 floor assemblage. Vessels are not to scale; see Figure 3.14 for size and type classification.

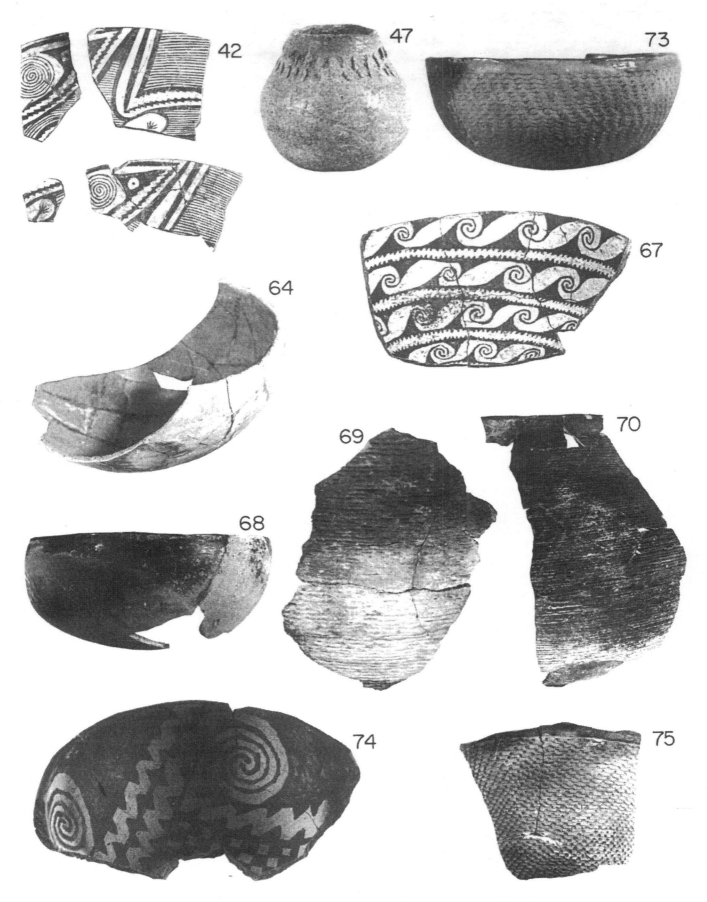

Figure 3.15. Vessels from pit houses and various proveniences. Vessels
are not to scale; see Figure 3.16 for size and type classification.

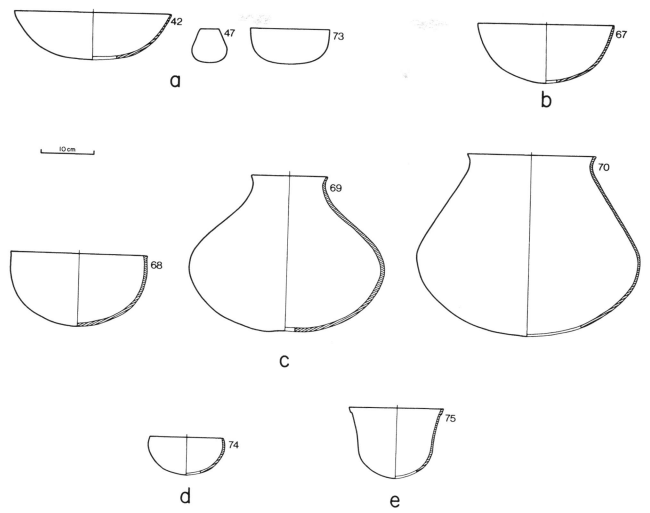

Figure 3.16. Profiles of vessels from Sub-B (*a*), Pit House 1 Fill (*b*), Pit House 3 Fill (*c*), probably Feature 14 in Room 4A (*d*), and unknown provenience (*e*). Hachure in section indicates portion of vessel present; vessels without centerlines are drawn from photographs. Style II black-on-white bowl (Vessel 42), Punctated jar (Vessel 47), Corrugated bowls with smudged and polished interiors (Vessels 73 and 75), Style I black-on-white bowl (Vessel 67), Plain bowl with smudged and polished interior (Vessel 68), Clapboard Corrugated jars (Vessels 69 and 70), Three Circle Red-on-white bowl (Vessel 74). Vessel 64 is the base of a white ware jar used as a scoop (no profile).

SUB-B
(Figs. 3.15, 3.16)

As noted above in the discussion of typological stratigraphy, the fill of the pit structures below Room Block B (grouped provenience Sub-B) contained a mixed sherd assemblage. Three vessels were recovered from or just above floors of the structures below Room 12 (Figs. 3.15, 3.16); these, too, represent a "mixed" assemblage. Two vessels associated with 12-NE are consistent with a Three Circle phase assemblage: part of a Style II Black-on-white bowl (Vessel 42) and a small, plain jar with punctate decoration around the rim (Vessel 47) containing a large cache of beads (recorded as Feature 75). Vessel 47 sat, upright, directly on the

floor of 12-NE, and may represent some form of abandonment ritual for that unit.

The third vessel (Vessel 73; Figs. 3.15, 3.16) from Sub-B came from the floor of 12-SW. The provenience of Vessel 73 is tenuous, and was determined (in 1987) through a process of elimination. Possible provenience error is important, in that Vessel 73 is an indented corrugated bowl with smudged-polished interior, a type normally associated with Mimbres phase or later assemblages. The presence of Vessel 73 on the floor of 12-SW is alarming, because Style III Black-on-white was rare or absent in lower levels of the structures below Room 12. The bowl may be part of the Style II assemblage of Sub-B, or perhaps it represents later materials deposited during the filling of 12-SW prior to Room 12 construction.

PIT HOUSE 1
(Figs. 3.15, 3.16)

Pit House 1 produced only one vessel, half of a Style I bowl that may have been used as a scoop (Vessel 67; Figs. 3.15, 3.16). It was found in the upper fill of the unit. No whole or partial vessels were found on the floor of Pit House 1.

PIT HOUSE 3
(Figs. 3.15, 3.16)

Three partial vessels were found in Pit House 3 fill (Figs. 3.15, 3.16): a plain bowl with smudged-polished interior (Vessel 68) and portions of two large corrugated jars (Vessels 69 and 70). All three vessels were in fill well above the floor. The excavator suggested that these were associated with roof fall from this structure.

LITHICS

Lithic artifacts from the Saige-McFarland Site included chipped stone, ground stone, stone slabs, minerals, and ornaments. The few shell artifacts recovered are described under ornaments.

Chipped-stone Artifacts

Over 15,000 pieces of chipped stone were inventoried from Saige-McFarland. The field inventory divided chipped stone counts into three material classes (Fitting and others 1971): "coarse," including volcanic rocks such as basalts and rhyolites; "agate," including cherts, chalcedonies, and other cryptocrystalline rocks; and "obsidian." Bifacially flaked tools (almost exclusively projectile points) were also tallied, but no further formal divisions were recorded.

The collection was subsequently arranged into projectile points, "finished artifacts," and "unmodified chippage." Projectile points were separated for a detailed analysis that was never completed, and they are now unfortunately lost. Drawings of some of the projectile points, made by me in 1971, are presented in Figure 3.17. "Finished artifacts" (mainly cores and retouched flakes) were boxed and stored separately from the "unmodified chippage." The "finished artifacts" from Room Blocks A and B were reunited with the collections in 1987, but the "finished artifacts" from Pit House 1 and Pit House 3 are apparently lost.

A descriptive analysis of most of the "unmodified chippage," using more detailed material and formal categories developed by James E. Fitting and David Anderson (Appendix C), was completed by George Sabo III during the 1970s. Sabo's data from Room Blocks A, B, and C, and parts of Pit House 1 form the basis for Appendix C. His analysis was supplemented by descriptive lists enclosed in the individual bags of "finished artifacts" (probably prepared by Sabo as well) and by a similar analysis of the floor and subfloor materials of Room 12 by Elizabeth Skinner (1974). A few additional bags that had never been analyzed (mainly from Pit House 1 Lower) were discovered in 1987. I completed the analysis of these materials.

The present discussion centers on the distribution of the kinds of lithic materials used and largely ignores tool assemblages, although comments are offered on individual tool types and their distributions throughout the site. This emphasis reflects my doubts about the completeness of tool data, particularly the "finished artifacts." Although almost all projectile points and other bifacially flaked tools are now missing, limited distributional and material data are available from the field tallies. Because both the analysis and the collection of tools are less than complete, I was disinclined to invest a great deal of time on tool assemblages beyond the few observations offered later.

Comparisons of field inventories and analysis counts indicate that items are missing from Rooms 4A, 7A and 7B, and from Room 12, Level 6 (the fill between Floors 2 and 1). The situation in the upper fills of Rooms 10 and 11 is also confused. The uppermost three levels of Room 10 are represented in the analyses by far fewer flakes than were recorded in the field inventories; the reverse is true in the uppermost two levels of Room 11. I suspect that some artifacts from Rooms 10 and 11 were mislabeled either on the bags, on the analysis forms, or both.

Despite these problems, lithic data are available from almost all of the grouped proveniences, the only important exception being Pit House 3. In discussions of *total numbers* of chipped stone items, I use the totals from the various analyses unless (1) no analysis exists or (2) the field inventory total is 15 percent or more larger than totals in the analyses totals, an arbitrary amount intended to correct for missing items or incomplete analyses.

Material Composition

The material types used in Upper Gila Project analyses were never lithologically defined in print. I have combined several of the Upper Gila Project material categories (Appendix C) to ensure comparability among the several analysts whose work is reported here and to make the Upper Gila Project's material types better conform with standard geologic definitions.

Table 3.9 summarizes the material composition of lithic assemblages for the grouped provenience units. The sample from Room Block C is exceptionally small; 31 flakes represent less than one-third of the flakes listed in field inventories, and the proportions of material types in the 1987 sample are at odds with those listed in the field inventory (Fitting and others 1971, Table 41). For these reasons, Room Block C data probably should be disregarded.

The sample from "Pit House 1 Fill" is not precisely the same as grouped provenience Pit House 1 Upper, the unit used in the ceramic analysis. Lithic data from the units combined in Pit House 1 Upper were not available in 1987. Data were available, however, from the East and West trenches and from the entrance of Pit House 1, and they are combined here as "Pit House 1 Fill." I believe that the lithics from these combined proveniences are representative of the lithics from the fill of Pit House 1.

Table 3.9. Percentages of Lithic Materials by Grouped Proveniences
(No data are available from Pit House 3)

Grouped provenience	Material					Number of specimens
	Basalt %	Andesite %	Chert %	Chalcedony %	Obsidian %	
Room Block C*	3.2	6.5	25.8	61.3	3.2	31
Room Block B	13.3	11.3	18.7	40.7	16.0	8681
Room Block A	16.3	18.0	20.5	36.1	9.1	1322
Sub-B	15.6	15.7	32.4	27.9	8.4	1125
Pit House 1 Fill†	36.7	25.2	11.7	23.1	3.3	961
Pit House 1 Lower	24.7	13.6	17.9	37.9	6.3	736

Note: Some trenches not included.
* Incomplete sample.
†Pit House 1 Fill consists of P1 East and West trenches, and Pit House 1 Entrance (see text).

Core materials reflect, in general, the proportions of materials used in the larger flake sample from each grouped provenience. In Pit House 1 Lower, Room Block A, and Room Block B, cores are predominately of cryptocrystalline materials, and "fine" materials equal about 75 percent to 80 percent of all cores. Sub-B has slightly more "coarse" material, with "fine" material making up 60 percent of the cores.

Pit House 1 Fill differs markedly in material composition from the other grouped proveniences. The small sample has higher proportions of "coarse" material cores; "fine" materials make up only one-quarter of the 15 cores from Pit House 1 Fill. By far the highest proportions of basalt and andesite were in this unit. This distribution is emphasized in Table 3.10, which contrasts "fine" (basalt and andesite) and "coarse" (chert, chalcedony, and obsidian) materials. Pit House 1 Fill is the only grouped provenience assemblage that is composed predominately of "coarse" materials.

Table 3.10. Percentages of Coarse and Fine Lithic Materials by Grouped Provenience

Grouped provenience	Coarse — Basalt, Andesite %	Fine — Chert, Chalcedony, Obsidian %
Room Block C	8.7	90.3
Room Block B	24.6	75.4
Room Block A	34.3	65.7
Sub-B	31.3	68.7
Pit House 1 Fill	61.9	38.1
Pit House 1 Lower	38.4	62.1

Note: No data available for Pit House 3.

In Table 3.10 there appears to be a temporal trend from high proportions of coarse materials to high proportions of fine materials. This trend is not perfectly linear. Pit House 1 Lower has considerably higher proportions of fine-grained materials than the later Pit House 1 Upper assemblage.

It is instructive to compare the proportions of "coarse" and "fine" materials at Saige-McFarland and other Cliff Valley sites to sites in the Mimbres Valley (Table 3.11). Data from the Mimbres Valley are taken from Margaret Nelson's analysis (in Anyon and LeBlanc 1984: 225–236, Table 16.3). "Coarse" and "fine" are defined almost identically in Nelson's study and in the present analysis.

In general, the proportion of coarse-grained materials decreases through time in both the Mimbres and the Gila Valley. The decrease is more obvious if the large sample from Mattocks (N = 2015) is taken as representative of the Mimbres phase, rather than the much smaller Galaz sample (N = 175), or if the two samples are averaged for a Classic Mimbres proportion of about 58 percent (Anyon and LeBlanc 1984, Table 16.3). The Gila Valley data show a similar decrease through time, with the Archaic sample at 61 percent, the Early Pit House sample at 47 percent, and the range of most later samples between 31 and 38 percent. Change in material assemblages does appear to have a temporal dimension.

Table 3.11. Percentages by Archaeological Period of Coarse Materials in Lithic Assemblages from the Mimbres Valley and the Gila Valley
(Coarse materials include basalt, andesite, and rhyolite)

Period	Mimbres Valley* % (site)	Upper Gila† % (site)
Post-Mimbres	44 (Disert, Stailey)	37 (Villareal II)
Mimbres	58 (Mattocks, Galaz)	24 (Saige-McFarland, Room Block B)
Mangas		34 (Saige-McFarland, Room Block A)
Late Pit House	53 (Galaz)	31 (Saige-McFarland, Sub-B)
		62 (Saige-McFarland, Pit House 1 Fill)
		38 (Saige-McFarland, Pit House 1 Lower)
Early Pit House	78 (McAnnally)	47 (Winn Canyon)
Archaic		61 (Eaton)

*Modified from Anyon and LeBlanc 1984, Table 16.3.
†Hemphill 1983 (Eaton), Fitting 1973 (Winn Canyon), Lekson 1978 (Villareal II)

Table 3.12. Frequency Distribution of Core Types

Grouped provenience	Core type	Basalt	Andesite	Chert	Chalcedony	Obsidian	Total
Room Block C	Blocky	1		1	1		3
	Plano-convex		1				1
	Biconvex						0
	Small Bipolar						0
	Total	1	1	1	1		
Room Block B	Blocky	7	2	20	29	3	61
	Plano-convex	7	7	14	11	4	43
	Biconvex	1	7	3	5		16
	Small Bipolar			7	16	19	42
	Total	15	16	44	61	26	
Room Block A	Blocky		10	7	8	3	28
	Plano-convex	1	1	5	6		13
	Biconvex	2	2	1	3		8
	Small Bipolar	1	1	1	10	1	14
	Total	4	14	14	27	4	
Sub-B total*		24	23	45	19	2	113
Pit House 1 Fill	Blocky	2	5	1	1		9
	Plano-convex	2	1		1		4
	Biconvex		1				1
	Small Bipolar					1	1
	Total	4	7	1	2	1	24
Pit House 1 Lower	Blocky	5	2	7	10		11
	Plano-convex	2	2	3	4		2
	Biconvex	1	1				14
	Small Bipolar			1	10	3	
	Total	8	5	11	24	3	
Total		56	66	116	134	36	

*Typological data not available for 90% of Sub-B cores, see text.
No lithic data from Pit House 3.

The one obvious exception in this apparent trend in the Gila Valley is, again, Pit House 1 Fill. The high proportion of "coarse" materials is almost identical to that from the Archaic Eaton Site. I will refrain from suggesting that Pit House 1 Fill is lithically "earlier" than its associated ceramics; however, the temporal trends seem real, and, as discussed above, Pit House 1 Fill is an evident anomaly.

Cores

Cores were classified into the same material categories described above and into a series of formal types defined by Fitting (1972a): blocky, plano-convex, biconvex, and small bipolar. Reasonably complete core data are limited to Room Blocks A and B. Counts from Pit House 1 are probably complete, but the cores from this provenience are now missing from the collections. Information from Sub-B is partially incomplete; although the totals by materials are accurate, most of the cores were not recorded by formal types. Data from Room Block C are definitely incomplete, since both material identifications and some counts are missing. Core data are summarized in Table 3.12.

Even with these difficulties, several distributional patterns are noteworthy. First, the number of cores per cubic foot of fill is similar in Pit House 1 Lower, Room Block A, and Room Block B (0.08, 0.07, and 0.05 respectively). Although it is difficult to make precise volume calculations for Pit House 1 Fill, the density of cores is in the same range or even slightly lower (my estimate for Pit House 1 Fill is about 0.04 per cubic foot of fill). In remarkable contrast to these low densities of cores is Sub-B (the only other unit with sufficient data), where density is 0.27 per cubic foot. There are a lot of cores from Sub-B, and 90 percent of those cores come from the pit structures below Room 12.

Unfortunately, formal typological data survive on only a few of the Sub-B cores. For the other grouped proveniences, there is surprising uniformity in the proportions of core types for both Room Blocks A and B and Pit House 1 Lower, with approximately 40 percent blocky cores, 25 percent plano-convex cores, 10 percent biconvex cores, and 25 percent small bipolar cores.

This percentage of bipolar cores, which seems high compared to many other Southwestern assemblages, probably reflects the small size of the raw materials involved. Over three-fourths of the small bipolar cores in Table 3.12 are of chalcedony and obsidian, which occur naturally as small (3-cm to 5-cm diameter) nodules. There are no direct data on core size, but the 1987 observations suggest that the vast majority of small bipolar cores are small nodules or pebbles broken by "bipolar" techniques; that is, setting the nodule on a flat cobble and smashing it, a reasonable way to deal with a rock the size of a golf ball.

The glaring exception to the 40-25-10-25 core formula is

Pit House 1 Fill. In this small sample there is a disproportionately high number of blocky and plano-convex cores, 13 of a total 15 cores.

Pit House 1 Fill cores differ markedly from other grouped proveniences in both material and formal types. The association of core form and material type is a simple function of the size of the raw material: "coarse" materials, available in large cobbles and blocks, were made into large blocky, plano-convex, and biconvex cores; and "fine" materials (generally restricted to smaller cobbles and nodules) were made into small blocky and small bipolar cores.

Projectile Points

Projectile points were the most frequent tool type at Saige-McFarland. About 200 were found. This seems a remarkable number compared to approximately 120 points from the 125-room Swarts Ruin (Cosgrove and Cosgrove 1932), but recovery techniques at the two sites were quite different. Saige-McFarland was screened and Swarts was not. A more appropriate comparison is the Galaz Ruin (Anyon and LeBlanc 1984). Data on artifact density per excavated unit volume are not readily available for Galaz, but it is possible to construct a useful comparative measure. At Galaz, the ratio of projectile points to pieces of chipped stone was 1:73; at Saige-McFarland, the ratio was 1:79. Thus the number of projectile points from Saige-McFarland is probably not remarkable when compared to Mimbres Valley sites.

Unfortunately, almost all of the Saige-McFarland points are now lost; only a few are present in the 1987 collections. Distributional and limited material data are available (from various inventories and counts), but no detailed information remains on form, size, or condition. Drawings of 35 points and one drill survive (Fig. 3.17), but these are not necessarily representative of the collection. Most of the points were small, side-notched forms similar to those found at the NAN Ranch Ruin (Shafer 1986, Fig. 9, groups 1 and 2). Narrowly concave bases were relatively common (Fig. 3.17*i*, *p*, *t*, *x*, *ff*).

The projectile points (Table 3.13) were made of obsidian or chert (the latter including the field inventory categories of chalcedony, jasper, and agate), with a few unidentified as to material. Over 75 percent of the points were made of obsidian, a proportion much larger than the proportions in two sites with comparable samples from the Mimbres Valley. At Swarts Ruin, of 121 points recovered (without screening) only 22 percent were of obsidian (Cosgrove and Cosgrove 1932). Of 108 points recovered by the Mimbres Foundation at the Galaz Ruin, about 35 percent were of obsidian (Anyon and LeBlanc 1984, Table 16.17).

Both Swarts and Galaz have substantial Pit House components, whereas most of the projectile points from Saige-McFarland came from Mimbres phase Room Block B. Is this difference in material selection chronological? Counting only those points with probable Mimbres phase assignments at Galaz, obsidian equals 39 percent of the total (54 points).

Projectile points from Swarts are not identified by time period. It appears that obsidian was used more often at Saige-McFarland than at comparable sites on the Mimbres River. This material selection may simply reflect the fact that Saige-McFarland is much closer to the Mule Creek obsidian sources than are the Mimbres Valley sites.

The distribution of projectile points across the site (summarized in Table 3.13) is noteworthy. Over three-fourths of the points were recovered in Room Block B, which contained only about one-half of the screened fill at Saige-McFarland. Within Room Block B, points were concentrated in the large front-row rooms, with 96 found in Rooms 11, 12, and 14. However, in terms of amount of screened fill *within* Room Block B, Room 12 produced numbers of points almost precisely proportional to its volume of screened fill, and most other rooms in Room Block B, like Room 12, produced points roughly in proportion to their volume of fill. Rooms 8 and 9 reflect a virtual absence of points. Room 11, Feature 33, was a remarkable case; the excavator noted:

At least 75% [actually, over 80%] of the points (for a total of 30) and a very high percentage of the chippage from this room occurred in a very localized area centered on the hearth [Feature 32] and extending four to five feet to the north, west and south (Brown 1971: 9).

Clearly at Saige-McFarland projectile points were most numerous in Room Block B, the latest of the excavated units. This concentration of points may have resulted from scavaging by the occupants of Room Block B of points from earlier units, or it may reflect different abandonment modes among the units at the site. Conversely, higher numbers of points may indicate a functional difference between Room Block B and earlier units, perhaps increased emphasis on hunting or warfare.

Choppers

Choppers were flat, oval river cobbles, on which uni-directional or bi-directional flaking produced a durable (if somewhat irregular) working edge. The remainder of these massive tools were left otherwise unmodified. Illustrations of choppers are in Burns (1972, Figs. 8 and 9), Fitting (1972a, Fig. 3 H and I), and Fitting (1973, Figs. 13 and 14).

No choppers remain in the 1987 collection. The records indicate that only seven were found, all in Room Block B. Intriguingly, all were in lower fill (floor fill), floor, or feature contexts (2 in Room 11 Level 6; 1 each in Room 12 Levels 4, 5, and 8; 1 in Room 12, Feature 49; and 1 on Floor 3, Room 15).

Other Tool Categories

I can only note, with fear and trepidation, the apparent absence of other classes of formal tools, particularly drills and knives. Drills were mentioned, rarely, in notes and field inventories, but they were never described. A single drill blade fragment was included in the small collection of projectile point illustrations (Fig. 3.17*r*). Larger bifaces

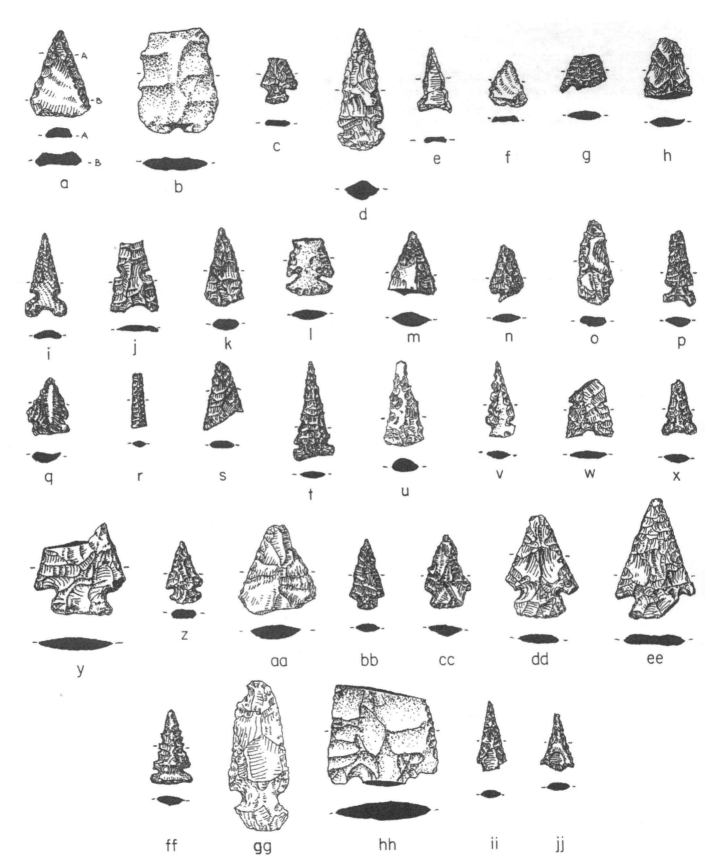

Figure 3.17. Selected projectile points and drill (*r*) from the Saige-McFarland Site. Provenience: Room 10, Level 4 (*a, b*), Level 5 (*c, d*); Room 11, Level 2 (*e*), Level 3 (*f–h*), Level 4 (*i–k*); Room 12, Fill (*l*), Level 3 (*m–p*), Level 4 (*q*); Room 13, Level 1 (*r–t*), Level 2 (*u*), Level 3 (*v, w*), Level 4 (*x, y*), Level 5 (*z, aa*); Room 14, Level 1 (*bb*), Level 2 (*cc*); Trench N650 E550, Level 3 (*dd, ee*); Trench N630 E550, Level 4 (*ff*); Pit House 1 Entrance (*gg, hh*); unknown (*ii, jj*).

Table 3.13. Frequency Distribution of Projectile Points

Grouped provenience Location	Material			% of total points	% of total screened fill
	Obsidian	Chert and chalcedony	Unknown		
ROOM BLOCK C	1			0.5	5.1
Block B trenches					
Room 8			7		
Room 10	4				
Room 11	5	3			
Room 12	30	7			
Room 13	38	7			
Room 14	5	5			
Room 15	11	3			
	17	3			
ROOM BLOCK B TOTAL	110	28	7	77.2	51.1
Block A surface	1	1			
Room 2A		1			
Room 5	1				
Room 6	2				
ROOM BLOCK A TOTAL	4	2		3.2	14.7
SUB-B	6	4		5.3	6.7
PIT HOUSE 1 UPPER	4	3		8.5	8.3
PIT HOUSE 3	5	2	9	3.7	3.4
PIT HOUSE 1 LOWER	2	1		1.6	10.7
Total	132	40	16		

Note: Excludes 17 projectile points from surface and unknown proveniences.

(knives?) must have been rare, based on the same sources.

Retouched flakes were definitely present, and included a variety of forms such as burins, perforators, and scrapers. These were noted on many of the lists included with the bags of "finished artifacts." I have serious doubts about the completeness of the retouched flake data and the criteria and consistency of their recognition. Therefore, retouched flakes are simply listed in Appendix C, counts that should be used with caution. No attempt has been made to separate and analyze utilized flakes, or to examine use wear on "finished artifacts." After years of cross-continental transportation and consequent "bag-wear," I question whether such a study would now be worthwhile.

Ground-stone Artifacts

Most of the ground stone in the 1987 collections was located in storage at Fort Burgwin at Ranchos de Taos. A few small pieces were with the collections in Michigan, and the infamous turtle effigy vessel is now in the collections of the Western New Mexico University Museum. Twenty-one manos and mortars were photographed by Klinger. Eleven of these ground-stone artifacts are now lost, and information presented here is taken from their photographs. For cross-referencing artifacts and contexts, each piece of ground stone was assigned an identifying number (for example, Ground Stone 3, listed in Table C.2).

The collections were first inventoried, and that list was compared to the field inventories (taken from Fitting and others 1971 for the first season and from a field laboratory tally kept during the second and third seasons). In addition, an anonymous preliminary analysis of the ground stone was completed during the early 1970s. The tables accompanying the manuscript report of this analysis were useful, but another table enumerating metates and metate fragments is, unfortunately, now lost.

Comparison of the field inventory, the 1970s analysis, and the 1987 collections indicates that many ground-stone artifacts, particularly metate fragments, are no longer with the collections. According to the field inventory and the 1970s analysis, between 71 and 82 manos should be present; 79 were located in 1987. Field inventories indicate at least 64 metates were recovered from Saige-McFarland, but only 21 remain.

Metates

About two-thirds of the metates are missing, perhaps edging the borders of some garden. Because so few whole metates were found, the missing pieces are probably almost all fragments. Figure 3.18c and e illustrate the only metates left in the collection that are reasonably photogenic.

Perhaps the most alarming discrepancy in metate counts occurs in Room 12 of Room Block B: 26 in the field inventory and only 4 in the collections. The field notes indicate that of the missing 22, 9 were incorporated in the walls of the two firepits of that room, Feature 40 (Floor 1) and Feature 52 (Floor 2). At least 6 more fragments were noted in wall fall. Thus at least 15 of the missing 22 specimens from Room 12 were fragments reused as architectural elements, and the location of several in upper room fill suggests that other metates could have been architectural elements as well. Similarly, all but one of the metate fragments from Room Block A were built into a single firepit (Feature 22).

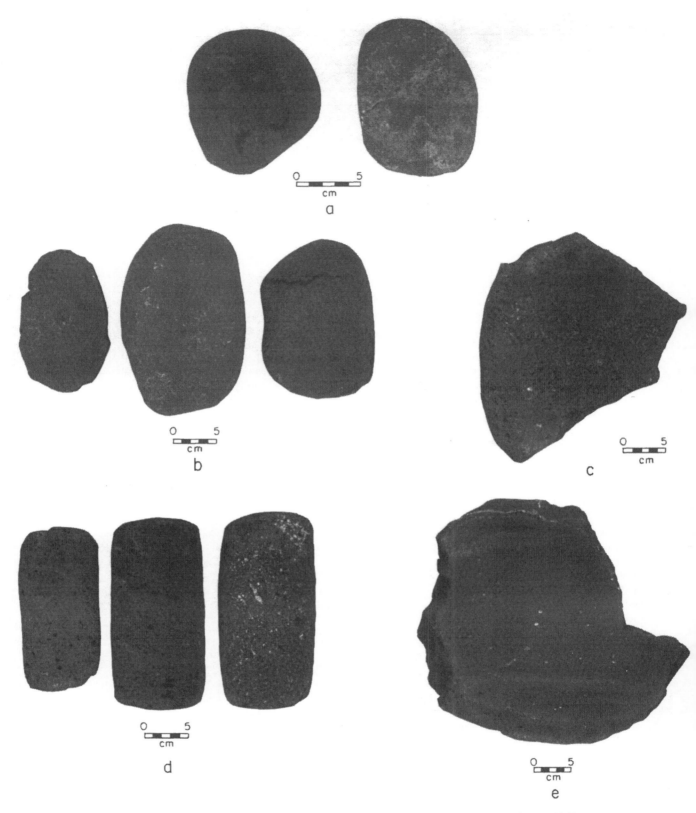

Figure 3.18. Selected manos and metates: *a*, oval-circular one-hand manos, Ground Stones 46 (Room 12, Floor 2) and 47 (Room 12 or 13); *b*, irregular manos, Ground Stones 39, 42, and 43 (all from Room 12, Level 8); *c*, basin metate fragment, Ground Stone 2 (Pit House 1, Fill); *d*, rectangular two-hand manos, Ground Stones 34 (Room 11, Level 4), 44 (Room 12 Fill), and 41 (Room 11, Level 2); *e*, trough metate fragment, Ground Stone 5 (Trench N604 E505, Level 2).

Notes indicate that at least five whole metates were found at Saige-McFarland. No whole metates came from Room Block A (Fitting and others 1971: 51). Three complete metates are listed in the field inventory from Room Block B. One was from the upper fill (Level 2) of Room 12 (Ground Stone 105, now missing) and another came from Room 14, Level 2. From a sketch included in the 1970s analysis, Ground Stone 105 was a trough metate on a massive boulder; the trough was quite shallow and the metate appeared "new," in the words of that analysis. No description survives for the metate from Room 14, Level 2, other than a reference in the field notes that it was complete. It may be Ground Stone 8 in the 1987 collection, about two-thirds of a trough metate on a round, thin boulder that currently has no provenience.

The third metate was listed from the firepit on the lower floor of Room 12 (Feature 52). This "complete" metate is almost certainly the combined fragments of a broken metate used to line the firepit (these pieces are now missing); although technically complete, this metate was not in usable condition.

A fourth metate (Ground Stone 5) from Pit House 1 fill is three-fourths complete. It is a basin type, on a minimally modified boulder. A fifth complete metate (Ground Stone 106) was reported in the notes from Pit House 3, Level 7. The metate is no longer in the collections, but a sketch of a cross-section of a metate (Ground Stone 106) in the 1970s analysis shows a rectangular (probably shaped) section on a massive blank and indicates that it was a closed trough type.

With only two exceptions, all the metates and metate fragments in the collection represent trough forms on minimally modified boulders or blanks; however, most fragments are so small that accurate description is difficult.

Included in the metate counts are three "expedient" metates: small (16 cm to 18 cm largest dimension), unmodified alluvial cobbles with one naturally flat or slightly concave surface used as a small grinding surface. Three remain in the 1987 collections (Ground Stones 40, 45 and 55, from the upper fill of Rooms 12, 11, and 15). The 1970s analysis hints that several more were recovered from unspecified proveniences.

Metate fragments clearly were concentrated in Room 12, which contained about 15 percent of the fill excavated at the site but produced over 40 percent of the metates. As noted, the metates of Room 12, with the exception of Ground Stone 105, were probably fragments reused in architectural contexts. Pit House 1, with the second highest number of metates (21% of the total) contained 19 percent of the screened fill plus large sections of unscreened fill, from which recovery of metates could reasonably be expected.

In summary, small sizes and wall fall contexts of most of the fragments suggest that many metates were used as architectural elements. Only three metates probably represent usable tools: the massive "new" metate in the upper fill of Room 12, the closed trough metate from Pit House 3, Level 7 and the (now lost) whole metate from the upper fill of Room 14, Level 2.

Manos

Despite the near agreement between the number of manos listed in field inventories and the number of manos in the 1987 collections, it remains possible that some manos are missing. The largest discrepancy concerns Room 12, where 31 manos were recorded in the field but only 22 manos were noted in subsequent analyses. It is possible that other soi-disant manos failed to survive the pitiless scrutiny of the lab. Some of the remaining 10 or so undocumented Room 12 manos may have been culled and discarded during the 1970s analysis.

For manos, the most basic (and perhaps most important) analytical distinction is between "one-hand" and "two-hand" types (Fig. 3.18). There is no reason to review the history and implications of these categories here, but for fragmentary specimens, the distinction between the two is by no means straightforward.

To place these distinctions on firmer ground, a measurable index of the types was formulated from a consensus of recent mano studies: "one-hand" manos are defined as any complete or nearly complete mano less than 13 cm maximum dimension, and "two-hand" manos are defined as any complete mano over 13 cm long (perpendicular to the presumed stroke) or any fragmentary mano over 16 cm long maximum dimension (the higher cutoff obviating uncertainties about stroke direction on fragments).

Since, by these criteria, fragmentary manos can be classified as two-hand but never as one-hand, these definitions obviously favor the former. Using these criteria, only about one-third of the manos can be assigned to either type, and two-hand manos outnumber one-hand manos by a ratio of four to one (Table 3.14).

Table 3.14. Frequency Distribution of One-hand and Two-hand Manos

Grouped proveniences		One-hand manos	Two-hand manos
Room Block B	Room 11		3
	Room 12	4	13
	Room 13		1
	Room 14		1
	Room 15		1
Room Block A	Room 2A		1
Pit House 1		1	
Total		5	20

Note: Counts are from the 1987 collections, defined by length; one-hand manos, any complete mano less than 13 cm long; two-hand complete manos, any complete mano more than 13 cm long and any mano fragment more than 16 cm long.

The distribution of complete manos across the site is of interest. Three-fourths (14 of 19) of the complete (or nearly complete) manos from the site were found in the upper fills of rooms in Room Block B; 12 of these were from the fill of the two largest rooms, Rooms 11 and 12. In a contingency

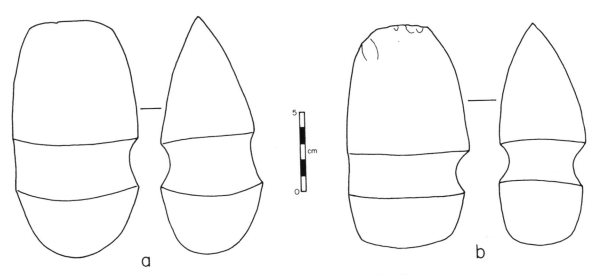

Figure 3.19. Axes of green metamorphic rock from Room
4A floor: *a*, Ground Stone 102; *b*, Ground Stone 103.

array of these two units compared to the rest of the site, the probability of this many whole manos being found in the fills of Rooms 11 and 12 is less than 0.001 (X^2 = 16.95, df = 1).

Eight whole manos in the fill of Rooms 11 and 12 form a fairly homogeneous group: they are rectangular in shape, of vesicular basalt, with an average length of about 21 cm (sd = 2.9) and an average width of about 11 cm (sd = 1.2). Although the notes and marked proveniences are not clear on this point, these manos all appear to have come from upper levels of the fill; that is, in the first two levels of each room. This cluster of similar manos may be associated with the two complete metates in the upper fills of Rooms 12 and 14 (noted above) and, like the group of corrugated jars found in the upper fill of Room Block A, represent a large group of whole artifacts in the upper fill of Room Block B. The remaining four whole manos from Rooms 11 and 12 include two one-hand oval manos and two irregular, probably two-hand manos.

Sub-B units produced three to six manos; the three in the 1987 collection are all complete, all irregular in shape, and all two-hand. Pit House 1 produced 10 or 12 manos, and Pit House 3 produced 5 or 8. Of the Pit House 1 manos, only one was complete, an oval, one-hand mano, found just above the floor. All of the Pit House 3 manos were small fragments in the fill, with the exception of one complete mano of unknown form on the floor.

Miscellaneous Ground-stone Artifacts

Saige-McFarland produced the usual array of other ground-stone artifacts: a pair of axes, a maul, palettes, pipes, small mortars, a large mortar, and a turtle effigy vessel.

A pair of fairly well-matched axes (Ground Stones 102 and 103) were found, side-by-side, in the center of the floor of Room 2A (Feature 5). These axes are now missing from

the collection, but a series of photographs (used to prepare Fig. 3.19) shows them as full-grooved, made of a green igneous or metamorphic stone, and not noticeably worn or damaged. The illustrations in Figure 3.19 were prepared from slides without scales; thus the outlines and grooves are accurate, as are the relative sizes, but the absolute sizes of the axes are only approximate. No other whole or fragmentary axes were found at the site.

An item described as a "full grooved maul" was in Room 14, Level 3, a fill deposit. This maul is not with the collections, and no illustrations of it survive. Several references make it clear that it was probably the only maul found at the site.

Fragments of four palettes (Fig. 3.20) were in Room Blocks A and B. The specimen from Room Block A (Ground Stone 98, Fig. 3.20c) was apparently associated with Burial 2; the others were found in room fill. Three of the four were of gray slate; the fourth (Ground Stone 97, Fig. 3.20a) was of a medium-grained sandstone. The slate specimens are intriguingly battered and worn. Both Ground Stones 95 and 98 have been split along the bedding planes of the slate. Ground Stone 96 (Fig. 3.20b) was ground and reshaped from an unknown original form and was marked by cutting or incising that scored its surface into tiny rectangles. In all three cases, it is possible that the slate material was being reworked into bead blanks and that palette fragments were being conserved for such a purpose.

Fragments of two pipes and a whole third pipe remain in the collection (Fig. 3.21). All are from Pit House 1: the two fragmentary specimens (Ground Stones 100 and 101) from fill and the complete example (Ground Stone 99) from the floor (grid N-4).

Small mortars (Fig. 3.22) are spherical or subspherical stone vessels with shallow basin (mortar?) grinding surfaces. Cross-referencing the several inventories produces a

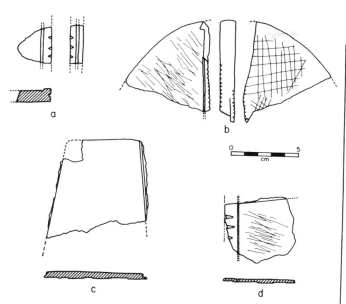

Figure 3.20. Palette fragments: *a*, sandstone, Ground Stone 97 (Trench N650 E550, Level 3); *b*, reworked gray slate, Ground Stone 96 (Room 12, Level 7); *c*, gray slate, Ground Stone 98 (Room 4A, Burial 2); *d*, reworked gray slate, Ground Stone 95 (Room 11, Level 2).

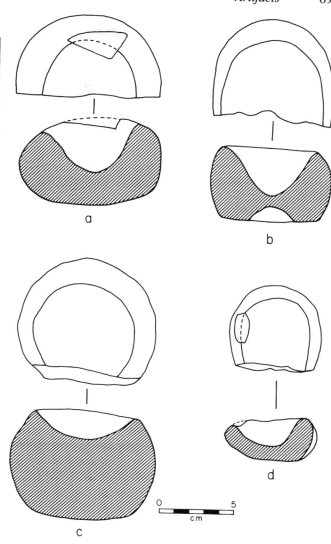

Figure 3.22. Small stone mortars: *a*, *b*, andesite(?) fragments, Ground Stone 11 (Trench N610 E510, Level 5) and 12 (Pit House 1, Grid M, Level 3); *c*, vesicular basalt fragment, Ground Stone 10 (Room 15, Level 4); *d*, pink volcanic rock, Ground Stone 94 (Trench N620 E520, Level 2).

list of seven to nine small mortars. The distribution of small mortars was evenly divided between Pit House 1 (four specimens) and Room Block B (three to five specimens). In addition to the four illustrated in Figure 3.22, small mortars were evidently also found in Room 12, Level 9 and N630 E510, Level 3. "Small mortars" are a heterogeneous group. They are made on a variety of materials, ranging from a very vesicular basalt (Ground Stone 10) to a soft pink volcanic rock, so soft that it may have been used as a pigment (Ground Stone 94). The mortars for which data are available average about 8.5 cm in diameter (sd = 1.9, N = 7), but only a few are truly round (Fig. 3.22).

A single large mortar was constructed into Feature 51, the adobe platform or ledge between Floors 1 and 2 of Room 12.

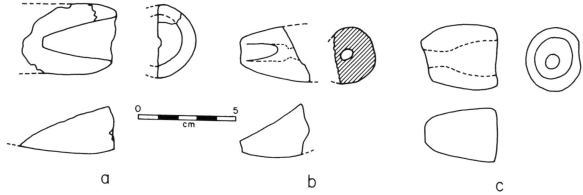

Figure 3.21. Stone pipes: *a*, *b*, sandstone fragments, Ground Stones 101 (Trench N610 E510, Level 4) and 100 (Trench N620 E510, Level 5); *c*, vesicular basalt, Ground Stone 99 (Pit House 1, Grid N, Level 4).

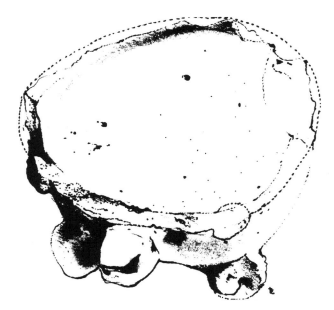

Figure 3.23. Stone turtle effigy vessel, Ground Stone 104 (Room 12, Floor 1). Maximum diameter is 19.5 cm.

This piece is no longer with the collection. It is described in the field notes as a massive, shaped disk, 25 cm in diameter and 13 cm thick. Basin-shaped grinding areas were pecked on both faces, meeting in the middle in a 3.8-cm diameter hole. One grinding basin was clearly larger and deeper than the other. There is no record of the type of material.

The turtle effigy vessel (Ground Stone 104, Fig. 3.23) was a part of Feature 43, the concentration of artifacts around the firepit on Floor 1 of Room 12. It has been described in enthusiastic detail (Lekson and Klinger 1973: 6):

> The vessel represented a zoomorphic form, possibly a turtle, with four bulbar legs and a projecting head with a shallow, straight slit marking the mouth. The area of the body was sub-hemispherical in shape, 19.5 cm in diameter and 3.6 cm deep. Rising from the body was a circular wall 1.4 cm thick. Two small lugs or knobs were located on the exterior of this wall flanking the head. . . . the dorsal side of the body was a flat, circular [grinding] surface 17 cm in diameter. The effigy vessel, manufactured of sandstone[?] with feldspar inclusions, was badly damaged. Three of four legs and one lug were broken; as was the vessel wall throughout its circumference. No other fragments of the vessel were found. . . .

Stone Slabs

At least 21 stone slabs were recovered at Saige-McFarland; none now remain with the collections. They were thin, subrectangular slabs, ranging from about 20 cm square to over 60 cm by 90 cm (Room 4A, Feature 12); most slabs were less than 30 cm by 45 cm. Only a few rough measurements survive in the field notes, supplemented by a few photos, and comments in a manuscript on ground stone

analysis. The edges were often chipped to shape, but little grinding was noted. With the exception of two fragments from Room 12, Level 8, all examples appear to have been complete. Only "a few" were discolored by fire or showed evidence of having been exposed to flames (one of them a complete slab from Room 12, Level 9). Similar slabs were common at Swarts Ruin, and examples are shown in that site report (Cosgrove and Cosgrove 1932, Plate 53).

In notes and analyses, these artifacts were called "hatch covers," "vent covers," and "door slabs"; in other cases (Room 11, Feature 31; Room 12, Feature 38) the excavators expressed doubt that the slabs served any such purposes.

More discouraging than the variety of suggested functions is the ambiguity surrounding the material of which the slabs were made. Fitting and others (1971) described the slabs of Room Block A as sandstone; notes from later excavations and analyses (in particular, the manuscript of the analysis of ground stone cited above) call the material tuff. The latter is probably correct. The first season's preliminary report was written before the Upper Gila Project became familiar with the lithic materials of the Cliff Valley. Sandstones in the Cliff Valley are limited to poorly consolidated, irregular lenses in the Gila Conglomerate. At least one slab from Room Block A was included in the later ground stone analysis and was identified there as tuff, as were all the slabs from Room Block B and Pit House 3.

Slabs have been treated as features in this report, because almost all the data about them come from architectural notes. In addition to those listed as features, slabs were apparently found in the following contexts (data from field inventory and the manuscript on ground stone analysis): Room 12, Level 8, two fragments; Room 12, Level 9, one complete small slab; Pit House 3, Level 7, one complete large slab.

The distribution of complete slabs was singular: with only two exceptions (Room 13, Feature 67, and a large slab from Pit House 3, Level 7), all were built into or lying flat on room floors or were in the fill immediately above the floor with one edge resting on the floor. That is, slabs were left lying on the floor when rooms were abandoned or were deposited (fell?) onto the floor before other major deposition took place within the room. The large slab from Room 13 may have been placed there after that room was largely ruined and filled. The large slab from Pit House 3, Level 7, was found amidst roof fall and was thought to be a roof hatch cover for that dwelling, the only rectangular, masonry-lined, pit structure excavated at the site. No such slabs are reported from the nearly identical pit structures at the Dinwiddie site, LA 6783 (Hammack and others 1966).

Every room of Room Block A had a small slab lying on the floor. Each of the three eastern rooms had slabs at the middle of the west wall. In the western rooms, this pattern was repeated in Room 2 (the slab was located near the middle of the west wall common to Rooms 2A and 2B). In Room 1, the slab was located at the middle of the longer of its exterior walls (the south), and in Room 4A. a slab of comparable size was located in the northeastern corner, perhaps related to the exterior north wall. If Rooms 3, 5, and 6 (all with firepits) were the front rooms of Room Block A, this pattern suggests that the small slabs covered or closed vents near the middle of the upper rear walls of the front row and in the middle of exterior walls of the rear row of rooms. With the addition of doorways near the middle of the now-reduced east walls of Rooms 3, 5, and 6, the system obviously would ventilate the room block.

Alternately, the uniform position of small slabs near the middle of the west walls of these rooms might indicate similar original placement on roofs, which deteriorated, fell, and deposited the slabs in identical fashion. Since the roofs were in part supported by common walls, a uniform pattern of deterioration is likely. In this case, the slabs in the front row of rooms may have covered hatchways or (more likely) smoke holes in the roofs. The slabs in the rear row of rooms may have covered other roof openings or vents or may, in fact, be unrelated to ventilation systems.

Slabs may have a different depositional history in Room Block B. The excavators believed that two slabs (Features 31 and 38) were partially plastered into the floors of Rooms 11 and 12 (respectively). If so, clearly these two slabs were not used to close openings. Two other complete slabs were found on the lower floors of Rooms 12 and 15; again, these were not used to block openings. This leaves only three slabs in Room Block B that may have served to close openings: the small slab (Feature 37) in the southwestern corner of Room 12, and the two slabs (Feature 28 and 68) on either side of the thin partition wall between Rooms 10 and 14. These slabs may have closed either side of a vent or opening in the upper part of that wall. The Feature 68 slab is sufficiently large that it could have functioned to close a small, elevated-sill door through that partition. Since the partition was badly reduced, it is impossible to know if any openings actually existed. Regardless, the pattern of one small slab on each floor of Room Block A is not present in Room Block B; out of eight rooms, five lacked small slabs lying on the uppermost floor.

The locations of at least two other slabs strongly suggest that they were used to block openings. Feature 12 in Room 4A, the largest slab at the site, lay directly at the base of the only door discovered at Saige-McFarland. (The door was blocked with masonry, and the excavator felt that the slab was therefore unrelated to the door.) In Pit House 3, Feature 104 lay directly below the lower opening of that pit structure's vent system, and it was precisely the right size to fit that opening. Although these two slabs probably did serve to close wall openings, their relevance to the function of other slabs is problematic, since the doorway of Room 4A and the ventilator system of Pit House 3 were unique among excavated units at the site.

Hammerstones

Hammerstones are conspicuous only by their absence. They are not mentioned in either field notes or analyses.

Secondary battering use was noted on two pieces of ground stone, but primary, formalized hammerstones are not recorded at Saige-McFarland.

Evidence from other sites suggests that the lack of hammerstones at Saige-McFarland is part of a larger pattern in the Cliff Valley: hammerstones are found in small numbers at earlier sites, but are rare indeed at Mimbres phase and post-Mimbres phase sites. At the Archaic period Eaton Site (Hemphill 1983), where about 2,225 flakes were recovered (a figure offered only as a rough index of collection size), 3 formalized, recognizable hammerstones were identified. At the Winn Canyon Site, dating to the Early Pit House period (Fitting 1973), there were 3,045 flakes recovered and 6 hammerstones were found. At the Classic Mimbres phase Heron Ruin (Burns 1972) and Riverside Site (Baker 1971) and the post-Mimbres Villareal II Site (Lekson 1978), with a combined flake collection of 2,740, only one possible hammerstone was recovered, and its identification was tentative. Thus it appears that hammerstones as formal, recognizable tools are virtually absent in later (Late Pit House through post-Mimbres phase) lithic assemblages in the Cliff Valley.

Hammerstones are a minor part of all Upper Gila lithic industries, both early and late, when compared to other areas of the Southwest. Cores may have been utilized or reutilized as hammerstones. Use wear and battering were not recorded in any of the several analyses of Saige-McFarland lithics. Any conclusions drawn from the absence of hammerstones should be tempered with the caveat that, although formal hammerstones are absent, de facto hammerstones may indeed be present.

Minerals and Odd Rocks

Oddly-shaped concretions, crystals, and blue-green "turquoise" were found throughout the site. In addition, a number of rocks were collected as "ochre." I am skeptical about this identification, and "ochre" is not discussed further here.

Intriguing distributional patterns are evident in these odd rocks (Table 3.15). In particular, there is a notable disparity in the distribution of quartz crystals, with a disproportionate number coming from the fills of rooms in Room Block A, Room Block C, and Sub-B. Relatively few were recovered from the much more extensive excavations of the fill and floors of Room Block B. Indeed, if crystals in burial and structural features (two from Pit House 1, one each from Room Blocks A and B) are eliminated, the disparity is even more pronounced. The total number of quartz crystals is too small for tests of association to be useful. However, their distribution is interesting and may, perhaps, relate to abandonment or postabandonment ritual. As discussed elsewhere, Room Block B was the last-used structure at Saige-McFarland. Large parts of Room Blocks A and C were probably standing abandoned during its occupation. The large numbers of quartz crystals in units that were abandoned prior to the end of the prehistoric sequence at the village suggest a nondomestic activity not evident in Room Block B.

Table 3.15. Frequency Distribution of Minerals

Grouped provenience	Location	"Turquoise"	Quartz crystals	Mica	Galena
Room Block C	Room 7A, Level 3		1		
Room Block B	Room 11, Level 4	1			
	Level 5	1			
	Level 6	1			
	Feature 16	1			
	Level 8	1			
	Room 12, Level 1	1			
	Level 2	1			
	Level 5	4			
	Floor 1	1			
	Feature 18	1			
	Feature 29	1			
	Level 7	1	1		
	Level 8		1		
	Level 9	2		1	
	Feature 27		1		
	Room 13, Level 2		1		
	Room 15, Level 6	2			
Room Block A	Room 1, Level 2		1*		
	Level 3		1		
	Floor	1			
	Room 2A, Level 1				1
	Level 2		1		
	Room 2B, Level 1	1*			
	Room 3, Level 1		1*		
	Room 4A, Feature 14		1		
	Room 5, Level 1		1*		
	Level 2	1*	1*		
	Subfloor		1*		
	Room 6, Level 3	2			
Pit House 1	Feature 13	1			
	Feature 20		1	1	
	Feature 33		1		
N640 E550	Level 2	1			

Note: "Turquoise" includes several blue and blue-green minerals.
*Not present in the 1987 collections.

In contrast to the distribution of quartz crystals, "turquoise" (variously described in the field inventories as malachite, turquoise, and chrysocolla) are more evenly distributed throughout the site, proportionately to the amount of excavated fill in each unit. The only exception is a notable absence of these minerals from Pit House 1; the only specimen there was a piece of worked turquoise from Feature 85.

A single piece of galena came from the upper fill of Room 2 in Room Block A. Two pieces of mica were recovered, both from pit structures (Pit House 1, Feature 20, and the floor of one of the Sub-B units).

ORNAMENTS

The inventory of ornaments in Table 3.16 is incomplete, but probably not too many items are missing from the list. Few data remain from Room Block A; 71 pieces of shell (now missing) were recovered from that provenience, but the preliminary report notes only that "at least one shell pendant and two shell bracelets were included in this count"

(Fitting and others 1971: 51). The field inventories confirm the presence of at least one shell bracelet fragment but do not mention the second bracelet fragment nor the pendant. Materials from Room Block B, Pit House 1, and Pit House 3 correspond to the field inventories (with the additions noted in Table 3.16).

The forms of ornaments represented were not unusual for Mimbres sites. Most common were shell bracelet fragments, similar to the shell bracelets from Swarts (Cosgrove and Cosgrove 1932, Plate 72), figure-8 shell beads (Cosgrove and Cosgrove 1932, Plate 70, Number 7), and small disk-shaped stone and shell beads.

If the data are even approximately correct, the distribution of shell bracelet fragments at Saige-McFarland (Table 3.17) is interesting, even though the total number is small. Excluding materials associated with burials, there are about 39 shell bracelet fragments in the fills of various units. Room Blocks A and B have about half of the bracelet fragments that would be expected from the amount of screened fill, whereas Pit House 1 Lower and Sub-B have considerably more than their

Table 3.16. Frequency Distribution of Ornaments

Grouped provenience		Shell			Unknown material, beads
		Bracelet fragment	Pendant	Bead	
Room Block B					
N640 E550	Surface (Pit House 4)	1		1	
N650 E550	Level 3	1			
Room 11	Level 2			1*	1**
	Level 3			1*	
	Level 4	4			
	Level 6	1			
Room 12	Level 1	1			
	Level 4			1	1**
	Floor 1			1**	
	Feature 45	1			
	Feature 49	3			9
	Feature 64	4			6
	Feature 65	1			10
	Sub Floor 2	1			5
	Level 7	1			1**
	Level 8	2			
	Level 9	1**			
Room 13	Level 2		1*		
Room 15	Level 4	1		1	
	Level 6	1			
Room Block A		1**	1**		
Room 3	Level 2	1**			
Pit House 1					
N610 E510	Level 5	1			
N620 E510	Level 2	2			
N620 E510	Level 5	1		1	
Grid K	Level 1	1			
Grid K	Level 3	1			
Grid Q	Level 1	1			
Grid T	Level 3	1			
Grid V	Level 2	1			
Grid X	Level 2	1			
	Feature 87	2			
Pit House 3	Fill	1			

*"Figure 8" bead, probably shell.
**Items not in the 1987 collections; data from Fitting and others 1971.

Table 3.17. Frequency Distribution of Shell Bracelets

Grouped provenience		Shell bracelets
Room Block B	Fill and Floors	7
Room Block B	Burials	9
Room Block A		2
Sub-B		5
Pit House 1 Upper		1
Pit House 3		1
Pit House 1 Lower		11
Total		36

share. Pit House 1 Lower produced a remarkable total of at least 11 shell bracelet fragments; if these artifacts were evenly distributed through the fill of the site, only 3 would be expected. The shell bracelet fragments were found mainly in the southern half of the unit, but apparently they did not constitute a concentration or cluster. In dramatic contrast was Pit House 1 Upper, with only one shell bracelet fragment. Sub-B also may have produced unusually high numbers of shell bracelet fragments, although the total number (5) is small. All but one came from pit structures below Room 12. In summary, it appears that shell bracelet fragments occur in higher proportions in the lower fill of pit house contexts than in the fill and floor contexts of masonry room blocks or in the upper fill of Pit House 1.

Two extraordinary finds of ornaments were a "bead cache" (Feature 75) on the floor of 12-NE, and a cache of pendants in a posthole of Pit House 1 (Feature 88).

A cache of 325 beads and pendants (Feature 75) was found in a small jar (Vessel 47), sitting on the floor of 12-NE. There was no indication that the beads were strung. The bead cache was described in a brief note (Klinger and Lekson 1973), a youthful indiscretion that has proven quite useful, because the "bead cache" is no longer with the collection. Four materials were noted: "turquoise," olivella shell, unidentified shell and "rose quartz." I suspect that the "rose quartz" of 1973 includes some worked shell. This description is quoted (and amended) here.

Olivella shells were most abundant, numbering 203 in all. Some were ground at the end, but most were simply punched through. Average length of the shells was 1.1 cm. Three forms of turquoise were present. Sixty-seven beads ranging from 0.1 to 0.7 cm wide with thicknesses from less than 0.1 cm to a maximum of 0.4 cm were found. All the turquoise beads were finely polished with holes drilled through the center. Ten turquoise pendants were also recovered, nine of which were rectangular . . . with off-center perforations. One of the turquoise beads was 0.7 cm long and 0.1 cm square with a hole drilled through its length. One other turquoise pendant, the largest of any present, measured 3.8 cm by 2.5 cm, finely polished and perforated at one end. Of the 27 rose quartz [pink shell?] specimens, nine were of pendant form with a mean length of 1.3 cm. . . . Eighteen rose quartz [pink shell?] beads were present, all circular, polished and perforated, with a maximum width of 0.5 cm. The assemblage included 17 unidentified shell specimens, seven of which were small circular beads, maximum width 0.6 cm. Ten shell pendants of "figure eight" form were present . . . perforated through one end and measuring from 0.2 cm to 0.6 cm in length (Klinger and Lekson 1973: 66–67).

The second unusual ornament find was a cache of pendants in Pit House 1, Feature 88, almost certainly strung when placed at the base of a large roof-support post seated in this hole. At the time of excavation, this was described as a "turquoise necklace." However, the material is not turquoise; rather the pendants are made of an unidentified chalky white material, probably a form of calcite, that had been smeared on both sides with a fugitive blue-green pigment, presumably to mimic turquoise. The pendants were oval to rectangular in shape and most were rectangular with rounded corners. Their average size was 25.35 mm long (sd = 2.53 mm, N = 78) by 20.56 mm wide (sd = 2.13 mm, N = 82). At least 95 elements were drilled for suspension, with holes of about 1 mm to 3 mm in diameter. The pendants ranged from 2 mm to 5 mm in thickness, and the drilled hole measured from 2 mm to 5 mm from one end.

CHAPTER FOUR

Archaeological Synthesis of the Saige-McFarland Site

Saige-McFarland is a large, multicomponent Mimbres site. It spans the Late Pit House to Mimbres periods, and probably includes the immediate post-Mimbres period, as well. Sites like Saige-McFarland are the key to understanding the prehistory of the Upper Gila region: the critical transitional periods and the bulk of the archaeology (however we care to measure it) are locked up in relatively few large sites, like Saige-McFarland.

Other Upper Gila excavations lack the time-depth of Saige-McFarland. Almost all professional excavations have been at single-component sites: Eaton, Winn Canyon, Lee Village, Heron, Dinwiddie, Ormand, and Kwilleylekia are all single component sites. A few excavated sites, such as Riverside and Villareal II, span two or more of the later ceramic periods, but these sites are much later than the critical Pit House to Pueblo period transition.

ARCHITECTURE

Pit Structures

Four to six pit structures were excavated or tested at the Saige-McFarland site; the range of numbers reflects my uncertainty about the pit structures below Room 12. Indeed, all the structures below Room Block B are, to varying degrees, problematic. Pit House 2 was only exposed in a small test, Pit House 4 was reconstructed 15 years after the fact, and 12-NE and 12-SW are completely mysterious. For these units, there is little to offer beyond the descriptions in Chapter 2. However, Pit House 1 and Pit House 3 deserve more attention.

Pit House 1
(A Large Communal Pit Structure)

Pit House 1 could be called a Three Circle phase Great Kiva, except that the term "Great Kiva" is currently out of favor in Mogollon studies. Anyon and LeBlanc (1980) substitute the ethnically neutral term "communal structure" for the older "Great Kiva." The Anasazi model, from which the Great Kiva comes, has played an enormous if inconstant part in Mimbres studies, and I support Anyon and LeBlanc's decision to clear the air of heavily encumbered Anasazi terminology.

Pit House 1, then, is a Three Circle phase communal pit structure. The characteristics of such structures have been catalogued by Anyon and LeBlanc (1980) and again in more detail by Anyon (1984). Compared to other such structures, Pit House 1 is unremarkable. At 563 square feet (52 square meters) it is on the small side, compared to contemporary structures. It has been suggested that the size of the communal structure is, in general, an index of village size (Anyon and LeBlanc 1980: 264). Extrapolating from Anyon and LeBlanc's (1980) Table 2, a communal structure the size of Pit House 1 could indicate a village between small (less than 20 pit houses) and medium (between 20 and 50 pit houses); and indeed, somewhere between 20 and 40 pit structures seems like a reasonable guess for Saige-McFarland.

Unlike several other Three Circle phase communal structures, the walls of Pit House 1 are not masonry lined; Anyon and LeBlanc (1980: 264) suggest that unlined walls are found early in the Three Circle phase. Like most Three Circle phase communal structures, Pit House 1 had an east-facing entrance, elaborate floor features, and was probably burned when abandoned.

Pit House 3
(A Small Masonry-lined Pit Structure)

Anyon and LeBlanc's terminological separation of Mogollon communal structures from the Anasazi model is commendable, not because there are no useful resemblances between the architecture of the two areas, but because the jargon of Anasazi archaeology is hopelessly laden with Puebloan implications. To graft that terminology on the Mimbres can only introduce false premises that will undermine the value of subsequent analysis. Although Anyon and LeBlanc were correct, in my opinion, to separate the discussion of Mogollon communal structures from Anasazi models, even they evidently could not withstand forever the siren call of the Plateau: in discussing "semi-subterranean kivas" (Anyon and LeBlanc 1980: 268), they fall at least partway into the trap they successfully avoided for communal structures.

Anyon and LeBlanc argue that at the same time large communal structures were superseded by plazas, "another series of structures appear: the small semi-subterranean kiva, . . ." (Anyon and LeBlanc 1980: 266), along with the large surface room and walled plazas, neither of which I discuss here. However, concerning small kivas, I have both opinions and data.

"Semi-subterranean kivas" are small, rectangular pit structures with ventilator systems and firepits; many "semi-subterranean kivas" in the Mimbres area were masonry-walled. Anyon and LeBlanc argue that "semi-subterranean kivas" were probably ceremonial structures, normally associated with single room blocks. They write, "Whether or not this roomblock oriented organization can be linked with any form of kinship, clan or other social grouping is unclear at present" (Anyon and LeBlanc 1980: 274), implying that some such linkage should become clear in the future.

The model, of course, is the Anasazi kiva. Anyon and LeBlanc (1980: 266) make explicit reference to the architectural criteria of Anasazi kivas in explaining their use of the term. By the list of features that traditionally define an Anasazi kiva, Mimbres "semi-subterranean kivas" (in the words of Anyon and LeBlanc 1980: 266) "barely qualify." In my opinion, recourse to the Anasazi "kiva" for Mimbres pit structures is unfortunate, since there are serious questions about "kivas" in the Anasazi area (Lekson 1988c). A case can be made that Pueblo II and Pueblo III Anasazi structures classified as "kivas" were simply pit houses, constructed a little differently than earlier pit houses. Modern archaeologists call these "kivas" because their teachers' teachers called them kivas, but there is no good evidence to support the use of the term, with all its Puebloan social and ceremonial implications.

Let us wipe the slate clean, as Anyon and LeBlanc did with Great Kivas and "communal structures," and start again. What is Pit House 3? A square masonry-walled pit structure with a hearth, a center post, a ventilator and (probably) a roof entrance. No in situ floor materials give us a clear picture of its function, either as a ceremonial structure or as a residence. Our best approach to this question is therefore architectural context. Pit House 3 was in close proximity to a small room block, partially covered now by a mobile home. This room block was the immediate reason for the trench in which Pit House 3 was discovered. We could not excavate this room block to test its "association" with Pit House 3, but Anyon and LeBlanc suggest such an association of "kiva" and room block in the Mimbres Valley.

At some Cliff Valley sites, and probably at many, units like Pit House 3 were associated with small room blocks (for example, the excavated Dinwiddie site near Cliff, Hammack and others 1966). This pattern was also evident at the Wind Mountain Site in nearby Mangas Creek. Pit House 3 was probably associated with the small room block beneath the mobile home, but this cannot now be demonstrated.

The reader will no doubt note the similarity of small Mimbres room blocks with pit structures (such as the Dinwiddie Site and the presumed association of Pit House 3) to the Anasazi "unit pueblo." But in neither the Anasazi case nor in the Gila Valley do I see the pit structure element of the "unit pueblo" as a kiva or "communal structure." It is difficult to envision the "communal" requirements of the inhabitants of a six-room surface unit. Just what "communal" functions were being served? What possible kin, or clan, or other social grouping that corresponds to just six rooms would require integration through the facility of a formal communal structure? These questions are not merely terminological hair-splitting; if no communal functions are housed in units like Pit House 3, then they are not kivas; if they are not kivas, then what are they? I suggest that they are pit houses, used contemporaneously with above-ground structures.

Room Blocks

There were at least four masonry room blocks at Saige-McFarland: A, B, C, and an undesignated small unit beneath a mobile home at the northern end of the site. About this last and about Room Block C, we know very little. Room Blocks A and B appear to have been chronologically sequent; A preceeded B. They are both small in size and alike in form.

Room Block A began as 4 rooms and grew to 6; Room Block B began as 5 rooms and grew to 10 or 12. Both were long rectangles, aligned north-south. Both were two-rooms wide and, in both units, larger rooms with firepits were located in the eastern row of rooms whereas the western row consisted of smaller rooms, generally lacking features and even (in the case of Room Block A) formal floors. Many of the techniques of wall construction and the use of stone slabs to close (ventilation?) openings were similar. Identifiable doors were either rare (Block A) or absent (Block B). Rooms of both units were internally subdivided and otherwise altered during the use of the structures.

Room Block A (minus later addition Room 6) is remarkably comparable to the initial construction of the southern half of Room Block B (that is, Rooms 8, 9, 10, 11, 13 and 14). These two units are similar in numbers of rooms, in total area, and in several apsects of room arrangement. Each includes a room or rooms in the eastern row with a firepit or hearth (Room Block A: Rooms 3 and 5; Room Block B: Room 11), a large room divided by a partition into lesser and greater halves (A: Room 2; B: Rooms 10 and 14), a small featureless room with a center post (A: Room 1; B: Room 8), and rooms with fixed basinlike features (A: Room 4; B: Room 10). The similarities are not isomorphic, nor should we expect them to be; however, the general pattern is striking.

In some details, however, the two units differed. Compare the irregular lines of Room Block A to the very regular plan of Room Block B. Even though this difference was enhanced by slightly varying mapping techniques used for each room block, the distinction is indeed real. Room size, too, is dramatically different: Room 12, the largest of Room Block B, is over three times the floor area of Room 5, the largest single room of Block A. The major difference, perhaps, lies in the number of rooms with firepits; Block A has two, whereas Block B initially had only one. However, the combined floor area of the two Block A rooms-with-hearths is about 210 square feet, not far off from the area of the initial Block B room-with-hearth (Room 11, with about

250 square feet). The implications are obvious, yet I hesitate to draw conclusions from them in the absence of a lengthy discussion of household development and family size, clearly inappropriate here.

Only a sample of the second, northern stage of Block B construction (Rooms 12 and 15) is evident. Significantly, the two rooms excavated were an even larger room-with-hearth (Room 12) and a room of undetermined original length with a fixed basinlike feature (Room 15). Surely a repetition of at least some of the earlier pattern is indicated. A significant part of the original floor of Room 12 may have been occupied by a large shelf or platform framework (Features 55–62), which would have reduced its floor space to an area almost exactly comparable to Room 11. We can speculate that with the addition of more rooms to the north, the shelf-platform was removed and a larger second floor installed; perhaps at the same time, Room 15 was converted from a room-with-basin to a small, featureless room with a center post. The pattern of one room with a hearth, one room with a large basinlike pit, and several featureless rooms is also repeated at the Dinwiddie site near Cliff (Hammack and others 1966).

A case can be made for architectural continuity in plan, arrangement of features, and other details, but with an increase in overall scale through time from earlier Room Block A to later Room Block B. The similarities are fundamental and striking, and suggest that roughly comparable groups occupied Blocks A and B. In terms of rooms and features there is no reason to believe that the two units represent qualitatively different social units.

Room Blocks A and B were small pueblos. Associated pit structures (if present, and it seems likely that they were) were not excavated. At the time of excavation, the conventional picture of the Mimbres did not include the Anasazi-like "unit pueblo," and pit structure-room block associations were not expected. No trenches were placed in front of the room block that might have located such structures, like the test trench that fortuitously discovered Pit House 3.

With or without pit structures, Room Blocks A and B are Mimbres pueblos. How do they compare to architecture in the Mimbres Valley? By far the most useful available summary of architecture at a large Mimbres site is Shafer's careful analysis of Mimbres architectural patterns at the large NAN Ranch Ruin (Shafer 1982, Shafer and Taylor 1986). After about A.D. 1070, architecture at NAN consists of room clusters defined by doorway patterns. A single room cluster generally consisted of two rooms: one large room (average area 204 square feet) with a stone-lined firepit complex, and one smaller room (average area 123 square feet) with or without an unlined hearth. Shafer interprets the larger room as a living room and the smaller as a storage room. With the exception of subfloor (storage?) pits, which were in both large and small rooms, no other fixed facilities were found in room clusters.

The room blocks of Saige-McFarland lack doorways, so we cannot define suites as was done at the NAN Ranch Ruin.

However, the small scale of construction at Saige-McFarland may offset this analytical limitation. Block A (minus later Room 6), the southern half of Block B, and the later northern half of Block B approach Shafer's room clusters. Clearly, the three units at Saige-McFarland are larger, in numbers of rooms, than the two-room clusters of NAN Ranch, and they may represent small groups of two-room units. The ratio of rooms with and without hearths in Block A is about 1:1, suggesting two two-room units; but in the fully excavated southern half of Block B, this ratio is 1:5.

Since doorway connections are lacking, it is possible that more than one room cluster may be represented by initial Room Block B construction. The presence of only one firepit argues against this possibility. If the two-room clusters at NAN Ranch Ruin indicate the basic household unit, then the "extra" rooms of Room Block B might answer functional problems solved, architecturally, above the household unit at NAN Ranch. The extra rooms of the Block B group represent types of facilities identified as "special activity rooms" at NAN Ranch (Shafer 1982), including granaries, processing rooms, and the like. At a large pueblo-style settlement, some of these rooms (particularly "activity" as opposed to storage rooms) might be used, with scheduling, by a number of different households; thus "special activity" rooms would make up a relatively small part of the NAN Ranch total. At smaller sites, such as Saige-McFarland, these rooms would necessarily represent a higher proportion of the total, and a lower ratio of rooms with hearths to rooms without hearths.

Room Block A and Room Block B are small, compared to 150-room Mimbres sites such as Galaz, NAN, and Swarts. Either room block, taken alone, would constitute a "small site," and to understand the place of such units in Mimbres archaeology, we must briefly review the "Mimbres Small Site Problem" (Nelson and others 1978; Laumbach 1982).

Mimbres Foundation surveys noted many small sites along the Mimbres River; "perhaps 5 to 6 times as many of these [small] settlements as large sites" (Nelson and others 1978). One of these sites, LA 12109, was tested. Two rooms in one corner of this 7- to 10-room unit were excavated. The two rooms produced an abundance of chipped stone but few sherds and were essentially featureless (Nelson and others 1978). Because the other five to eight rooms belonged to a different and uncooperative landowner, those two rooms were all that could be excavated. Thus the small sample was no fault of the Mimbres Foundation, but the conclusions drawn from that small sample were not tempered by its obvious limitations.

Based on the LA 12109 excavations, LeBlanc (1975: 13) argued that "this type of site was utilized for a set of specialized activities and/or occupation, and is not simply a permanent Mimbres residence site that happens to be small." The two-room sample was cited, repeatedly, as evidence that small sites throughout the Mimbres Valley were all "special activity" sites (LeBlanc 1983: 105; Blake and others 1986: 459, 464). It was even argued that the "cut-off point" for small sites might go higher than 7 rooms (presumably to 10, the upper limit of the lowest size class used in the survey analysis; Blake, LeBlanc, and Minnis 1986: 464). However, in 1983 (p. 105) LeBlanc implies an upper limit of 25 rooms.

These statements may all be true. But I submit these conclusions regarding Mimbres small sites ask a great deal from a two-room sample, structured by the whims of a landowner. Other evidence indicates that some small sites (that is, of less than 10 rooms) had features and characteristics of larger Mimbres residential sites. The Montoya Ruin, in the Mimbres River drainage, had only five rooms; three had firepits (Parsons 1955). The Berrenda Creek site, one drainage over from the Mimbres, had nine rooms; at least four had formal firepits and a total of nine burials beneath their floors (Gomolak and Ford 1976). And then there was Saige-McFarland; Room Block A had been described in preliminary reports (Fitting and others 1971). None of these sites were obscure or mysterious, yet two rooms at LA 12109, for some reason, were more real than three completely excavated small sites.

Not all small Mimbres sites are Swarts *en petite*. Many probably were non-residential, special activity sites, such as one-room field houses. The Mimbres Foundation concluded that *all* small masonry units in the Mimbres region were limited activity sites (Blake and others 1986: 459; Nelson and others 1978: 205). By classifying all structures with less than 7 to 10 rooms as non-habitations, they eliminated any possibility of recognizing the small room block, a fundamental unit of Mimbres architecture, when it appears as a distinct small site. The small room block and small site problems are tied up in taxonomic debate over the Mangas phase, to which I return in the Epilogue.

ARTIFACT DEPOSITION

Densities of chipped stone, decorated ceramics, and "utility" (nondecorated) ceramics in room fill are shown in Table 4.1. The lowest density of artifacts, about three per cubic foot, is found in the two rooms of Room Block C, both presumably rear-row rooms of a larger room block now destroyed by the highway. The highest densities for grouped proveniences are Pit House 1 Upper and Lower, with 17 to 18 artifacts per cubic foot. Falling between these two extremes are Room Blocks A and B, and Sub-B.

The differences between Room Block A and Room Block B (including Sub-B) are of interest; these units were excavated over several seasons under different supervision, and variations in densities may reflect different collection procedures. Framed in terms of cubic feet, the difference of the two mean densities is statistically significant (at the 0.01 level); however, this test is probably meaningless, since N (the unit of volume) is an arbitrary measure and may be large or small as one wishes. Lower densities in Room Block A may reflect in part the partial recovery of artifacts from the uppermost level of the southern rooms of Room

Table 4.1. Density of Artifacts per Cubic Foot of Excavated Dirt

Grouped provenience Location	Chipped stone	Decorated sherds	Utility sherds	Total artifacts
Room Block C				
Room 7A	0.29	0.41	1.85	2.55
Room 7B	0.40	0.65	3.09	4.14
Total	0.33	0.51	2.38	3.22
Room Block B				
Room 8	0.57	1.45	3.83	5.85
Room 9	1.08	1.27	5.21	7.56
Room 10	6.78	3.39	23.62	33.79
Room 11	3.60	2.89	11.18	17.67
Room 12	2.43	1.69	7.36	11.48
Room 13	2.89	2.01	8.07	12.97
Room 14	5.02	3.47	17.34	25.83
Room 15	3.66	2.52	10.92	17.10
Total	2.87	2.16	9.52	14.55
Room Block A				
Room 1	1.38	1.23	5.54	8.15
Room 2A	2.56	2.62	10.76	15.94
Room 2B	1.17	1.94	8.14	11.25
Room 3	1.22	1.41	8.14	10.77
Room 4 (A and B)	2.35	2.73	13.75	18.83
Room 5	1.47	1.78	9.76	13.01
Room 6	0.91	1.20	4.92	7.03
Total	1.68	1.82	9.27	12.77
Sub-B	2.50	2.06	9.52	14.08
Pit House 1 Upper	1.44	1.69	15.02	18.15
Pit House 3	*	1.93	*	*
Pit House 1 Lower	1.26	2.20	13.54	17.00

*Insufficient data

Block A because of frozen ground. Some of the highest densities of artifacts in Room Block B came from the uppermost levels of room fills, and this type of distribution may have been present in the southern rooms of Room Block A, as well. With that single caveat, the differences between Block A and Block B densities probably do not represent varying strategies for artifact recovery. Nearly all dirt went through one-fourth-inch screens, and since a great deal of noncultural material like rocks made it to the laboratory, we can be fairly certain that those screens were overcollected.

Pit House 1 Upper and Lower have the highest densities of any grouped provenience, about 17 to 18 artifacts per cubic foot. Some and perhaps most of the fill of Pit House 1 probably represents intramural trash.

Although Pit House 1 densities are high, its densities are lower than some individual rooms in Room Blocks A and B. The range of density values within individual rooms at Saige-McFarland is not particularly large, with two striking exceptions. Artifact densities in rooms in both Room Blocks A and B range from 5.85 (Room 9) to 18.83 (Room 4, A and B), with two extremely high values of 25.83 and 33.79 in Rooms 10 and 14, respectively.

Rooms 10 and 14 were contiguous: they represent a single large room with a partition wall, perhaps of less than full height. High densities of sherds in Room 14 may reflect, but only in part, the vessels of Feature 69, the utility vessels on the floor of that room. Room 10 (with the highest density of

Table 4.2. Density, in Items per Cubic Foot, of Various Artifact Classes at Cliff Valley Sites and Selected Proveniences at the Saige-McFarland Site

Phase	Provenience	Decorated sherds	Utility sherds	Flakes	Manos	Choppers	Projectile Points
Cliff	Villareal II	0.5	5.1	2.6	0.009	0.002	0.020
Late Mimbres-Cliff	Riverside	0.5	2.8	0.6	0.003		
Late Mimbres	Heron	0.6	2.8	0.4	0.004	0.009	0.005
Late Pit House-Mimbres	Saige-McFarland Total	2.0	10.0	2.2	0.009	0.001	0.024
Mimbres	Room Block B	2.2	9.5	2.9	0.015	0.002	0.045
Mangas-Mimbres	Room Block A	1.8	9.3	1.7	0.007		0.006
Late Pit House	Pit House 1 Upper	1.7	15.0	1.4	0.007		0.008
Late Pit House	Pit House 1 Lower	2.2	13.5	1.3	0.007		0.003
Late Pit House	Lee Village†	1.7	4.0	*	*	*	*
Early Pit House	Winn Canyon		4.3	*	0.003	0.003	0.020

Note: Densities for bulk artifacts computed for screened fill only; densities for larger artifacts (manos, choppers, points) computed for entire excavated fill.
*Insufficient data
†Not screened

artifacts on the site) had no similar deposit of whole vessels. In addition, decorated pottery and lithic densities (neither of which reflect Feature 69 per se) are also high in both rooms. It seems reasonable to conclude that the high densities of artifacts in the fills of Rooms 10 and 14 reflect a related depositional process. If high densities of sherds and lithics in fill indicate trash, then both Rooms 10 and 14 may have been trash-filled, over the partially collapsed partition and over the broken vessels of Feature 69.

How do these densities compare to other sites in the Cliff Valley? Several excavated sites provide some density data (Table 4.2). Statistics for bulk artifacts (decorated sherds, utility sherds, and flakes) in Table 4.2 reflect *only* the screened portions of those sites (and the total fill of the unscreened Lee Village). The statistics for manos, choppers, and projectile points are for the entire excavated fill (screened or not), since high proportions of these rare artifact classes were probably recovered under all excavation strategies.

The sites and proveniences in Table 4.2 are arranged in approximate chronological order, beginning at the bottom with two large pit house sites (the Early Pit House period Winn Canyon site and the Late Pit House period Lee Village), followed by the grouped proveniences at Saige-McFarland, two apparently short-occupation Classic Mimbres sites (Heron and Riverside), and ending with a small Salado pueblo (Villareal II).

Saige-McFarland has the highest artifact densities of any of these sites, but densities similar to those at Saige-McFarland may also have been present at Lee Village, the only site on Table 4.2 comparable in scale to Saige-McFarland. Densities of decorated sherds are probably the best index for comparison, because Lee Village was not screened. Although the recovery of painted ceramics was surely more complete than of utility sherds, equally certain is that the density of decorated sherds at Lee Village shown in Table 4.2 is still too low. Those densities, from unscreened collections, are comparable to densities at Saige-McFarland. Thus the den-

sity figures for Saige-McFarland may not be (and probably are not) extraordinary for large residential sites of this time period.

Densities at Saige-McFarland are markedly higher than those at most later sites. Only Villareal II, the latest site in the series, equals or exceeds Saige-McFarland densities (and then, intriguingly, only for manos and flakes). In only one artifact class, choppers, is Saige-McFarland lower than other sites; significantly, both older and younger sites have higher densities of this artifact class.

Lower densities at earlier and later sites undoubtedly reflect any number of currently uncontrolled variables, such as functional differences in the sites excavated for each period, or functional differences in the use of the Cliff Valley during each time period. Earlier pit house sites, for example, may represent a less sedentary occupation than Saige-McFarland; the excavated later sites (Heron, Riverside, and Villareal II) arguably represent much shorter term sedentary occupations. At present, arguments attempting to relate these suggestions to artifact density would necessarily be circular.

Vertical Distribution

Although architecture and architectural stratigraphy are reasonably well documented, few notes describe the fill of architectural units. Internal stratigraphy was recorded only in the fill of Pit House 1 and Pit House 3; the fill of other units was seldom remarked upon, presumably because it was unremarkable. Vertical control and screening of fill (with the exceptions noted for Room Block A, Pit House 1, and Pit House 3) make it possible to test the uniformity of fill by looking at the vertical distribution of artifacts.

At least three patterns of vertical distribution are apparent: first, relatively even distribution between levels, hereinafter referred to as "I" (this and the following symbols refer to graphic representations of the distributions, as in a strip graph seriation); second, a distribution with higher densities in lower levels ("A"); third, a distribution with higher densities in upper levels ("V").

**Table 4.3. Artifact Densities and Vertical Distribution
of Materials in Rooms at the Saige-McFarland Site**

	Density	
	Low (<17)	High (>17)
Distribution	Room No.	Room No.
I Even density in all levels	3, 8, 12, 13	2
A Higher density in lower levels	1(?)	4
V Higher density in upper levels	5(?), 9	10, 11, 14, 15

Note: Room 1 appears to be an "A" distribution, but the upper levels
of this unit were removed without screening. Room 5 had an
excessively thick first level which almost reached the floor; its
levels probably are not comparable. Room 15 appears to have
high densities in both uppermost and lowermost levels, more of
an "X" than a "V," but it is similar to Rooms 9 and 11 (see text).

Vertical distribution patterns are related to total density
(Table 4.3). In general, rooms with low total densities have
"I" distributions, and rooms with higher densities have "V"
distributions; only Rooms 1 and 4 have "A" distributions.
Low density "I" distributions may represent "background
noise," sherds and flakes, in relatively low densities, found
evenly distributed in the fill of every architectural unit. If
so, then higher density "V" distributions represent different
and perhaps more interesting depositional processes. High
density "V" distribution rooms include 10, 11, 14, and 15.
Room 9 could be added to these four; although low in density, Room 9 has the most dramatic "V" distribution of any
room.

Over half of the rooms in Room Block B had "V" distributions; that is, concentrations of materials in upper fill levels.
The fill of Room 12 had a low density, "I" distribution, but
contained a number of whole manos and metates in its uppermost levels. These complete artifacts in upper fill may reflect
the "V" distributions of sherds and lithics in nearby Room
Block B rooms. Thus, there appears to be a pattern of use
and discard over much of Room Block B, with higher densities of bulk artifacts and complete ground-stone artifacts
in the fill 2 feet or more above the floors of the rooms.

To anticipate the discussion of ceramic chronology, the
distribution of late (post-1100) intrusive pottery types is also
of interest here. In Room Block B, post-1100 pottery occurred in the uppermost level of Rooms 8 and 12, and in
Room 15. Similarly, post-1100 sherds were found only in
the uppermost fill of rooms in the southern half of Room
Block A.

These patterns suggest postabandonment reuse, an ex-
planatory scenario of long standing in the Mimbres. Parsons
used this argument to explain certain characteristics of the
Montoya Ruin, a small Mimbres site in the Mimbres Valley
(Parsons 1955). Late (post-Mimbres) sherds in the upper fill
of some Mimbres phase rooms at the Mattocks Site in the
Mimbres Valley have been attributed to "camping out"
reuse, according to Patricia Gilman in 1987.

CHRONOLOGY

No absolute dates were obtained during the original excavations and analysis of the Saige-McFarland Site. A series
of dendrochronological specimens from the site (including
almost all of the center posts and larger beam fragments
mentioned in Chapter 2) were submitted for dating in 1972,
but none could be dated. All these specimens are now lost.
No datable materials survived from Pit House 3 or Room
Block C.

Tree-ring Date

The few surviving fragments of charred wood were
examined by the Laboratory of Tree-ring Research at the
University of Arizona in 1988. A roof-support post from late
construction in Room Block A (Room 6, Feature 23; NMM-
3) was successfully dated to A.D. 1126vv. This post probably
represents the latest construction or repair in Room Block
A. No other datable materials were available from this room
block.

Carbon-14 Dates

A small collection of macrobotanical samples provided
materials for carbon-14 dating. Carbon-14 dates are calibrated (Stuiver and Reimer 1986), and the intercept(s) and
the one sigma range are presented.

One sample, from Pit House 1, came from a probable
roof element (Pit House 1, N610 E510, Levels 8–9; Beta-
20512). The date of 1320 ± 60 B.P. calibrates to A.D. 672
(645–770). The burned pinyon roof beam, about 10 cm in
diameter, should date the construction of Pit House 1. The
quantity of material from this beam was insufficient to allow
a conventional age determination from outer rings alone;
thus the sample represents inner and outer portions of the
beam and therefore may produce a date slightly earlier than
actual construction.

Two samples were dated from Room Block B. The first
consisted of carbonized twigs and small wood fragments
(unknown species) from a subfloor hearth beneath Room 11
(Feature 34; Beta-20513). This sample produced a date of
910 ± 60 B.P., calibrated to A.D. 1070, 1085, 1127, 1137,
and 1154 (1024–1209). Feature 34 should immediately pre-
date construction of the floor of Room 11 and, by extension,
construction of the southern half of Room Block B.

The second sample consisted of carbonized corn from the
fill immediately above the floor of a room in Room Block B
(Room 8, Level 6; Beta-20514). It produced an uncorrected
date of 640 ± 80 B.P. Unfortunately, carbon-13 corrections
were not determined for this sample, but M. Tramers of Beta
Analytic, Inc. advised me in 1987 that "this would add about
200 years on to the date," producing a date of about 840
B.P., calibrated to A.D. 1212 (1074–1260). This calibrated
date of 1212 is late for the Mimbres phase, which is generally dated 1000–1150. The date is probably not worth a great

**Table 4.4. Intrusive Pottery Types
Grouped into Temporal Ranges**

Pottery Type	Suggested Date A.D.
	1100–1200+
El Paso Polychrome	early-1100s–1400+
Chupadero Black-on-white	(?)1100–1400+
Casa Grande Red-on-buff	1100–1350
Starkweather Smudged-decorated	1050–1150+
Late Reserve-Tularosa Black-on-white	mid-1100s–early 1200s
Encinas Red-on-brown	900–1150 to 1200
	950–1100
Sacaton Red-on-buff	(?)950–1100+
Reserve Black-on-white	950–1150
Red Mesa Black-on-white	950–1050
	800–950
Late Santa Cruz-Early Sacaton Red-on-buff	about 950
Early Red Mesa Black-on-white	875–950
Kiatuthlanna Black-on-white	800–early 900s
San Marcial Black-on-white	?–950

Note: Date estimates made by Stephen Lekson, Peter McKenna, Bruce Masse, and Bruce Huckell.

deal of worry, however, considering the approximate nature of the carbon-13 correction and the substantial overlap of the one-sigma range with the accepted Mimbres phase dates.

Non-Mimbres Pottery Types

"Trade" or non-Mimbres sherds were comparatively rare in the Saige-McFarland collections. Intrusive pottery types and suggested dates for them are listed in Table 4.4. I have assigned dates to these types in consultation with several individuals: Bruce Masse, Bruce Huckell, and Peter McKenna. Alternate datings are available for every type listed, but in general, the intrusive pottery segregates into three broad temporal ranges: A.D. 800–950, 950–1100, and 1100–1200+.

The earliest provenience, in terms of dated intrusive ceramics, is Pit House 1 Lower. Sherds of Kiatuthlanna or early Red Mesa Black-on-white indicate a date in the early A.D. 900s. Pit House 1 Upper, Pit House 3, and Sub-B each have one or two sherds in the 950 to 1100 span; these are all Red Mesa Black-on-white with one sherd of late Santa Cruz or early Sacaton Red-on-buff in Pit House 1 Upper, all types that probably date to the earlier half of this span (about 950 to 1000–1050).

In the discussion of deposition, above, I suggested that materials high in the fill of Room Blocks A and B may represent reuse of these units. To further examine this possibility, I divided Room Blocks A and B into fill and floor units, as defined in Table 4.5. Floor materials from Room Block A included a sherd of Sacaton Red-on-buff from the subfloor fill of Room 4, a type that probably spans the period A.D.

950 to at least 1100. Unfortunately, this range is too long to offer much help in precisely dating floor materials in Room Block A. The fill of Room Block A contained intrusive types with a wide range of dates, from one sherd of Kiatuthlanna or early Red Mesa Black-on-white dating to the 800s or early 900s, to El Paso Polychrome and late Reserve or Tularosa Black-on-white that may date as late as the 1200s and early 1300s. These late types indicate that at least part of Room Block A fill was deposited no earlier than the mid-1100s.

Room Block B floor and fill contained sherds of both the A.D. 950 to 1100 and the 1100 to 1200+ ranges. In floor contexts, sherds dating 950 to 1100 were all Reserve Black-on-white, and post-1100 sherds included late Reserve or Tularosa Black-on-white, Starkweather Smudged-decorated, and El Paso Polychrome. Sherds in Room Block B fill included Red Mesa and Reserve Black-on-white (both dating to the 950 to 1100 span) and late Reserve-Tularosa Black-on-white, Chupadero Black-on-white, and Casas Grandes Red-on-buff (1100–1200+). Later (1100–1200+) ceramics indicate at least some of the Room Block B floor area was still in use in the early 1100s, and perhaps even later. Encinas Red-on-brown, a type tenuously dated from about 900 to as late as 1200, was found only in the upper fill of Room Block B.

The distribution of non-Mimbres pottery types in Room Blocks A and B supports the idea of late reuse of the upper fill of these units, but the evidence is not entirely clear. Although most sherds of later types were found in upper fill, types dating to later post-1100 periods were also found on the floor of at least one room in each room block.

Mimbres Series Pottery Types

The stratigraphy of the Mimbres white wares has been discussed in Chapter 2. The chronology of those types is considered here.

Shafer and Taylor (1986) proposed a detailed chronology for Mimbres series black-on-white types in the Mimbres Valley. With the caveat that the ceramic stylistic chronology in

Table 4.5. Occurrence of Dated Intrusive Ceramics

Grouped provenience	Date A.D.		
	800–950	950–1100	1100–1200+
Room Block B Fill		+ +	EEEE + + +
Room Block B Floor*		+ + +	+ + + +
Room Block A Fill	+	+	+ + +
Room Block A Floor*		+	
Sub-B		+ +	
Pit House 3		+	
Pit House 1 Upper	+	+ +	
Pit House 1 Lower	+ +		

Note: Each + indicates one sherd. EEEE indicates four sherds of Encinas Red-on-brown.
*"Floor" includes the level immediately above the floor, floor contact, and features associated with the floor.

Table 4.6. Synthesis of Absolute and Ceramic Dates for Selected Events at the Saige-McFarland Site

Grouped proveniences	Event	Absolute date (A.D.)	Intrusive pottery types (A.D.)	Mimbres pottery types (A.D.)	Suggested date of event (A.D.)
				1050–1100	1050–1100
Room Block C	Fill			1100–1150	1100–1150
Room Block B	Last use-fill	1074–1260*	1100–1200+	1050–1100	1050–1100
	Subfloor burials				1050–1100
	Initial construction	1024–1209*		1050–1100	mid 1100s
Room Block A	Last use-fill		1100–1200+		1126+
	Last construction	1126vv			950–1000
	Subfloor burials			950–1000	950–1000
	Initial construction		(?)950–1100		950–1100
Sub-B	Fill		950–1100	950–1100	950–1000(?)
	Initial construction				950–1050
Pit House 1 Upper	Fill		950–1050(?)	750–950+	about 950
Pit House 3	Fill		950–1100	750–950+	pre 950
	Initial construction				early 900s
Pit House 1 Lower	Last use		early 900s	750–950	800s
	Initial construction	645–770*			

* Carbon-14 date, one-sigma range.
vv Tree-ring date.

the Mimbres may differ from that in the Gila, their ceramic chronology can be applied to Saige-McFarland. The I-II-III stylistic sequence and a series of subdivisions of Style III were discussed in Chapter 3. The dating of these styles and subdivisions, supplemented with dates from Anyon and LeBlanc (1984) for Style I follows.

Style I	A.D. 750–950
Style II	A.D. 950–1000
Style III unborderd	A.D. 1000–1050
Style III framed	A.D. 1050–1100
Style III extended rim line	A.D. 1100–1150(?)

Room Block A has proportionately more unbordered Style III than does Room Block B, which has proportionately more framed Style III. The distribution of extended rim line sherds is limited to fill and floor contexts in Room Block B. Chronological estimates, based on the stratigraphy of the style I-II-III series and finer subdivisions of Style III, are given in Table 4.6.

Chronological Synthesis

Five types of datable events are indicated in Table 4.6: (1) initial construction; (2) last construction; (3) subfloor burials; (4) last use (floor assemblages); and (5) post-occupational fill. "Fill," of course, is the least precise target event, since multiple fill events are possible and even likely. "Last use," similarly, may represent a palimpsest of last use and initial fill events. "Burials" are direct associations of pottery and event; countering the problem of "heirloom" vessels are multiple burials or multiple pots with a single burial. "First" and "last" construction are variably precise; a tree-ring date

on a roof beam is certainly the most precise date possible, but other techniques for dating construction events are subject to a well-known catalogue of woes.

Pit House 1 Lower, the floor and lowest fill units of Pit House 1, includes an absolute date relating to construction and ceramic dates for last use of this structure. The carbon-14 dated roof beam (Beta-20512) has a calibrated date of A.D. 672 (645–770); as suggested above, this date may be somewhat earlier than actual construction. The upper end of the range, 770, precedes the "last use" intrusive ceramic date, early 900s, and falls within the earliest span of Style I Mimbres series dates. A likely date for construction of Pit House 1 is in the late 700s or early 800s, with "last use" in the early 900s. Two centuries seem far too long for use of a pit structure (even a "Great Kiva"). The use life of construction timbers in pit structures is relatively short, more likely two decades than two centuries. Either the date of the intrusive ceramics (900s) is too late or the carbon-14 date of the beam (645–770) is too early. The two-sigma range on the carbon-14 date extends the span only up to 862, so a date in the late 800s seems likely.

Pit House 1 Upper, the fill of Pit House 1, has an almost exclusively Style I ceramic assemblage. Later styles and later intrusive ceramics appear in the uppermost levels and a span of A.D. 800 to 1000 is suggested for the whole unit.

Pit House 3 is poorly dated. The lowest levels of Pit House 3 fill are predominately Style I, with some Style II and one sherd of Style III. I suggest dates of A.D. 750 to 950+ for the Mimbres series types. The intrusive ceramics are limited to one sherd of Red Mesa Black-on-white, in the fill well above floor. The fill may date to around 950, with construction and use of this feature at some time (shortly?) before that date.

The fill of Sub-B is almost certainly mixed with later materials related to construction and use of Room Block B. A Style II bowl (Vessel 42) was found on the floor of a pit structure below Room 12, indicating last use of Sub-B between A.D. 950 and 1000. Mimbres series and intrusive pottery types in the fill date to the 1050 to 1100 range. The fill of Sub-B likely was deposited between 950 and 1050–1100, and initial construction may have been at the earlier end of the range from 950 to 1000.

Based on the Style I and Style II vessels of subfloor burial Feature 14, Room Block A probably was constructed initially about A.D. 950 to 1000, or even earlier. A single intrusive Hohokam sherd is not inconsistent with construction within this range. Much later, the presumably last construction in Room Block A was the addition of Room 6 sometime after about 1125 (1126vv, NMM-3), and last use ceramics are not inconsistent with that date. The whole and partial vessel assemblage on the floor of Room Block A included framed Style III. Pottery in the fill dates to the mid-1100s, or later, suggesting that parts of Room Block A may have been used for trash fill at the time of Room 6 final construction and use. These dates indicate a span (perhaps intermittent) of at least 150 years for Room Block A, a use-life much longer than I would have thought likely or even possible for this crudely constructed masonry dwelling.

Room Block B has bracketing absolute dates: carbon-14 intercepts of A.D. 1070–1154 (1024–1209) on a subfloor hearth (Beta-20513) and a problematic carbon-14 date of 1212 (1074–1136) on burnt corn from a room floor (Beta-20514). The two dates are late and in the correct stratigraphic order, but the length and overlap of their ranges makes more precise chronological conclusions impossible. Subfloor burials offer the best dating of early use and provide an upper limit for initial construction: either during or immediately prior to 1050–1100, a date not inconsistent with the carbon-14 date of the preconstruction, subfloor hearth. Burials from Room 12 probably date to the 1050–1100 span; whole vessels are Style III, with either flare rims or framer lines. Floor vessels are also of Style III, with flare rims or framed designs. Sherds from last use and fill ceramics appear to be later, with sherds of Mimbres Style III extended rim line (dating to 1100–1150) and sherds of intrusive types dating from 1100 to as late as the 1200s and 1300s. I suggest a probable date of 1100 to 1150 for last use of Room Block B.

Room Block C is poorly dated. Mimbres pottery types suggest a date for fill of Room Block C of A.D. 1050–1100.

To summarize the data in Table 4.6, Pit House 1 was prob-ably built and used in the late A.D. 800s and early 900s. The abandoned Pit House 1 was filled with trash in the 900s and perhaps early 1000s, with small amounts of later materials deposited in the uppermost fill.

Based only on fill ceramics, Pit House 3 may have been contemporaneous with or slightly later than Pit House 1. The Mimbres white ware assemblage in the fill of Pit House 3 is similar to the lower fill of Pit House 1.

Parts of Sub-B, and perhaps all of that grouped provenience, date to 950–1000. The fill of Sub-B was probably in part related to the construction of Room Block B and may date to that time.

Initial construction of Room Block A was also in the A.D. 950 to 1000 range. Parts of the unit may have been in partial ruin in the late 1000s and early 1100s; however, rooms in the northern half of this unit were open and used between 1050 and 1100, and probably even later. Last construction of Room 6 took place sometime after about 1125; the walls of Rooms 4 and 5 presumably were standing and architecturally useful at that time. Last use of upper fill levels of the southern half of Room Block A probably also occurred at this time.

Construction of Room Block B took place during the latter portions of A.D. 1050 to 1100. The unit continued in use until the mid-1100s, and perhaps later.

The fill ceramics of Room Block C suggest use during the 1050 to 1100 span, with construction (obviously) prior to that time. There is no indication of later use or reuse of this unit.

Pit House 1 dates to the late A.D. 800s and early 900s. Pit House 3 may have been contemporaneous or slightly later than Pit House 1. Both Room Block A and Sub-B were probably constructed between 950 and 1000. Room Block B was built later, perhaps 1050 to 1100. Room Blocks A, B, and probably C were all in roughly contemporary use during the mid-1000s to late 1000s. Final use of parts of Room Blocks A and B was in the early to mid-1100s.

The transition from the Late Pit House period to the early Mimbres phase may be the Upper Gila's most interesting archaeology. It appears to be the Upper Gila's most extensive archaeology. Saige-McFarland provides our only excavated data from a site that spans this transition. We have only a sample of Saige-McFarland; the rest of the site is now gone. I have tried to rescue that sample from oblivion and to make the data from Saige-McFarland available to Southwestern archaeology. I also have made contentious arguments and odd observations based on these data; now it's your turn.

CHAPTER FIVE

Mimbres Archaeology of the Upper Gila

Three major projects have surveyed the upper Gila below the Mogollon Mountains. The first and most extensive was James E. Fitting's Upper Gila Project survey along the Gila and its tributaries in the Cliff Valley (Fitting 1972). The second was my survey of the Gila valley in the vicinity of Redrock (Lekson 1978a). The third, and most recent, was the Upper Gila Water Supply Study Class II (UGWSSII) sample survey of the Cliff Valley for a proposed dam (Chapman and others 1985).

A fourth project on the Upper Gila, a survey of the Gila Cliff Dwellings area (Anderson and others 1986), was 20 airline miles away and separated from the Cliff Valley by the rugged Mogollon Mountains. Although the Gila Cliff Dwellings area is also on the upper Upper Gila, it is not considered further here.

Fitting's Upper Gila Project continued the University of Michigan Mimbres Area Survey, which visited several Cliff Valley sites in 1967. Fitting returned to the Cliff Valley in 1971. Along with a number of major excavations, site-oriented survey began in that year and continued through 1973. Fitting recorded over 225 sites in the 21-mile long Cliff Valley (from where the river leaves the Mogollon Mountains to its narrows through the Big Burro Mountains) and in a number of the river's tributaries: Mogollon Creek, Duck Creek, Lobo Creek, Sycamore Creek, Mangas Creek, Greenwood Canyon, and Bear Creek. The total area surveyed approached a hundred square miles; the density of sites was thus less than three per square mile, reaching four sites per square mile only along the Gila River valley itself. A brief article (Fitting 1972) summarized the initial survey (including only 79 sites), but analysis of all the survey data has never been presented in print. I have used the unpublished site records from Fitting's survey in the following analysis of Mimbres archaeology in the Upper Gila. Ceramic data from Timothy C. Klinger's 1970s analysis were framed in the Boldface-Classic typology of that time; efforts to relocate these collections for reanalysis using the current Style I-II-III typology were, unfortunately, unsuccessful.

My Redrock survey in 1974 was an attempt at total coverage of about 22 square miles along a 16.5-mile reach of the Gila Valley above and below the town of Redrock. About 175 sites were recorded, for a site density of about 8 sites per square mile. My unrealistically detailed ceramic chronology (Lekson 1978a, 1982) discouraged subsequent comparative use of these data. By way of penance, I have re-sorted the decorated ceramics from the Redrock Survey into the

Style I-II-II typology (used in this report) and reassigned the sites into more useful chronological groupings, described below.

The Upper Gila Water Supply Study Class II survey (UGWSSII) was a well-designed 15 percent sample of a total study area of about 90 square miles of the Gila in the Cliff Valley and the Burro Mountains narrows, Duck Creek, and Mangas Creek, completed in 1983. About 90 prehistoric sites were recorded, or a site density of roughly 7 per square mile. About 15 percent of these sites had been discovered by Fitting's Upper Gila survey, but the UGWSSII records and maps of these sites are far more useful than the original notes. The Upper Gila and Redrock surveys targeted landforms along the river valley, but the UGWSSII survey included samples of uplands away from the river valley. UGWSSII data used in this analysis come from the published report (Chapman and others 1985) and from the field ceramic counts (on file at the Bureau of Reclamation offices in Phoenix).

These three surveys of the Upper Gila were all slightly different in method and focus. Fitting's Upper Gila Project survey was the most extensive, but probably the least rigorous in method. Fitting's survey could be described as an intensive reconnaissance, with reasonably complete discovery of structural sites along the terraces of the Gila and its tributaries. (The UGWSSII survey later confirmed that ceramic period structural sites are almost exclusively found on these land forms.) Site recording was minimal, limited to a brief description, estimated room counts, and a grab-sample of ceramics. The data from the Upper Gila Project survey are very useful for "big-picture" questions, but less useful for more detailed analyses.

The Redrock survey also focused on river valley landforms, but attempted to be more complete in coverage and more systematic in recording than was the Upper Gila Project. Sites were carefully mapped and large, proportionate samples were recorded of lithics and ceramics. This survey provided reasonably complete data on the Gila's valley at Redrock, but it did not include tributaries or nonriverine areas.

The methods and field techniques of the UGWSSII survey were the most rigorous of the three, but the UGWSSII study area was defined by nonarchaeological, engineering requirements and then the area was sampled. As with any sample survey, some of the variation in the sites recorded may be attributed to the vagaries of sampling. For example, the high number of Salado sites recorded by UGWSSII reflects the inclusion in the sample of a small enclave of Salado sites on Duck Creek. Comparison with Fitting's survey data demonstrates that Salado sites are less abundant in the Cliff Valley, as a whole, than might be estimated from the 15 percent UGWSSII sample. Conversely, the large number of aceramic pit house sites on a minor side drainage of Duck Creek is not represented in either Fitting's or my surveys, perhaps because similar areas were not investigated by the Upper Gila or Redrock projects. The UGWSSII survey is a fine modern survey and can be used best as a "fine tuning" of Fitting's much less rigorous survey of the same area and as a healthy corrective to riverine-focused surveys.

The combined strength of the three surveys is in the record of ceramic-period structural sites. The UGWSSII sample confirmed the location of such sites along the major stream channels, and thus suggests that the area focus of Fitting's survey coverage was appropriate for the landforms on which such sites are found. The Redrock Valley survey provides a nearly complete set of riverine sites to which Fitting's less systematic Upper Gila data can be compared. Combining data from the three surveys provides a context for understanding the place of the Saige-McFarland Site in Upper Gila archaeology. The following sections discuss the extent to which the three rather different surveys can be made comparable.

CERAMIC ASSEMBLAGES

Pottery is the primary tool for dating sites located in survey but, as all archaeologists know, surface ceramics often do not directly represent the range or extent of features actually present at sites. I do not believe that we control either the correspondence of surface with subsurface archaeology or absolute chronology in southwestern New Mexico. Although I once attempted to reconstruct population history in the Redrock Valley from surface data (Lekson 1978a), I now see that effort with its reliance on surface ceramics for fine-grained chronology as misguided. As a result of my disenchantment with my own past follies, I am also skeptical about momentary population estimates for the Mimbres area, such as those offered for the Mimbres Valley by Blake and others (1986). Population history may ask more of the surface record in the Mimbres area than we can realistically expect it to show.

Rather than read more into a surface archaeological record than it might support, a system of descriptive surface ceramic assemblages, similar to that developed for the eastern Mimbres area (Lekson 1989; Mills 1986), provides a reasonable summary of both the survey data and their limitations. For the three Upper Gila surveys, the ceramic assemblages cross-cut the varying typologies and techniques underlying the primary data (Table 5.1). Because decorated sherds from the Upper Gila survey could not be relocated and reanalyzed using the Style I-II-III system, Assemblage IVA for the Upper Gila Survey refers only to those sites with pueblo architecture and Boldface Black-on-white. Thus As-

Table 5.1. Ceramic Assemblages and Chronological Periods

Chronological period		Ceramic assemblage
Salado	VI	0–5% Classic (Styles II-III, III) 95–100% Salado series
Multicomponent Mimbres-Salado	V	0–15% Transitional (Styles I-II, II) 30–50% Classic (Styles II-III, III) 50–55% Salado series
Mimbres	IVB	0–5% Boldface (Style I) 0–5% Transitional (Styles I-II, II) 95–100% Classic (Styles II-III, III)
Mangas(?)	IVA	65% Transitional (Styles I-II, II) 35% Classic (Styles II-III, III)
Multicomponent Pit House-Mimbres	III	UGWSSII Survey: 40% Mogollon Red-on-brown and Three Circle Red-on-white 35% Boldface (Styles I, I-II, II) 25% Classic (Styles II-III, III)
	III	Upper Gila, Redrock surveys: 5% Mogollon Red-on-brown and Three Circle Red-on-white 45% Boldface (Styles I, I-II, II) 50% Classic (Styles II-III, III)
Late Pit House	IIB	50% Boldface (Style I) 50% Three Circle Red-on-white
Late Pit House	IIA	0–5% Boldface (Style I) 95–100% Mogollon Red-on-brown
Early Pit House	I	No decorated ceramics 0–5% Red ware 95–100% Alma series
Late Archaic		Ceramics absent

semblage IVA is underrepresented for the Upper Gila Survey collections.

The basic temporal units used in Table 5.1 reflect the Mimbres Foundation chronology, presented in Table 1.1. The Animas phase, familiar from the literature on the Upper Gila (Lekson and Klinger 1973), fails to appear in the surface archaeology or, for that matter, in excavation (Lekson 1984a, note 1). The assemblage system in Table 5.1 recognizes that a great many sites cannot be placed into single chronological periods. In my opinion, we lack the tools to partition specific features at long-lived sites into the various phases and stages. Analytical units that accommodate multi-component sites are more reasonable than phase systems that force sites into tightly defined chronological taxons.

SITE SIZE

It is possible to compare numbers of sites for each area or each survey, but numbers of sites do not reflect any archaeological reality beyond the size of areas that archaeologists felt comfortable recording. Some dimension independent of the "site" is necessary for describing and comparing the archaeology of the Upper Gila. With my current doubts about population estimates, the reasonable dimension to use is site size.

The only measure of site size common to all three surveys is estimated room count (surface and pit rooms). In each

**Table 5.2. Survey Room Counts Expressed as a Percentage
of Total Rooms by Chronological Periods**

Chronological period	Ceramic assemblage (Table 5.1)	UGWSSII survey 997 rooms %	Upper Gila survey 3744 rooms %	Redrock survey 864 rooms %
Pueblo Period	Unknown	2.9	8.3	2.2
Salado	VI	2.3	4.6	17.4
Mimbres-Salado	V	29.9	7.0	4.2
Mimbres	IVB	5.0	21.2	17.4
Mangas(?)	IVA	5.5	7.4	6.3
Pit House-Mimbres	III	27.9	43.0	34.7
Late Pit House				
Three Circle	IIB		3.0	8.8
San Francisco	IIA	3.5		
Early Pit House	I	6.7	4.3	9.0
Late Archaic		16.3	1.2	0.0

survey, room counts were estimated in different ways: in Fitting's Upper Gila survey, room counts were simply a guess; in my Redrock survey, room counts were estimated by dividing the mapped architectural area by an average room size; in the UGWSSII survey, room counts were estimated during the mapping of each site. Despite these differences, room counts are a consistent index of site size *relative to each survey data set* and, I believe, a reasonable comparative measure among surveys. Despite hand-wringing concerns over comparability, room counts are Hobson's Choice: they are the only available measure.

Table 5.2 summarizes total site size for each survey. Site sizes have been reduced from absolute values to relative values by presenting these data as percentages of the summed total site area recorded for each survey. If, for example, total site area doubled in each of three temporally sequent assemblages (A, B, and C), the total room count (100%) would have a percentage distribution of Assemblage A, 14.3 percent; Assemblage B, 28.5 percent; and Assemblage C, 57.2 percent.

Table 5.2 shows the distribution of visible, surface archaeology in the three surveys. Fitting's Upper Gila survey is the most extensive and presumably offers the most complete picture of Cliff Valley archaeology. The Upper Gila survey shows that most of the surface archaeology, as measured by room counts, is associated with a ceramic assemblage (III) that spans the Pit House period and the Mimbres phase, an assemblage that includes the Saige-McFarland Site. Assemblage III together with Mangas(?) and pure Mimbres phase ceramic assemblages (IVA and IVB) account for almost three-fourths of the visible archaeology. Pit House period and Archaic (aceramic) sites constitute less than one-tenth of the visible archaeology; sites with either Salado series alone or mixed Mimbres-Salado Assemblages V and VI make up another tenth.

The Redrock survey, a more systematic coverage of the same target landforms as the Upper Gila survey, in general

recorded a similar surface archaeology. Pit House period sites were estimated to have, proportionately, twice as many rooms as those evident in the Upper Gila Survey area, and rooms on sites with Salado assemblages made up twice as large a fraction of the total room count as similar assemblages in the Cliff Valley. Proportionately, sites with earlier and later ceramic assemblages contributed more to the Redrock surface archaeology than the Cliff Valley (as recorded by the Upper Gila Survey); the two surveys are otherwise in close agreement.

The UGWSSII survey differs from the Redrock and Upper Gila surveys in three ways. First, the discovery of an extensive complex of aceramic pit house sites on a minor tributary of Duck Creek produced the remarkable proportion of Late Archaic rooms in the UGWSSII sample. Similar settings were not included in the Upper Gila and Redrock surveys. Second, the fortuitous placement of survey sampling on a tight cluster of Salado sites on Duck Creek resulted in a much higher proportion of Mimbres-Salado (Assemblage V) archaeology than in the other two surveys. Third, the total size of Mimbres and Mimbres series assemblages (III and IV) is much lower than the Upper Gila and Redrock totals. In part, this is a simple mechanical function of higher proportions of earlier and later sites, but to a greater extent this reflects the failure of the sample to include the rare, large sites that contribute most of the room totals to the Upper Gila and Redrock surveys. Huge Assemblage III sites (the Woodrow Ruin in the Cliff Valley and the Cemetery and Redrock Village sites in the Redrock Valley) contributed sizable numbers of rooms to the total surface archaeology of these areas; no similar sites were recorded by the UGWSSII sample.

Use of the UGWSSII data must be tempered by the knowledge that very large Assemblage III sites are missing from the UGWSSII sample. Conversely, the UGWSSII sample survey demonstrated the existence of an extensive aceramic pit house archaeology and a substantial occurrence of sites with both Mimbres and Salado ceramics, both phenomena lacking or underrepresented in the Upper Gila and Redrock surveys.

SURFACE ARCHAEOLOGY

Based on survey data, the record begins with aceramic, presumably Archaic, pit houses. Archaic pit houses have been excavated at the Eaton site (Hemphill 1983) and the Ormand site (Hammack and others 1966) in the Cliff Valley, and at LA 29397 in the Redrock Valley (Laumbach 1980). Early Pit House period sites appear in all three surveys, ranging in size up to about 40 rooms. The partially excavated Winn Canyon site (Fitting 1973) is of this size. Some sites of both Late Archaic and Early Pit House periods are located away from the river terraces, either on high "defensive" mesas or on minor tributaries. We can be reasonably certain that both aceramic and Early Pit House components are also present in the larger, multicomponent river terrace sites (see Lekson 1989: 52–56 for development of this argument).

Late Pit House components are also represented in large Assemblage III and, rarely, Assemblage V sites. Single component Late Pit House sites are rare, and I suspect that the major portion of Late Pit House archaeology exists in multicomponent sites. If my assessment is correct, then there is little point to extended discussion of Late Pit House settlement in the Upper Gila. Excavations at large Assemblage III sites on the Mimbres support this interpretation (Anyon and LeBlanc 1984; Shafer and Taylor 1986), as do the data from Saige-McFarland.

The importance of large, multicomponent Late Pit House and Mimbres sites is dramatically illustrated by the Redrock and Upper Gila survey data. In both cases, large sites (100 to 150 or more rooms) contribute approximately one-third of the *total* room count in each survey, and almost half of the room count totals for sites with Mimbres series assemblages.

The huge Woodrow Ruin is the single most important Mimbres site in the Cliff Valley. The other large multicomponent sites in the Upper Gila survey are both much smaller than Woodrow and are almost all located on tributary creeks, away from the main river valley. Woodrow dominates the Gila, with at least 300 rooms in 16 separate room blocks built over an extensive Late Pit House period component. Two masonry-walled great kivas appear to be contemporary with the pueblo room blocks. About one-fifth of the site was destroyed by commercial pothunters; Woodrow has never been scientifically investigated.

As in the Mimbres Valley, large multicomponent sites are the central matter of Upper Gila archaeology. The formation and structure of these sites varies: whereas Galaz, Swarts, and NAN have large pit house components overlain by much larger Mimbres pueblos (Anyon and LeBlanc 1984; Cosgrove and Cosgrove 1932; Shafer and Taylor 1986), the large Mimbres phase Mattocks ruin does not appear to have substantial earlier pit house period occupation, according to Patricia Gilman in 1988. With the extensive excavations in the Mimbres Valley, it may be possible to characterize the individual histories of each of the dozen large sites there, and then to attempt more detailed reconstructions of that valley's prehistory. We are nowhere near this degree of resolution in the Upper Gila, where we can contrast the large Pit House period and smaller Mangas and Mimbres components at Saige-McFarland with the obviously extensive Mangas and Mimbres components at the Woodrow Ruin, but beyond recognizing that variability exists, we dare not go.

In terms of sites, not room counts, small sites are much more frequent than large sites. If sites from Assemblages III and IV are combined with masonry pueblo sites of indefinite Mimbres series affiliation (usually small sites with few decorated ceramics), the pattern is clearly one of many small sites and only a few large sites. In all three surveys, Assemblage III, IV, and "indefinite" pueblo ruins of less than ten rooms make up from about 70 percent (Upper Gila Survey,

Redrock) to 80 percent (UGWSSII) of the total number of sites with these assemblages. By far the majority of total room counts (visible architecture) is concentrated on the few largest sites, but from the survey data, the "typical" Upper Gila Mimbres site could be characterized as a rubble mound of about five rooms and a pit structure depression (see also Chapman and others 1985: 357–358, 379–380). I have argued elsewhere that the larger Mimbres sites are, in general, aggregates of these units (Lekson 1988a, 1989).

A number of small Upper Gila puebloan sites have ceramic assemblages characterized by approximately two-thirds Transitional and one-third Classic Black-on-white (Assemblage IVA). Like larger Assemblage III sites, these sites could represent multicomponent situations. All but 3 of the 38 Assemblage IVA sites recorded by the three surveys are less than 20 rooms and most are less than 10 rooms. The small size of many of these sites suggests another explanation. I have argued above and elsewhere (Lekson 1988a) for the existence of the Mangas phase, a transitional span between the pit house villages of the Late Pit House period and the large pueblos of the Mimbres phase. I do not insist on the term Mangas phase or on a rigid definition, but Assemblage IVA on the Upper Gila does reiterate the surface reality of an archaeology that looks like what once was called Mangas. The Saige-McFarland Site demonstrates the subsurface reality of the Mangas phase at one site, at least.

The Mangas phase issue pales to a mere quibble compared to the dramatic difficulties of the post-Mimbres sequence. There appears to be a major break between the Mimbres phase, as it is understood from the Mimbres Valley, and the Saladoan Cliff phase. If Mimbres Black-on-white ceases to be made by A.D. 1150 (LeBlanc 1983) and Gila Polychrome, the hallmark of the Cliff phase, is not produced until after 1300 (Doyel and Haury 1976, Lekson 1984c), there appears to be no likely surface assemblage that fills that 150-year gap. It is possible that marker ceramics for that period are not decorated types and so are not recognized in the decorated-ceramics assemblage system; it is possible that sherds of rarer 1150 to 1300 types are found only at large sites, where sampling might tend to preclude their discovery; or it is possible that the Cliff Valley was abandoned during this interval. I have argued elsewhere for continuity between Mimbres phase and post-Mimbres phase populations in the eastern Mimbres area (Lekson 1988b), and I have suggested above that late re-use of the Saige-McFarland Site may date to this span. However, no post-Mimbres, pre-Salado presence can be defined from the surface archaeology of the Upper Gila (see Chapman and others 1985: 161, for a similarly bleak conclusion).

The Saladoan Cliff phase is represented by both single-component (Assemblage VI) and multicomponent (Assemblage V) sites. Notably, Assemblage VI sites are either very large (200+ rooms) or very small (5 rooms or less). Multicomponent Mimbres-Salado sites in the Redrock and Upper Gila surveys are of intermediate size (less than 40 rooms) and lack extensive time depth; their ceramic assemblages are limited to Mimbres Style III and Salado series types. The multicomponent Salado sites recorded by the UGWSSII survey differ in having evidence of even earlier occupation (Late Pit House period ceramic types) in addition to Mimbres Style III and Salado types. The UGWSSII Salado sites were primarily located along Duck Creek. The longer time depth of these sites, when compared to other Upper Gila Mimbres-and-Salado sites, may reflect conditions specific to that drainage.

Salado pottery is either rare or all-but-absent at the largest multicomponent (Assemblage III) sites in the Upper Gila. I suggested above that the largest Assemblage III sites may have had occupations reaching back to Late Archaic or Early Pit House; but they lack the latest, Cliff phase. This absence, combined with the single-componency of the very largest Salado Cliff phase sites, suggests a remarkable shift in settlement location between the Mimbres and Salado periods, and makes the apparent hiatus between them all the more significant.

REGIONAL CHRONOLOGY

Compared to the Mimbres Valley, much less excavation has taken place in the Cliff Valley and little of that has been fully reported. The most extensive excavations in the area were those of Richard Ellison, an archaeologist from Silver City, and of the Museum of New Mexico Cliff Highway Salvage Project. Ellison has been generous in discussing his data (from Mimbres sites and from an important late Salado site, Kwilleylekia), but no reports have been published. The Museum of New Mexico prepared brief descriptive reports of its excavations at the Lee, Ormand, and Dinwiddie sites, but beyond Bussey's use of the Lee and Dinwiddie materials in his dissertation (Bussey 1973, partially reprinted in Bussey 1975) no analyses of these extensive excavations have appeared. Excavations by avocational archaeologists have produced brief reports (for example, Mills and Mills 1972; Brunett 1972, 1986) but as yet no full analysis. The most extensive series of excavation reports from the Cliff Valley were produced by Fitting's Upper Gila Project (Baker 1971; Burns 1972; Fitting 1973; Fitting and others 1971; Hemphill 1983; Lekson and Klinger 1973). Even these are usually presented as "preliminary" reports or are brief master's theses.

The sketchy, preliminary nature of so much of the Cliff Valley literature makes the interpretation of the few absolute dates from the area very difficult. An initial failure of tree-ring dating for Cliff Valley samples led Fitting to rely on carbon-14 dating, a much more expensive (and therefore more limited) and much less precise process. Recently, tree-ring dates have been successfully determined in a series of 12 samples; however, all but one (from Saige-McFarland) come from undescribed, unpublished sites. Thus we are left with a handful of carbon-14 dates, a dozen tree-ring dates,

and several unpublished, unconfirmed archaeomagnetic dates with which to build a 2,000 year-long chronology for a major section of the Mimbres region (Table 5.3).

Only three architectural units have tree-ring dates: a Mimbres room block at the DeFausell site (Brunett 1986), which dates after A.D. 1108; Room 6 at Saige-McFarland, which was added to Room Block A sometime after 1126; and an unknown site on Duck Creek, which produced two cutting dates at 1243. All other dates are either carbon-14 dates or early archaeomagnetic determinations (dated by Robert DuBois; I have only secondary references for these dates). Carbon-14 dating is an exercise in sampling, and suites of dates are far preferable to single dates, which are problematic at best. Because of expense, only one carbon-14 date was obtained from any single unit on the Upper Gila. The only exception to this pattern of parsimony was Room 6 at Winn Canyon with two dates, which, rather than increasing the precision of the dating, illustrate the problems of interpreting carbon-14 dates. It is tempting to dismiss any discussion of Upper Gila chronology as premature; we simply do not have enough dates to seriously tinker with chronology. But I have yet to meet an archaeologist who could walk away from a list of dates. At the very least, the Upper Gila dates may be compared to the Mimbres Valley chronology (Table 1.1).

The two earliest dates from the Upper Gila are almost identical: 383 B.C. (401–208 B.C.) from the Eaton site and 393 B.C. (757–135 B.C.) from Winn Canyon. The Eaton site is a Late Archaic site; Winn Canyon is an Early Pit House site. Either we have an unusually tight date on the Late Archaic-Early Pit House transition and, incidentally, an extension of the Early Pit House period some 600 years earlier than its traditional dating (Table 1.1), or something is wrong.

The same pit room (Room 2) at Winn Canyon produced a second date of A.D. 411. The two dates fail, by almost 200 years, to overlap at the two-sigma range. It is possible to average the dates, but the average is meaningless. I suspect that there is an archaeological explanation for Room 2, which was a large, shallow "Great Kiva." The earlier, 393 B.C. date came from a subfloor feature (Feature 10), described as a pit house within a pit house. Feature 10 was a basin-shaped depression, 4.0 m in diameter, 0.7 m deep, with a series of interior postholes around its circumference and a central hearth, a feature that closely resembles the Late Archaic house excavated at the nearby Eaton Site. Feature 10 was filled and the floor of Pit Room 2 was built over it. It seems possible that Feature 10 was, in fact, an earlier Late Archaic pit structure incorporated into a later Early Pit House great kiva. This scenario would explain the close agreement of the Feature 10 and Eaton carbon-14 dates. Room 2, the Early Pit House great kiva, could then be associated with the later A.D. 411 date (one-sigma range 262–535), and all would be well with the world. Arguing against this interpretation is the symmetrical placement of Feature

Table 5.3. Absolute Dates from the Upper Gila

Method	Number	Date	Provenience
		A.D.	
Carbon-14	B-20514	1300–1380 (1280–1380)	Saige-McFarland, Room 8 corn, corrected: 1212 (1074–1260)
Tree-ring	(45 dates)	1276rLG–1287rLGB	Gila Cliff Dwellings (Anderson and others 1986)
Tree-ring	DCR-2, -3	1243 cG	Site on Duck Creek (Bannister and others 1970: 53)
Archaeomag	OK-665	1175 ± 23	Riverside Site, Feature 11 (Fitting and others 1982: 76)
Archaeomag	OK-664	1155 ± 24	Riverside Site, Feature 11 (Fitting and others 1982: 76)
Tree-ring	NMM-3	1126vv	Saige-McFarland, Room 6
Tree-ring	NMM-12	1108 + vv	DeFausell Site, D-16 (Brunett 1986)
Tree-ring	NMM-14	1102vv	DeFausell Site, D-16 (Brunett 1986)
Tree-ring	NMM-15	1102v	DeFausell Site, D-16 (Brunett 1986)
Tree-ring	NMM-18	1100vv	DeFausell Site, D-19 (Brunett 1986)
Tree-ring	NMM-10	1098 + vv	DeFausell Site, D-16 (Brunett 1986)
Tree-ring	NMM-9	1091vv	DeFausell Site, D-16 (Brunett 1986)
Tree-ring	NMM-8	1083vv	DeFausell Site, D-16 (Brunett 1986)
Tree-ring	NMM-13	1074vv	DeFausell Site, D-16 (Brunett 1986)
Tree-ring	NMM-16	1063vv	DeFausell site, D-16 (Brunett 1986)
Carbon-14	B-20513	1070–1154 (1024–1209)	Saige-McFarland, Room 11
Carbon-14	N-1588	1023 (984–1157)	Villareal II, Pit House 1 (Lekson 1978)
Archaeomag	?	950	Lee Village (Bussey 1975: 17)
Carbon-14	N-1554	778–800 (687–938)	Black's Bluff, Pit House 1 (Brunett 1972)
Carbon-14	B-20512	672 (645–770)	Saige-McFarland, Pit House 1
Carbon-14	N-1556	411 (262–532)	Winn Canyon Site, Room 6, floor (Fitting 1973)
Carbon-14		408 (258–533)	LA 29397 roasting pit and pit house, averaged (Laumbach 1980)
Carbon-14	JRIA	383 B.C. (401–208 B.C.)	Eaton Site (Hemphill 1983)
Carbon-14	N-1555	393 B.C. (757–135 B.C.)	Winn Canyon Site, Room 6, subfloor (Fitting 1973)

Note: Carbon-14 dates calibrated according to Stuiver and Reimer (1986).

10 within Room 2, which seems unlikely if the construction of the two was separated by 800 years.

Two dates from an aceramic site (LA 29397) in the Redrock Valley bear on this problem. These dates may be legitimately averaged, producing a date of A.D. 408 (one-sigma range 258–533). The range on this date suggests that the Late Archaic continues at least into the late A.D. 200s, reinforcing the anomaly of a 393 B.C. beginning for the Early Pit House period at Winn Canyon.

Two carbon-14 dates relate to the Three Circle phase: A.D. 672 (645–770) from Pit House 1 at Saige-McFarland and 778–800 (687–938) from Pit House 1 at Blacks Bluff. Both structures (and both dates) are clearly associated with Boldface Black-on-white (Style I) assemblages. These dates and their one-sigma ranges are consistent, if a trifle early, with the Mimbres Valley dates for the Three Circle phase (Table 1.1). A third date, a reported archaeomagnetic date of 950 from Lee Village (Bussey 1975: 17), also falls into the traditional range for the Three Circle phase.

Dates from Mimbres contexts range from a carbon-14 date of A.D. 1023 (984–1157) from Pit House 1 at Villareal II to a tree-ring date of 1126vv from Saige-McFarland. Most Upper Gila carbon-14 and tree-ring dates from Mimbres contexts fall within the 1000–1150 span suggested by the Mimbres Foundation chronology. Two archaeomagnetic dates from superimposed hearths at the Riverside Site date to 1155 ± 24 and 1175 ± 23. The dates were in reverse stratigraphic order (Fitting and others 1982: 76), suggesting an approximate date of the hearths to a span of 1150–1175. This dating is late for the associated Classic Mimbres Black-on-white ceramic assemblage (Baker 1971), but not so late as to cause archaeologists to defenestrate. Indeed, for hearths a slightly later archaeomagnetic dating (which likely represents late or last use) than tree-ring dating (which usually is obtained from construction timbers that represent initial use) should be expected.

The single apparent anomaly is a late carbon-14 date from Saige-McFarland: an uncorrected date of A.D. 1300–1380

(1280–1380) on corn from the floor of Room Block B. This date probably represents a corrected date of about 1212, with a one-sigma range of 1074–1260. The one-sigma range includes the final century of the Mimbres phase as dated in the Mimbres Valley (Table 1.1).

The only possible Salado dates from the Upper Gila are two cutting dates of A.D. 1243 from a site on Duck Creek. "The site is reported to yield Gila Polychrome" (Bannister and others 1970: 53). These dates are of special interest. Gila Polychrome is generally considered to postdate 1300. If the 1243 dates are in fact associated with Gila Polychrome, they represent one of the few pre-1300 dated contexts for pottery of this type. It is worth noting that the Gila Cliff Dwellings are well dated to a span from 1276 to 1287, but Gila Polychrome pottery was lacking in the Cliff Dwellings assemblage (Anderson and others 1986).

A number of Salado sites are known from Duck Creek, but the two A.D. 1242 tree-ring dates cannot be definitely associated with any single site. If we accept a post-1300 dating of Gila Polychrome, it seems unlikely that the 1242 dates are from Salado contexts. But if these dates are not from a Salado site, then from what site are they? I noted above the apparent hiatus between the Mimbres phase and the Saladoan Cliff phase. There are at present no site candi-

dates dating to the transitional interval between the Mimbres and Salado phases, but the only two cutting tree-ring dates from the Upper Gila fall right into this nonexistent period. The bulk of Saladoan archaeology is represented by late, single-component sites and the relatively rare multicomponent Mimbres-Salado sites are clustered on Duck Creek. With these mysterious tree-ring dates and the occurrence of multicomponent Mimbres-Salado sites on Duck Creek, it seems reasonable to conclude that if evidence for continuity between Mimbres and Salado exists, it will be found in the Mimbres-Salado sites of Duck Creek.

In summary, absolute dates from the Upper Gila conform to the accepted Mimbres chronology. The Mimbres Valley chronology is not supported by an over-abundance of dates, and the Mimbres regional chronology is thin indeed when compared to many other areas of the American Southwest. Many more dates are needed before we can begin to construct detailed regional prehistories for the Mimbres. "More dates" may seem like a cheap and easy exit, but it is not. It is, I believe, a statement of fact: in the Mimbres area we simply do not have sufficient chronological control to play the kinds of demographic games our Anasazi colleagues take for granted.

Mimbres Taxonomy

In an area like the Upper Gila, with limited excavation and sparse dating, archaeological taxonomy is much more important than in better-studied districts. With few absolute dates and only a tentative network of ceramic cross dating, phases and periods become primary chronological tools. Arguments over phase taxonomy, which might seem quaint and even embarrassing in well-dated Anasazi archaeology, are still central in a less well-studied region like the Mimbres.

The early work of Haury (1936) and the Cosgroves (1932) established the initial phase system that was used until more recent excavations broadened the data base. The basic archaeological taxonomy of the Mimbres region now in use is the Mimbres Foundation system (Anyon and others 1981; Anyon and LeBlanc 1984; Nelson and LeBlanc 1986), developed primarily from Mimbres Valley data (Table 1.1). The archaeology of the Upper Gila region does not always gracefully conform to this system (for example, LeBlanc and Whalen 1980). Some archaeologists working in the area have rebelled against what sometimes appears to be a Procrustean application of the Mimbres Valley taxonomy to the Upper Gila area (Fitting and others 1982; Lekson 1988a). The Saige-McFarland Site is at the center of some of these disagreements.

Pit House 1 at Saige-McFarland can be assigned to the Three Circle phase without argument. It may be possible to dispose of the pit structures below Room Block B with similar taxonomic ease, as other Three Circle phase structures. But Pit House 3 is more of a problem. Based on the ceramics found in its fill, I suggested that this unit was built sometime prior to A.D. 950. Pit House 3 is a deep, square, masonry-lined pit structure with a ventilator system. According to the guide book (Anyon and LeBlanc 1980; Anyon and LeBlanc 1984: 137) this kind of structure should date to the Mimbres phase, or after A.D. 1000. Perhaps the sherds in the fill of Pit House 3 were redeposited from earlier contexts; or perhaps Pit House 3 is an early example of this kind of structure, straddling the taxonomic fence between the Three Circle phase and the Mimbres phase. There is a taxonomic term for the gray area on the cusp between the Pit House and Pueblo periods, but it is a term filled with contention and fraught with difficulties: the Mangas phase.

The Mangas phase is a taxonomic association of small pueblos with Boldface Black-on-white pottery. The Mimbres Foundation concluded that the Mangas phase was at best illusory and at worst bogus (LeBlanc and Whalen 1980; LeBlanc 1986). I have maintained that the association of little pueblos with early Mimbres white wares was real, at least on the Gila and perhaps all over the Mimbres region (Lekson 1988a). Moreover, many of these little pueblos appear to have associated pit structures, some of which are notably like Pit House 3 (for example Hammack and others 1966).

Room Block A began, both in prehistory and in the archaeological literature, as a Mangas phase unit. A subfloor burial with a large cache of Style I and Style II vessels (Feature 14) was clearly associated with the small masonry-walled pueblo. At least the initial construction of Room Block A was thus definitely associated with ceramics that in an earlier time would once have been called Boldface. But the ceramic arguments about Room Block A extended beyond this burial. Fitting (in Fitting and others 1971) argued that the total ceramic assemblage of Room Block A was predominately Boldface Black-on-white, indicating the Mangas phase.

This phase assignment sparked a lively debate (Fitting and others 1971; Gilman in LeBlanc and Whalen 1980; Stuart and Gauthier 1981; Fitting and others 1982; LeBlanc 1986; Lekson 1988a; Anyon 1988), and consequently the ceramic assemblage of Room Block A holds some interest for enthusiasts of taxonomy. Fitting and others (1971) published the proportions of Boldface to Mimbres Classic in Room Block A as 86 percent Boldface and 14 percent Classic. In fact, this high proportion of Boldface to Classic was the original reason for proposing a Mangas phase designation, since the vessels from Feature 14 had not been reconstructed and studied at the time the 1971 report was prepared.

Gilman challenged these proportions, suggesting that the ceramic assemblage of Room Block A was mixed and that "Fitting typed early Classic sherds as Boldface Black-on-white" (Gilman in LeBlanc and Whalen 1980: 212). Both of her points are correct: the total ceramic assemblage from Room Block A spans at least 150 years, from the Mangas phase through the Mimbres phase, and Fitting indeed typed some "early Classic" (Style II) as Boldface. Style II had not yet been defined when Fitting was flipping the sherds from Room Block A. Style II was carved out of what earlier typologies called Boldface. LeBlanc (1986) accepted Gilman's analysis and declared the Mangas phase morally, legally, physically, and spiritually dead.

As a matter of historical interest, the Room Block A Mimbres white wares, reclassified in the Style I-II-III series, fall into the following percentages: 37 percent Style I, 20 percent Style II, and 43 percent Style III. This reanalysis shows about three times as much Classic Black-on-white as Fitting's original counts, but still the majority of the Mimbres white wares were what Fitting (and other ceramicists of the pre-I-II-III era) called Boldface, Styles I and II.

Gilman was right, but she was also wrong. Whatever the shortcomings of the total Room Block A ceramic assemblage, the initial construction of Room Block A, "Classic period architecture" (Gilman in LeBlanc and Whalen 1980: 212) was unquestionably associated with Style I and, more importantly, Style II ceramics. This association is not unknown in the Mimbres Valley. Shafer's excavations at the NAN Ranch Ruin in the Mimbres Valley demonstrated pueblo-style, above-ground construction was in fact associated with Transitional (Style II) Black-on-white (Shafer and Taylor 1986).

The NAN Ranch Ruin had a long occupational history, beginning with an extensive Pit House period occupation, spanning the transition to the Mimbres phase. Thus evidence for Transitional pueblo-style building, if it existed at all, could be expected to be present at NAN. The two major excavations of the Mimbres Foundation, at Mattocks and Galaz, apparently did not encounter the Transitional period pueblo-style building, perhaps because transitional deposits of any kind were either very limited or outside the Mimbres Foundation's sample at these sites. The Mattocks Site apparently did not have an extensive Pit House component, according to Patricia Gilman in 1988. Lacking a major Pit House period component, Mattocks presumably might not have had much evidence for a Transitional occupation between the Pit House period and the Mimbres phase pueblo. Excavations at Galaz were limited almost entirely to the salvage excavation of Pit House period structures (Anyon and LeBlanc 1984). Transitional pueblo-style houses (if any) would almost certainly have been destroyed by pothunters bulldozing the Galaz Mimbres phase pueblo ruins. Perhaps the Mimbres Foundation rejected the Mangas phase because it was not present in their excavations, but pueblo-style building with Style I and (more importantly) Style II Mimbres ceramics is present at NAN and at Saige-McFarland. Call it Transitional, call it Mangas, call it (as I have often wanted to call equally problematic "Great Kivas") a duck, it matters little to me what we call it as long as we can agree that it really exists.

Whatever conclusions are reached on the Mangas matter, there should be little argument over the assignment of the later occupation of Room Block A and all of Room Blocks B and C to the Mimbres phase. The pottery is Mimbres Black-on-white (made who-knows-where) and the architecture is identical in form and detail to that of the large Mimbres Valley sites; it should be hard to deny the Mimbres phase on the Upper Gila. Unfortunately, the history of research in southwestern New Mexico fosters the notion that "the Classic Mimbres appears only to have been *classic* in the Mimbres Valley . . ." (Stuart and Gauthier 1981: 204), and that the Mimbres of the Upper Gila is something different, related to real, Mimbres Valley Mimbres, but essentially a separate research domain.

I have argued elsewhere that this Mimbres-centric view is mistaken (Lekson 1984b, 1986a, 1988a). More than simply mistaken, this narrow view of the Mimbres is pernicious, and illustrates the real importance of taxonomy: I am concerned not so much with classificatory hair-splitting as with the way taxonomy influences our thinking. If one wants to investigate the ancient Mimbres, what is the appropriate scale in which to frame one's research?

To understand Mimbres ecology and economy (prerequisite to the headier realms of Mimbres social structure, iconography, and ritual), the necessary research scale must include all of southwestern New Mexico, much of southeastern Arizona, and great huge areas of northern Chihuahua (Lekson 1986a). River valleys, such as the Mimbres and the Gila, are convenient ways to classify modern archaeological data, but I see no reason to assume that prehistoric societies structured the geography of their lives and adaptations hydrologically. This short study presents data from the Mimbres of the Upper Gila area, in contrast to the many volumes on the Mimbres of the Mimbres Valley. But I submit that neither valley, alone, will prove sufficient for us to understand the societies that made Mimbres pottery and built Mimbres pueblos.

Burials

Eleven burials were given separate numbers at the Saige-McFarland Site. Two of these burials (numbers 5 and 8) are now interpreted as portions of the same individual, leaving a total of 10 burials. At least one, Burial 1, is only a fragment; the remainder probably represent formal interments of both inhumations and cremations. Data are available from Burials 4 through 11, all from Room 12, which were analyzed by me as a student project for an osteology class. None of the other three burials were studied, or if they were the records have not survived. Nor have any of the burials themselves survived with the 1987 collections. Weight of bone recovered from three cremations is given in Table A.1, and artifacts associated with the burials are summarized in Table A.2.

Burial 1

Burial 1 was found in the approach trench to Room Block B, during the first season at the site. "This burial, and this is a very liberal use of the term 'burial', was found scattered over Room 9 and in the area beyond Room 9 to the north [a room between Rooms 9 and 15 that had been pothunted]. This was a scattering of badly decayed bone and teeth found in an area at least six feet long, five feet wide and within a foot of the surface. It probably represents a late intrusive burial into the site, made long after the rooms of Room Block B had fallen into ruin" (Fitting and others 1971: 31).

Burial 2 (Feature 14)

Burial 2 was an extended inhumation, positioned on its back with the head to the east, accompanied by a spectacular cache of ceramics (Feature 15, Figs. 3.5–3.8). It was found below the floor of Room 4A. "The pit [Feature 14] had been dug into hardpan [substrate] and the upper portions of the body, which were badly decayed, were one foot lower than the lower portions. The long bones of the legs and the small bones of the feet were in excellent condition" (Fitting and others 1971: 20). Unfortunately, we know very little about the osteology of this individual, other than it was clearly a large adult.

Burial 3 (Feature 26)

Burial 3 was a portion of an inhumation that had been partially destroyed by the road cut. It was observed eroding out of what was left of a subfloor pit, below the unnumbered room south of Room 7. Very little was left of the individual;

Table A.1. Weight in Grams of Bone Fragments from Three Cremations

Skeletal fragments	Burial 6	Burial 7	Burial 10
Cranial	69.0	157.4	225.1
Vertebrae	8.3	29.3	18.4
Ribs	5.1	37.1	
Pelvis	2.7	18.2	
Long bones	34.1	223.9	288.6
Unidentified	27.5	162.0	360.2
Total	146.7	627.9	892.3

Table A.2. Materials Associated with Burials at the Saige-McFarland Site

Burial number	Feature number	Vessel number	Other Artifacts
1		None	None
2	14, 15	11–32	"Small clay effigy" in Feature 15, quartz crystal "near throat," palette fragment (Ground Stone 98)
3	26	None	1 projectile point(?), 2 Mimbres Black-on-white sherds
4	47	46, 49	None
5 + 8	48, 50	None	None
6	49	43, 51, 52	5 stone beads, 1 shell bead, 1 shell pendant, 3 shell bracelet fragments, 1 projectile point, a piece of "turquoise," 6 concretions, numerous pieces of worked red shale
7	65	41, 48	6 stone beads, 1 shell figure-8 bead, 1 shell bracelet fragment
9	66	None	None
10	64	50, 71	21 shell figure-8 beads, 15 stone beads, 4 shell bracelet fragments, 1 quartz crystal
11	45	44, 45	1 turkey gastrolith(?), 9 shell beads, shell bracelet on left arm, 1 piece of worked turquoise

only the navicular and calcaneous, and the distal ends of the tibia and fibula (of unspecified side) were recovered. They appeared to be from an adult individual. No further details survive in the field notes.

Burial 4 (Feature 47)

Burial 4 was poorly preserved; based on size and the delicacy of the few remaining bones, it was probably a pre- or neo-natal individual. No diagnostic osteological features were recognized.

Burials 5 and 8 (Features 48 and 50)

These two burials, as well as other human bone, were found in a single rodent-disturbed pit (Feature 46). Since these "burials" are not from obviously different individuals and since neither represents more than a fraction of one person, all the material from Burials 5 and 8 is assumed to be from a poorly preserved inhumation of one adult. Material recovered consists of the lower portion of the skull, the left foot, and lower leg bones; however, soil stains indicated the locations of the ribs and the lower vertebrae. From the relative locations of the skeletal material and the stains, it appears that the individual was on his or her back, lying southwest-northeast with the head to the southwest, and at least one leg slightly flexed.

Cranial material included the basal portion of the occiput, part of the left temporal, and fragments of the left maxilla. Postcranial material included one cervical vertebra, a poorly preserved fragment of a humerus (side unknown), part of the left radius, fragments of the left tibia and fibula, and parts of the left ankle (that could not be removed intact).

The left maxilla, which was not in immediate proximity to the other cranial materials, included incisors one and two, canine, and premolar one; near the maxilla was an upper right incisor one. The teeth displayed heavy wear and caries appeared on mesial left incisor one and lingual left canine.

In view of the poor condition of the bones and the possible mixed associations, interpretation of this material is limited; Burials 5 and 8 represent an adult, age and sex unknown.

Burial 6 (Feature 49)

Burial 6 was a cremation of a child about six or seven years old, sex unknown. After the individual was completely incinerated, the remains were placed in Vessel 52, which was then covered with Vessel 51. Partial Vessel 43 was also associated with this burial, but its precise location relative to Vessels 51 and 52 is unknown. Vessels 51 and 52 were intact, so the cremated remains are probably complete (vessels in Figs. 3.9, 3.10). The bone fragments weighed 147 grams (Table A.1). The largest fragments were two pieces of parietal measuring about 10 mm by 17 mm and 8 mm by 13 mm; most fragments were considerably smaller. Specific identifications of bone fragments were often impossible, but several observations can be made.

1. No completely closed sutures were recognized in the cranial materials.
2. One wormian bone was located in the right parietal-occipital suture.
3. The iliac and ischium were not fused.
4. No fused vertebral arches were observed; however, these would be fragile and may not have survived.
5. Distal ends of both the left and right humerus were identified, plus the proximal ends of both tibias. It is possible that none of these epiphyses were fused, but this was difficult to determine with assurance.
6. Loose teeth included both lower canines, upper right incisor two, upper left incisors one and two, and upper left canine. They all appeared to be primary dentition. In addition, one lower incisor germ was identified.

Burial 7 (Feature 65)

Burial 7 was a cremation of probably a young adult of undetermined sex. After the individual was completely incinerated, the remains were placed in Vessel 48 and covered with Vessel 41 (Figs. 3.9, 3.10). Both were broken; some loss of cremated material is possible, but unlikely. The cremated materials weighed 628 grams (Table A.1). The largest fragments were of the parietal (15 mm by 17 mm), sphenoid (10 mm by 22 mm), and a tibia (5 mm by 22 mm). Heads of all nondigital longbones were present, as were both patellas; only one calcaneous was identified. The iliac crest was apparently not fused on identifiable fragments. Three teeth were present, but only as root fragments. Two were single root and two bifurcate.

Burial 9 (Feature 66)

Burial 9 was an inhumation of an infant, less than a year old, sex unknown. The body was placed on its left side with the legs flexed and the arms straight along the sides, head to the southwest. Little cranial material survived, but the postcranial skeleton was surprisingly well preserved, including diaphysial long bone, vertebral bodies, and unfused portions of the pelvis.

Burial 10 (Feature 64)

Burial 10 was a cremation of an individual at least 10 years old, sex unknown. The cremated bone was placed in Vessel 71, which was covered with Vessel 50 (Figs. 3.9, 3.10). Both vessels were inverted when buried. They were broken, and the pit may have been disturbed by rodents. Burial 10 weighed 892 grams (Table A.1). The largest fragments were a parietal (18 mm by 13 mm) and an unidentified long bone (20 mm by 5 mm). In general, the material was much more fragmentary than the cremations of Burials 6 and 7. No pelvic or coastal material, as identified in Burials 6 and 7, could be recognized in Burial 10. Some observations were possible.

1. Both proximal and distal ends of both humeri appeared to be fused.
2. The proximal ends of both radii were also fused.

3. A number of phalanges, with both proximal and distal heads fused, were identified.

4. Fragments of two capitates and two lunates were present.

5. Only one patella was found.

6. Teeth were represented only by 10 single-root and 8 double-root fragments. The latter figure may reflect extreme warpage of upper premolar roots.

Burial 11 (Feature 45)

Burial 11 was an inhumation of a child about seven to eight years old, sex unknown. The individual was placed on the back, oriented nearly north-south with the head to the north and the legs slightly flexed. Preservation was poor, but the right pelvis was well represented. The iliac and ischium were not fused. Only the condylar regions of the occiput remained of the crania; both axis and atlas bodies were present, as were several cervical and thoracic vertebral bodies. No vertebral arches were fused. Several upper ribs were recovered, along with small fragments of both femurs and unidentified long bones of both arms, apparently without epiphysial fusion. Similarly, none of the several phalanges appeared to have fused epiphyses. Teeth, found in the fill above the occiput, included lower left incisor two, right and left upper incisor two, and an indeterminate premolar two. All of these were permanent teeth. Also recovered were two upper first molar germs.

Ceramic Sorting Categories and Sherd Counts

The ceramic sorting categories used at the Saige-McFarland Site include various levels of typological identifications. Timothy C. Klinger first analyzed the pottery at the time of site excavations (1971–1973). I reanalyzed the decorated sherds using Style I-II-III categories developed more recently by the Mimbres Foundation. The utility types (the last four categories below) are those used in the original analysis, and utility sherd counts are from Fitting and others (1971) and from Klinger's unpublished analysis. Table B.1 presents my counts for decorated sherds and original analysis counts for utility sherds.

Provenience (Table B.1) lists room, pit house, or grid unit and Location indentifies the Level or Feature. Level numbering in Pit House 1 varied from unit to unit (Figs. 2.8, 2.9). Level 3 in one unit may be equivalent to Level 7 in another. For ease of comparison, I have substituted a capital letter code for the numbered Pit House 1 levels. The new level codes are as follows: A, 0–0.30 m; B, 0.30–0.46 m; C, 0.46–0.61 m; D, 0.61–0.76 m; E, 0.76–0.91 m; F, 0.91–1.07 m; G, 1.07–1.22 m; H, 1.22–1.37 m; I, 1.37 m to floor (usually at about 1.52 m).

For the analysis of rim sherds and vessel form assemblages (Table B.2), I included an additional utility category for vessels with smudged and polished interiors. Proveniences are combined into grouped proveniences, described in Chapter 3.

The numbers below are used to identify the sorting categories in Table B.1. Categories 31–35 duplicate, as closely as possible, the Mimbres Foundation typology (Scott 1983; Anyon and LeBlanc 1984: 151–152). Full descriptions and definitions have not yet been published for these types, but I worked closely with Anyon and believe that my classification of sherds into categories 31–35 parallels his. Some of the temporal distinctions within Style III developed by Shafer and Taylor (1986) require larger fragments of the design than were available on all sherds and I have not incorporated their categories in the sherd reanalysis. One of their temporally sensitive attributes, the "extended rim line," was recorded in the rim sherd analysis and is discussed in Chapter 3.

CATEGORY DEFINITIONS

20   Plain white wares. White-slipped sherds of the Mimbres series lacking any painted decoration.

21   Mogollon Red-on-brown (Haury 1936). Mogollon Red-on-brown, identified as an early type in the Mimbres sequence, occurs in varying (but not decreasing) amounts through the seriation (Table 3.4). Although the unit (Pit House 3) with the highest proportion of Mogollon Red-on-brown is early, the type makes up over 12 percent of the later Mimbres phase assemblage of Room Block B. Either the type is longer-lived than heretofore suggested, or I mistyped later red-on-brown sherds. It appears that red-on-brown vessels form a consistent part of all assemblages at Saige-McFarland, early and late, and that sherds from these vessels cannot be typologically differentiated from Mogollon Red-on-brown. Although early and late varieties of red-on-brown could not be defined, these sherds may prove useful in future attempts to do so. Change from the dimpled finish of San Francisco Red to a smoother surface finish may prove important.

22   Three Circle Red-on-white (Haury 1936; Anyon and LeBlanc 1984). Differentiated from misfired Boldface by the exterior dimpled finish on bowls and creamy slip. Three Circle Red-on-white appears to decrease through time (Table 3.4).

30   Undifferentiated Mimbres series black-on-white. Any decorated sherds of the Mimbres series with designs too fragmentary to assign to the next seven categories. Primarily sherds with a single line or a fragment of a solid motif.

31   Style I (Mangas or Boldface) Black-on-white (Cosgrove and Cosgrove 1932, in part; Scott 1983; Anyon and LeBlanc 1984). The most common motifs include crudely painted interlocked spirals, free elements (in particular, "F" elements), thick zigzag lines (Anyon's "wavy" lines, see 41 below), scalloped bordered solids, and "squiggle hachure" (wavy-line cross-hachure).

32   Indeterminate Style I-II. Sherds indeterminate between Styles I and II. The category is seldom used and is combined with Category 33 in the manipulations of the data.

33   Style II (Transitional) Black-on-white (Scott 1983; Anyon and LeBlanc 1984). The most com-

mon motifs include thin linear hachure (and less commonly cross hachure and checkerboard hachure between thick framing lines, with or without well-executed interlocked spirals, and thick zigzag lines opposed to solid elements. Most designs reach the rim, but a frequently seen variant had a rim band of opposed scalloped lines (as on the exterior of Vessel 23).

34   Indeterminate Style II-III. Sherds indeterminate between Styles II and III. This category is used for rim sherds with designs classifiable as Style II, but that stop just below the rim on a thin line. This arrangement is often seen on late Style II (Anyon and LeBlanc 1984: 151). In the manipulations of the data I have combined Category 34 with Category 35.

35   Style III (Mimbres Classic) Black-on-white (Cosgrove and Cosgrove 1932, in part; Scott 1983; Anyon and LeBlanc 1984). Thin-line cross hachure within thin framing lines, and thin-line parallel hachure, both in oppostion to solid elements; complex negative designs; rim bands or framers; flare rims. More extensive motif descriptions are in the cited references.

36   Mimbres Polychrome (Cosgrove and Cosgrove 1932). The one sherd of this type in the collections came from the surface of Room Block A.

37   Thick parallel lines, black-on-white (Style I or II?). Multiple, thick (greater than about 2 mm width) parallel lines; thick-line checkerboard pattern. Fragments of these patterns found alone or, rarely, in opposition to fragmentary solid elements.

38   Thin parallel lines, black-on-white (Style II or III?). Multiple, thin (less than about 2 mm width) parallel lines; thin-line checkerboard pattern. (If motif was in opposition to solid elements, sherd was classified as Category 35).

39   Thick-line spiral, black-on-white (Style I or II?). Single or interlocked spirals with lines more than 2 mm wide.

40   Thin-line spiral, black-on-white (Style II or III?). Single or interlocked spirals with lines less than 2 mm wide.

41   Zigzag and scalloped black-on-white (Style I or II?). Anyon's "wavy" line motif (Anyon and LeBlanc 1984: 151), and solid elements edged with wavy lines.

42   Negative design, black-on-white (mostly Style III?). Small fragment of an apparently negative design, usually consisting of a single white "line" running through a black field.

OT   Other non-Mimbres decorated types (see Table 4.4).

PLAIN   Alma Plain and related types (Haury 1936). There are differing opinions on the precise definition of Alma Plain; here the category refers to plain, unslipped brown ware pottery.

SCORED   Alma Scored, Alma Punctate, and related types (Haury 1936). Plain, unslipped wares modified by scored and punctated designs; very rare.

CLAP   Clapboard corrugated (Mimbres Corrugated). Vessels with exposed corrugations, usually slightly flattened in a "clapboard" manner. This category may include sherds from neck-corrugated vessels, although almost no neck-banding, neck-corrugation, or even corrugation of only the upper half of jars were observed in the collection. At Saige-McFarland it appears that vessels were either entirely plain or entirely corrugated (with the exception of necks of corrugated jars), an observation much at variance with the customary understanding of Mimbres series utility types. Perhaps neck or upper-body-corrugated vessels broke along the corrugation-plain juncture, eliminating most sherd evidence. Almost all the whole or partial corrugated vessels were Mimbres phase or later. Most of the utility pottery counts are taken from the 1971–1973 analyses, and a reanalysis of utility sherds might discover more nonrim, partially corrugated or neck-corrugated pieces.

INDENT   Indented corrugated. Corrugation with patterned indentations or tooling; rarely observed.

RED   Slipped red wares, including San Francisco Red (Haury 1936). In 1971–1973, all red-slipped pottery was classified as San Francisco Red and it was recorded in astonishing quantities in late Classic Mimbres assemblages. I did not reanalyze all the red wares, but the rim sample offers some typological control of this situation. True San Francisco Red is most abundant in the earliest (Pit Houses 1 and 3) assemblages. Polished red-slipped wares continue to be made and produced, although they decrease in proportional frequency through time.

Table B.1. Sherd Counts

Sorting Categories span columns 20 through OT.

Provenience	20	21	22	30	31	32	33	34	35	36	37	38	39	40	41	42	OT	PLAIN	SCR	CLAP	IND	RED
ROOM																						
1 Level 1	3	2	1	3	3	1					2	2	1									
1 Level 2	7			9	12	2	6	1	7	1	5	1			1			80		27	1	6
1 Level 3	6	3		22	12	2	4	5			11	1	3	2		1		189	2	81	4	15
1 Floor					1		1	1			2							195		65		18
1 Below Floor											2											
2A Level 1	28	2	1	34	8	1	1	4	5		15	5	8		1			2		11		
2A Level 2	13	2	2	25	10	1	3	3	9		8	11	3		1	1	2	312	2	97	34	40
2A Level 3	22	5	6	49	17	2	13	3	4		16	3	5	13	4	1		385		96		14
2A Level 4	2	2		12	4	1		1	1		8	2	2		2	1		504	6	113	15	33
2A Below 4	7	2		2	1	2		1			5		1					102		23	1	3
2B Level 1	9	2	1	6	2			5	1	7	4	2	4		1			76		6		
2B Levels 2&3	9			20	13		5	2	10		18	6	4		6	2	1	186		39		15
3 Level 1	13			23	3		5	2	1		9	5	4		6	2		257		88		16
3 Level 2	28	1		25	6	1	8	3	20		14	9	6		3			259		19	1	3
3 Floor																		673	3	171	1	32
3 Below Floor					1			2	1		5		2		1			9		5		1
4A Level 1	20			9	4	1	2		2		3	2			1			8		7		3
4A Level 2	25	1	3	27	8		8		13		3	6	1		1	1		213	4	59		13
4A Floor							8				13	6	3		6			360	1	99		15
4A Feature 14	63			38	5	3	9				11	9	4		5			2				
4A Below Floor	12	3		17	14	1	4	1	6		9	4	4		5							4
4A Level 3	17	1		28	8		5		9		15	3	3		5	1		556	8	108	1	29
4A Level 4	8			11	13	1	1	5			3	3			6			403		110	1	29
4B Level 1	4	1		9	4			2	6		1	2					1	131		30		8
4B Level 2			1	1					3			1			1			119		29		5
5 Level 1	36	4		74	4	1	6	3	23		20	10	5		3	1		65		11		7
5 Level 2	28	1	2	27	17		3	1	17		9	4	6	2	5			720	13	259	8	36
5 Below Floor	1			1					2									398	19	270		17
6 Level 1	6			13	3	3		1	6		5	1	3		1	1		8		4		2
6 Level 2	11	1	1	9	3	1	3	1	4		13	3	2	1	3	4		151	5	62	2	4
6 Level 3	6			5	1		1	1			1	1	2					149		49	1	12
7A&B Level 1	12	2		3			2	2	11		4	7	1		1			36		12		2
7A Level 1	2	1	2	6	4			2	4		4	2			4			116	7	42	2	3
7A Level 2	3	•		3	2	2			2				3					105		44	1	
7A Level 3	3	1		4				1	2				2					59	3	23		2
7B Level 1													2					37	5	8		1
7B Level 2	3				1		1	1	1		3	2						102	5	22		
7B Level 3	7	1		14	6		2	5	7		4	5	3					25	1	13		1
8 Levels 1&2	10	3		15	8		2	1	17		14	9	6		4	2	1	132	10	44	5	1
8 Level 3	15	1	1	12	5	1	4	1	8		3	5	4		3	1		120	1	69	3	5
8 Level 4	9	3		18	5		1	3	14		8	10	3			2		201		33	6	10
8 Level 5	19			10	7	1			14		7	3	2		3	1		170	1	72	11	8
8 Level 6	30			31	13		11	3	48		17	14	5	1	5	4		145	4	80	4	6
8 Floor	5			5	1		2	2	2		6	3	2		1			278		90		11
8 Level 7	20			18	11		4		16		11	5	6		9	3		133	2	52	3	16
9 Level 1	51	6	1	59	14		8	1	20		21	42	12		9	2		40		11		
9 Level 2	7	2		15	2		3	1	4		6	10		1	9	2		916	8	140	15	18
9 Level 3	3	1		3			1				1	4			2	2		182		32	2	7
9 Level 4	1			2				3			1	4			1	1		65		19		
9 Level 5	3	2		5	2		1	1	4		2	4	1	1				46		9		
9 Level 6	5			5	3		4		2		5	1	1	3	1	1		64	4	27		
9 Floor	1			9			3	2	6		3	1	1	1	2	1		76	3	13	2	
10 Level 1	9	1	2	13	4	1			5		5	12	1		3			52	3	22		
10 Level 2	20	4	2	33	4		2	2	7		8	6	9		2			499	19	115	2	36
10 Level 3	13	10	1	31	10		5	3	18		6	21	9		2	3		574	9	96	1	27
10 Level 4	11	4	1	28	11		2		8		4	17	3		2	1	1	720	34	134	1	35
10 Level 5	9	2		20	8		4		13		6	7	3		4			255	2	22		
10 Level 6	10	1	1	18	4		5	3	3		6	9	6	1	2	3		244	2	63	1	9
10 Level 7 (PH4)	2	1	1	4	4	1		1			2	5	1	1	1			256	3	44		
10 Level 8 (PH4)	7	1		13	12			1	3		7	2	2		3	3		39		16		
11 Level 1	102	14	5	141	30		14	17	42		30	79	15	8	21	10		237		38		
11 Level 2	79	14	3	198	54	3	22	11	41		45	83	20	13	24	5	1	1622	10	460	9	7
11 Level 3	19	6	2	30	11		8	8	10		6	23	7	3	3	2		1760		445	19	78
11 Level 4	23	8	2	60	16		6	5	20		21	22	13	2	12	3		446	2	118	4	32
11 Level 5	15	1	1	1	30		1	5	7		3	11	2		6	2		606		151	2	34
11 Level 6	10	4		25	11		8	7	1		9	16	7		1	2		132		35	2	9
																		387		49		14

Table B.1. *(Continued)*

Provenience	20	21	22	30	31	32	33	34	35	36	37	38	39	40	41	42	OT	PLAIN	SCR	CLAP	IND	RED
11 Floor				8	3		7	2	3		6	5	1		1	2						
11 Feature 32									2									3		3		
11 Feature 34								11	2									4	1	1		
11 Level 7 (PH2)	13	1		12	7	1	1	2			2	5	2					233		24	3	3
11 Level 8 (PH2)		1		1				5			1		1					118		2		4
11 Level 9 (PH2)				1				1										103				
11 Level 10 (PH2)	2	5		4	12						3		2		1			105				
12 Level 1	46	7	4	62	21	1	17	3	25		7	36	8	4	3	6	2	619	*	215	3	33
12 Level 2	31	7	3	42	5	1	4	4	13		10	18	7		6	3		669	*	134		36
12 Level 3	38	13	5	66	15	1	12	4	21		13	38	6	1	7	5		486	*	139	3	42
12 Level 4	30	6	6	64	18		10	5	18		4	45	8	5	12	2	1	855	*	219	4	33
12 Level 5	41	10	5	107	14	3	22	8	33		11	48	6	5	6	12	1	1211	*	271	3	27
12 Feature 43	7	2	2	7	5		3		3		4	14	2		3		1	201		124		7
12 Feature 44	3		2	4	5						1	3		1	1			18		2		2
12 Feature 46	11	6	3	21	1		2	2	6		6	18	3	2	6	2		374		91		1
12 Feature 49		2	1	6					1		4	2						102		7	1	5
12 Feature 50			1								2	1						45		1		2
12 Level 6	28	13	4	61	12	1	14	8	29		31	30	10	5	5	8		596	*	140		20
12 Feature 52								1										102		7		5
12 Below Floor	2			3				2	5		1	5			1	1		50		15		7
12 Level 7	41	17	3	122	38		27	8	35		24	57	14	10	18	4		1457	*	142	2	73
12 Level 8	21	8	9	37	13	3	14	4	4		11	19	3	2	14			669	*	38		33
12 Level 9	16	5	3	25	28	1	13	1			10	18	8		9		2	771	*	34	3	41
12 Below Pit Structure Floor																		7		1		1
13 Level 1	3	4	1	19	4		5	4	11		5	8	2	1	1			165		61		8
13 Level 2	2	3		14	7		1	1	14		5	6		2	1	1		289	1	93	1	21
13 Level 3	4	3		13	6	2	4	3	16		3	6	3		2	4		169		44		12
13 Level 4	6	4	1	16	3	2	6	8	15		2	14	1	4	6	3		244		77	2	16
13 Level 5 (PH4)				4	1		1	3			1	3	1		3	1		94		9		6
13 Level 6 (PH4)		1	1	3	1		2	2	2		3	2				1		82		8	1	1
13 Level 7 (PH4)	1	2		4	4		1	1	2		3	3	1		1			259	1	17		14
13 Feature 74	3			1	3				5		1	2						59		10		
14 Level 1	65	10	4	140	26	3	28	11	39		46	50	17	12	17	5	2	1741		420		52
14 Level 2	6	7	2	34	4		4	5	12		6	10	1	1	3	1	1	372		89		11
14 Level 3	13	9		27	10		12	3	9		12	11	5	3	6		2	357		175		9
14 Level 4	5			3				1			1	3			2			117		102		
14 Feature 69	19	2	2	36	4	1	7	4	7		6	15	4	2		1	1	560		505		
14 Floor	2			1	1		1	1			4		1					(NOT SORTED 71–72?)				
14 Below Floor	8	4		24	10		7	3	5		11	6	3	4	2			(NOT SORTED 71–72?)				
15 Level 1	26	9	1	43	7		8	2	14		14	32	6	1	7	1		655		115		2
15 Level 2	12	5		29	5		5	1	12		3	14	4	1	3	1		314		54		1
15 Level 3	15	8	4	29	1	2	3	13			11	19	2	1	2	5		435		59	3	
15 Level 4	16	6	2	22	6		4		15		7	25		1	3	3		635		106		2
15 Level 5	26	14	2	34	7		3				14	14	4	1	3	3		519		66		
15 Level 6	7	2	3	19	3	2	3	3	7		10	13	4	4	5	1	3	245		30		
15 Floor 3	30	8	2	53	4		7	2	21		12	38	9	3	11	6		503	2	90	4	52
PIT HOUSE 1																						
Level A		7	2	1	14	1		1	2			2	1		3			(NOT SORTED 71–72?)				
N604 E505																						
Levels A&B	1			16	5	2	4	2	7		4	7	2		1	1		787	7	42	4	11
N604 E515																						
Levels A&B	10	3		52	17				4		9	18	4		9			2207	6	132	4	160
N610 E510																						
Level A	2	1		16	1			1	1		6	6	2	1	1			295		32		
Level B	2	1	1	6	7			2			3	1		1				329	10	53	2	6
Level C				2					2			9				1		252		27	4	
Level D	1	1	1	3	8		1				3	4		1				167	15	17		13
Level E	1	4	3		14	1	3	1			7	9	2	4	5	1		302	2	21	2	17
Level F		1	1	2	19	1	4				8	6	7	2	3			202	2	17	1	12
Level G	3	3		9	26	2	4	1			7	2	3		2			194		14		14
Level H	1	2	2	3	39	1	5				13	6	11	1	10			607	1	33		16
Level I		3	6	11	8						2	2	3	1	1			274	3	14	3	19
N620-630 E510																						
Levels A&B	2	6	2	9	27		12	5	17		7	18	2		12	6	1	747	2	100	2	25
N620 E510																						
Levels C-F	2	3	2	13	92	3	49	8	2		8	39	18	2	24		1	1051	6	108	4	36
Level G			5	3	15	3	4				5	2	1		2			247		24	1	8
Level H				4	17	2	1				5	4	1		4	1		105		10		9
Level I		4	4	3	31	2					6		6		1		1	164		9		6

Table B.1. *(Continued)*

Provenience	20	21	22	30	31	32	33	34	35	36	37	38	39	40	41	42	OT	PLAIN	SCR	CLAP	IND	RED
N630 E510																						
Levels C-F		7	3	3	25	4	1	2			2		3	2	13	1		488	2	44	3	39
Level I		1			5	2					2				2	1		157	1	6		9
Grid																						
A Level I	1																					
B Level I				1	1													2				1
C Level I											1	1						21				2
F Level I		3			10										1			7				
G Level I		1	1	3	5						2	2	1					125		6		13
H Level I					1						5	1	3					233		6		18
I Level I		2			2						2				1			27				4
J Level I	1	1	1	7	4	1					2							145		11		17
K Level G		3	1	15	15	5	4				6		3		1			181		7		14
K Level H	2	2	2	12	13	3	2				6	7	1		3	2		255		11	2	5
K Level I	2	4	1	17	17	4	2				3		5		3			142		5		
L Level G		2		6	11	3	1				4	2	6		1			212		8		
L Level H		3	4	4	1	1					3	2			3			136		9		3
L Level I	1	3	2	3	15	1	1				3	1	1	1				180		11		8
M Level G		1		3	6	1					9	2	2					260		4		1
M Level H		1	1	4	6						1	1	1					125		3		2
M Level I		3	1	12	11						1	1	2	1	1			201		5		8
N Level G		2		18	22	2	3				2		4	1	2			182		1		3
N Level H	4	1	1	10	7		1				7	2	10		7			317		8		6
N Level I	6	2	1	16	14	1					9		3		4			218		20		8
O Level I		1		2	3						6	2			2			267		11		2
P Level I	1	7	1	4	5						4							191	1	4		21
Q Level G	2	1			2						1	2			3			78		6		11
Q Level H	1		1	4							5	1			2			145		3		
Q Level I	1		3			1						1			3			146		4		
R Level G									1			1	1					56		2		6
R Level H	2	2	2	8	18	2	2											39				2
R Level I		1		5	6	2					3	1	4		5			159		8		4
S Level G				21	16	2	1				3	1	4	1	1			159		3		12
S Level H	2	2		11	20	1					5	2	4	1	3			269		7		8
S Level I	1	5	4	11	14	2					6	1	4	1	1			168		8		
T Level G	2	2	2	5	3	1					7	1	6	1	3			256		10	7	18
T Level H											5	1	3	1	1			86		1		4
U Level G	1			5	3						2							17				
U Level H	1	5	4	2		2					2		1	1	1			66		7		
U Level I			3		2						3	1			1			79		5		
V Level G	2	4	2	5	5						2							20				3
V Level H	1	1	1	4	11	1					2	3	2		1			99		5		5
V Level I		2	2	5	5						10	1	10		1			215		8		8
X Level G	1	1	1	3	5	1					3	2	2	1	1			80		1		9
X Level H		4			2	1					1	1	1		2	2		102		4		1
Y Level G		4	2	3	3	1							1		3			70		4		3
Y Levels H&I	2	1		8	6	1	1				2	3	4		2			309		2		17
Z Level G		2		3	7	1					2	2			2			305		6		30
Z Level H			6	6	9							1	1		1			90		7		2
Entrance											3	1	3					187		4		
Features																		1069		38		15
81																		140				21
83																		40		5		9
85		5	1	5	27	1					7	3	3		5	1		179		9		5
86	2	4		1	3	2	1				1	5	5		6			113		4		25
87		1	2		2										1			86		3		13
88					1		1				2				1			42		3		3
91				1							3				1							3
97		1	1	1							1											
PIT HOUSE 3 **											1							82				4
Level 6		7	1		16	6	2	2			8	7	3	2	7	4	1					
Level 7		7	8	1	22		3				11	9	7		6							
Level 8	1	5	2	2	20	2	6	3			28	14	7	2	2	2						
Level 9		9	1	6	17	2	1			1	15	10	4	2	2							
Level 10		10	1	4	6	11	2				8	6	6	2	4							
Level 11		2	2	7	11		3				5	7	6		2							

*Scored apparently not used as a sorting category for these proveniences.

**For Pit House 3, partial 1972 counts list only 66 utility sherds in Level 6, 12 sherds in Level 7, and no utility sherds in Levels 8 through 11. Both field tallies and utility sherds are now lost.

Table B.2. Summary Rim Form-Ware Data

Grouped provenience Ware	Bowls	Undifferentiated Jar	Large Jar	Small Jar	Seed Jar	TOTAL
ROOM BLOCK A						
Plain	24	51	9	3		87
Corrugated		20	17	9		46
Red ware	29	2		1	3	35
Smudged-polished	39					39
White ware	111				1	112
ROOM BLOCK B (excluding Sub-B)						
Plain	90	209	58	36	26	419
Corrugated		22	68	23		113
Red ware	130			7	12	149
Smudged-polished	121					121
White ware	844	10	7		7	868
SUB-B						
Plain	15	24	6	1	12	58
Corrugated		3	9	1		13
Red ware	23			1	2	26
Smudged-polished	6					6
White ware	100		3	2		105
ROOM BLOCK C						
Plain	2	7	3	2	1	15
Corrugated		4	2	3		9
Red ware	1					1
Smudged-polished	3					3
White ware	26		1	1		28
PIT HOUSE 1 UPPER FILL						
Plain	5	37	11	1	4	58
Corrugated		10	48	1		59
Red ware	25	1		2	3	31
Smudged-polished	1					1
White ware	141	1	4	6	2	154
PIT HOUSE 1 LOWER FILL						
Plain	33	31	7	12	5	88
Corrugated		9	38	3		50
Red ware	97	1		1	3	102
Smudged-polished	3					3
White ware	202	1	5	3	5	216
PIT HOUSE 3						
Plain	26	22	10	10		68
Corrugated		5	6	7		18
Red ware	36			3	4	43
Smudged-polished	4					4
White ware	65					65

Table B.3. Non-Mimbres Pottery Types
(Each entry indicates one sherd)

Provenience	Pottery Type
Room Block A, Fill	Starkweather Smudged-Decorated
Room Block A, Fill	Red Mesa Black-on-white
Room 2A, Level 1	El Paso Polychrome
Room 2A, Level 1	Late Reserve-Tularosa Black-on-white
Room 2B, Level 1	Early Red Mesa Black-on-white
Room 4A, Level 4	Sacaton Red-on-buff
Room 8, Level 1	Chupadero Black-on-white
Room 10, Level 3	Undifferentiated Hohokam buff ware
Room 10, Level 4	Reserve Black-on-white
Room 11, Level 2	*affinis* Encinas Red-on-brown
Room 12, Level 1	*affinis* Encinas Red-on-brown
Room 12, Level 1	Casa Grande Red-on-buff, Safford var.
Room 12, Level 4	Reserve Black-on-white
Room 12, Level 5	Reserve(?) Black-on-white
Room 12, Level 9	Red Mesa Black-on-white
Room 12, Level 9	Red Mesa Black-on-white
Room 12, Feature 43	Reserve Black-on-white
Room 14, Level 1	White Mountain(?) red ware
Room 14, Level 1	*affinis* Encinas Red-on-brown
Room 14, Level 2	*affinis* Encinas Red-on-brown
Room 14, Level 3	Red Mesa Black-on-white
Room 14, Level 3	Late Reserve-Tularosa Black-on-white
Room 14, Feature 69	Late Reserve-Tularosa Black-on-white
Room 15, Level 6	Starkweather Smudged-Decorated
Room 15, Level 6	Undifferentiated Hohokam buff ware
Room 15, Level 6	El Paso Polychrome
Pit House 3, Level 6	Red Mesa Black-on-white
N610 E510, Level 4	Late Red Mesa Black-on-white
N610 E510, Level 7	Early Red Mesa Black-on-white or San Marcial Black-on-white
N620 E510, Level 1	Early Red Mesa Black-on-white
N620 E510, Level 4	Unknown carbon-painted black-on-white
N630 E510, Level 2	Early Sacaton Red-on-buff
Pit House 1, Grid T, Level 1	Early Red Mesa Black-on-white
Unknown	Late Red Mesa Black-on-white
Unknown	Undifferentiated Hohokam buff ware
Unknown	Late Reserve-Tularosa Black-on-white

Lithic Definitions and Artifact Counts

MATERIALS

Lithic material types used for Upper Gila Project analyses were originally devised by Fitting and Anderson (Fitting 1973), and were subsequently modified by Skinner (1974), Lekson (1978b), George Sabo (who worked on the lithics in the 1970s), and Hemphill (1983). In most of these references, materials were simply named and not defined. Hemphill's definitions are the most complete, but none of the material categories have been defined lithologically. I combined a number of sorting categories to ensure comparability among the various analyses and to bring the material categories in line with standard geologic definitions. With the exception of obsidian, all materials are available either at the Saige-McFarland Site or within 5 to 7 km. Codes used in the tables are given in parentheses.

Basalt (BAS)

Fine-grained to coarse igneous material, usually dark gray to almost black. Flakable basalts occur as large cobbles in the terrace gravels at the site and outcrop nearby in the Datil Formation.

Rhyolite (RHY)

The terms andesite and rhyolite were evidently misapplied in most of the Upper Gila Project analyses. The term "rhyolite" was used for reddish porphyritic fine-grained igneous rocks; "andesite" was used for tan or buff porphyritic fine-grained igneous rocks. In terms of color, these names are the reverse of the usual geological usage. Hemphill concluded that "the two are the same rock with differences only in color" and identified that rock as rhyolite. I have combined andesite and rhyolite as used in the initial analyses. Rhyolites occur as large cobbles in the terrace gravels at the site and outcrop nearby in the Datil Formation.

Chert (CHERT)

"A broad category of cryptocrystalline material with a concoidal fracture pattern. Dull and glossy opaque material, waxy to gritty in texture, good to moderate flaking properties. In color, from gray, brown or black to white or yellow; frequently green or red (jasper), and often mottled or variegated" (Hemphill 1983: 36). This category combines chert, jasper, and agate as used in the initial analyses. Most varieties of chert occur as small cobbles in the terrace gravels and underlying alluvial deposits at the site, but some varieties may have originated elsewhere.

Chalcedony (CHAL)

A waxy, smooth cryptocrystalline material, usually translucent. The color is white to grayish white. This distinctive material commonly occurs in the local terrace gravels. It has a distinctively textured white cortex, referred to by local residents as "alligator" chalcedony.

Obsidian (OBS)

A black to green volcanic glass, translucent to transparent. The nearest well-known obsidian is the Mule Creek source, about 45 km northwest of the site. Obsidian at Mule Creek occurs as small (generally less than 5-cm diameter) nodules in perlite. Similar, undocumented sources are known to occur along much of the Mogollon Rim in New Mexico, and occasionally nodules are found in the terrace gravels of the Cliff Valley. Larger cobbles of low grade, green obsidian have been observed in the bed of nearby Turkey Creek.

CHIPPED-STONE TYPOLOGY

The formal typology used for most of the Upper Gila Project lithic analyses was developed by Fitting (1972a, 1973). The typology was rather subjective, and most flakes were classified as either "blocky" or "flat," with basically eponymous definitions. A third category, "bifacial retouch flakes," was defined by criteria similar to those used in many other lithic analyses. The following definitions are paraphrased from George Sabo's unpublished analysis, with my additions marked by brackets. (For illustrations of core types, see Fitting 1972a, 1973.) The abbreviations used in Table C.1 are given in parentheses.

Blocky Flakes (BIF)

Blocky flakes are squarish, uneven, thick chunky flakes, with unprepared striking platforms and angles of about 90° between the platform and the inner face of the flake. They are massive and irregular in longitudinal section and rectangular in cross section. Sabo also includes "shatter" and blocky decortication flakes as well.

Flat Flakes (FlF)

Flat flakes (defined by Fitting 1972a: 53) included flakes produced through a variety of chipping techniques. [In the 1987 analysis, flat flakes are those that are neither blocky nor bifacial retouch flakes.]

Bifacial Retouch Flakes (BiF)

These flakes were produced during the manufacturing or resharpening of bifacial implements (Fitting 1972a: 53). They are characterized by an acute angle between the striking platform and the exterior surface of the flake and by flake scars on the outer face. Flakes removed from cores with highly acute angles could not be differentiated from bifacial retouch flakes. [Flake scars may be present on the striking platform.]

Block Cores (BlC)

Fitting (1972a: 14) describes block cores as "large, blocky chunks of raw material from which flakes have been struck in a random manner. There does not seem to be any intentional preparation of a striking platform."

Plano-convex Cores (PlC)

These are conical or pyramidal cores on which the flat base was used as a striking platform. As flakes were removed, the angle between the striking platform and the convex face became greater. This condition was repaired by the removal of small flakes from the edge of the striking platform or by the removal of a single, large "core rejuvenation" flake. These cores were used occasionally as scraping tools.

Biconvex Cores (BcC)

Biconvex cores are similar to plano-convex cores except that flakes were removed from both faces of the core, resulting in a striking platform ridge around the medial plane of the core.

Small Bipolar Cores (SBC)

Small bipolar cores are small pebbles or cobbles on which flakes were removed by bipolar techniques, producing two opposed zones of percussion.

Retouched Flakes (ReF)

Some of the Upper Gila Project lithic analyses developed an impressive typology of retouched flakes (for example, Fitting 1973). As discussed in Chapter 3, I combined these subdivisions into a single category that includes scrapers, perforators, and burins, as well as less formalized retouched pieces.

GROUND-STONE TYPOLOGY

Ground-stone artifacts were assigned a "GS" number (Table C.2) in order to compare collections, original lists, and photographs. Some items assigned "GS" numbers were later eliminated as duplicates or non-ground stone; these numbers are omitted from Table C.2.

Data recorded for ground stone in the 1987 collections follow the analysis of Lancaster (in Nelson and LeBlanc 1986). Only data from manos and metates are tabulated here (Table C.3); other unique or unusual ground-stone artifacts are described in Chapter 3.

Attributes recorded for manos (Table C.3) and metates (Table C.4) are listed below. For this analysis, Lancaster's observation of "finger grooves" on manos is not included because no specimens at Saige-McFarland had finger grooves.

Number (GS)
 The serial number assigned to the ground-stone artifacts (identified in Table C.2).

Material (MAT)
 BAS   Basalt
 VBAS Vesicular basalt
 RHY   Rhyolite
 SAN   Sandstone
 GRA   Granite

Type and Cross section (TY/X)
Manos
 TAB   Tabular
 TUR   Turtleback
 WEG   Wedge
Metates
 BAS   Basin
 IT   Indeterminate trough
 SLA   Slab
 T   Trough
 TT   Through trough
 EXP   Expedient metate; grinding surface on an unmodified cobble.

Shape (SHP)
 R/S   Rectangular-square
 O/C   Ovoid-circular
 O/I   Oblong-irregular

Grinding Surfaces (SUR1, SUR2)
 A   Absent
 B   Beveled
 CV   Convex
 FL   Flat
 SB   Slightly beveled
 SC   Slightly convex

Striation Orientation (STR1, STR2)
 A   Absent
 R   Random
 X   Parallel to short axis

Y   Parallel to long axis
XY   Parallel to both axes

Secondary Usage and Exterior Modification (2nd/EXT)
Mano
   HS   Hammerstone
   ED   Chipped edge, edge damage
Metate
   A   Absent
   P   Pecked
   P/G   Pecked and ground
   R   Reworked

Length (LEN): + indicates measurement of incomplete dimension

Width (WID): + indicates measurement of incomplete dimension

Thickness (THI): + indicates measurement of incomplete dimension

Portion present (POR)
   W   Whole or nearly whole
           (fractions indicate estimate of portion present)

Grinding surface depth (GSD): Metates only

Grinding surface width (GSW): Metates only

Table C.1. Data for Chipped Stone
(Only proveniences with items are listed)

Provenience	MATERIAL TYPES					FORMAL TYPES							
	Bas	Rhy	Chert	Chal	Obs	BIF	FIF	BiF	BIC	PIC	BcC	SBC	ReF
ROOM													
1 Level 1	3	2	6	8	3	8	9	1		1			
1 Level 2	1		6	14	3	9	9	3				1	2
1 Level 3	6	15	32	49	7	38	44	23	1			1	3
2A Level 1	29	27	24	30	5	54	47	2	2	3	1	1	2
2A Level 2	21	17	15	46	22	52	38	9	3	5	1	4	2
2A Level 3	26	23	28	49	10	66	43	1	6	2	2	3	10
2A Level 4	8	7	4	9	3	21	10						16
2A Below 4	3		3	1		2	5						
2B Level 1	7	8	8	21	2	25	17					1	3
2B Levels 2&3	3	7	5	14	7	9	20	2	1			1	3
3 Level 1	19	29	9	16	4	25	44						6
3 Level 2	18	21	17	22	12	36	42	5	3	1	1		4
3 Feature 7		1		1		1	1						
3 Below floor	1	1	2			2	1						
4A Level 1	4	6	15	15	6	21	15	7	1				1
4A Level 2	15	16	9	35	5	31	37	8	2			2	2
4A Feature 14		1	4	12	2	5	11		3				
4A Below floor	4	2	10	11	2	13	10	1		1	1		3
4A Level 3		2	2	2		3	2				1		
4B Level 1	2		6	7	4	14	4						1
4B Level 2		3			3	2	2			1			1
5 Level 1	37	44	35	69	13	74	99	19					5
5 Level 2	6	5	15	27	3	28	19	2	1			1	5
5 Below floor			1			1							
6 Level 1	3	2	12	2	4	9	8	2	2		1		1
6 Level 2	1	1	1	2	2	3	3		1		1		
6 Level 3	2	1	1	8		9	3						
7A Level 2				3	1	2	1		1				
7A Level 3		1	1	3		2	1		1	1			
7B Level 3	1	1	7	13		6	13	2	1				
8 Level 1	3	5	6	7	2	12	7	1		1			2
8 Level 2	1	1		8		3	3	1	1				2
8 Level 3	3		10	19	8	11	19	1	1		1	1	6
8 Level 4	5	1	9	20	6	18	14	4	1			1	3
8 Level 5	2	1	4	9	7	7	12	2			1		1
8 Level 6	5	8	8	17	5	22	13	2	3	1		1	1
8 Floor		1	2	6		3	3				2	1	
8 Level 7		1	2	3	3	5	4						
9 Level 1	28	28	58	107	32	86	130	13	5	3		5	11
9 Level 2	6	2	7	14	6	15	17	2					1
9 Level 3			1	2		3							

Table C.1. *(Continued)*

Provenience	MATERIAL TYPES					FORMAL TYPES							
	Bas	Rhy	Chert	Chal	Obs	BIF	FIF	BiF	BIC	PIC	BcC	SBC	ReF
9 Level 4		1				3	9				1		1
9 Level 5	1	1	3	4	4	17	15	3	2				
9 Level 6	2	1	9	18	7	3	3	1					2
9 Floor	1	1	2	5		26	46	7				1	5
10 Level 1	10	14	23	29	9	103	151	17	4		1	1	11
10 Level 2	48	42	52	115	30	57	125	13		1			7
10 Level 3	18	26	37	97	26	34	45	4	1		2		4
10 Level 4	3	4	18	50	15	32	50	9	1		2		4
10 Level 5	13	8	18	45	14	50	59	7					5
10 Level 6	30	24	23	37	7	5	6	2	3	1			1
10 Level 7 (PH 4)	2	2	5	7	2	15	20	1					1
10 Level 8 (PH 4)	4	5	6	16	6			1					14
11 Level 1	79	70	143	306	74	240	391	20	4	1		2	33
11 Level 2	107	110	162	246	180	375	344	47	1	3		1	9
11 Level 3	17	17	53	97	42	93	103	17	2	1			14
11 Level 4	6	8	58	107	58	94	113	16					4
11 Level 5		2	19	21	17	30	24	1					9
11 Level 6	5	6	28	36	16	37	38	3	1	3			4
11 Feature 32		1	3	6	5	7	4						2
11 Feature 34	4	1	1	3	1	1	6		1				6
11 Level 7 (PH 2)		1	11	20	7	16	15	2					3
11 Level 8 (PH 2)	1	1	7	8	2	5	10	1					2
11 Level 9 (PH 2)		1	3	12	1	8	7						1
11 Level 10 (PH 2)		1	3	3		3	3						
12 Level 1	71	54	73	167	50	191	177	22	2	5	1	2	15
12 Level 2	32	22	43	101	31	92	116	7	2	1	1	1	9
12 Level 3	28	9	34	80	50	66	104	11	2	4		6	8
12 Level 4	47	37	68	123	64	119	184	13	4	5		8	6
12 Level 5	47	38	81	161	86	145	232	16	4	3	1		12
12 Feature 43	27	10	5	43	13	33	57	4	2				2
12 Feature 44	2	2		4		4	4			1			
12 Feature 46	19	13	19	64	18	43	80	9			1		
12 Feature 49	10	8	9	7	1	18	14		1				2
12 Feature 50	4		4	11	2	7	11		3				
12 Level 6	21	30	82	35	11	23	148	1	4*				3
12 Floor 2	3	6	2	8	4	8	11	3					1
12 Feature 52	1	1	8	11	5	11	13	1					1
12 Below Floor 2	4	9	16	3	2	6	25	1	1*				11
12 Level 7	79	105	171	150	45	50	392	30	67*				2
12 Level 8	49	21	65	27	13	14	131	6	22*				3
12 Level 9	27	17	64	27	14	12	122	1	11*				
12 Floor	2		1	10		2	11						
13 Level 1	13	9	12	48	9	28	54	2	3	2		1	1
13 Level 2	16	13	26	59	22	37	92	4		1		3	2
13 Level 3	13	7	15	39	17	29	52	4	1	1	1	3	1
13 Level 4	13	12	14	43	11	34	52	2	1	1		1	
13 Level 5 (PH 4)	4	8	3	10		7	14	2	1	1			
13 Level 6 (PH 4)	1	3	2	5	1	7	4				1	2	1
13 Level 7 (PH 4)	1	11	7	15	2	12	20	1	2	1			
13 Feature 74		3			1	3			1				
14 Level 1	118	73	91	258	109	181	421	28	3	4		1	11
14 Level 2	19	22	19	51	13	32	78	10	2				2
14 Level 3	32	19	40	76	31	53	138	3			1	1	4
14 Level 4	3	2	7	24	10	15	29			1	1		
14 Feature 69	41	45	39	107	37	84	161	16	2		1		6
14 Below floor	11	4	10	15	3	20	21	1	1				4
15 Level 1	6	6	34	182	59	96	182	5					4
15 Level 2	9	7	12	35	18	33	44	4					
15 Level 3	26	21	24	68	39	60	108	7				1	3
15 Level 4	14	20	31	97	37	82	112	5			1		1
15 Level 5	43	41	29	67	31	75	132	2				1	
15 Levels 6&7	67	65	42	130	38	124	207	10					

Table C.1. *(Continued)*

Provenience	MATERIAL TYPES					FORMAL TYPES							
	Bas	Rhy	Chert	Chal	Obs	BIF	FIF	BiF	BIC	PIC	BcC	SBC	ReF
PIT HOUSE 1													
N610 E510													
Level G	13	5	5	4	1	18	4		4				
Level H	9	3	9		2	15	4		2			1	1
Level I	4	1	2	8		12	2		1	1		1	
N620 E510													
Level G	3	1	1	2	2	5	2						
Level H	2		1	2	2	1	1			3			2
Level I	7	3	4	7	1	16	2	1	2	1			
N630 E510													
Level I	4	3	6			6	5		2				
Grid													
B Level I	2	2	1		1	5	1						
C Level I	1		1			2							
F Level I	2	1	4	1		2			1				
G Level I	7	4	4	3	1	2	5		4				
I Level I	1	2	1	4	1	10	8	1					
J Level I	2	2	5	7	1	6	2				1		
K Level G	4		6	1	1	7	9		1				
K Level I	2			2	1	6	5			1			
L Level G	5	2	1	3	3	2	2						
L Level H	4	3	5	7	1	7	6			1			
L Level I	24	12	2	16		11	8		1				
M Level G	1	1	1	2		30	24						
M Level H	3	2	9	10	2	3	1	1	1				
M Level I	3		6	16	4	12	11	2	1				
N Level H	1		1	2		15	14						
N Level I	5	2	4	2		3	1						
O Level I	10	3		8		10	3						
P Level I	3	2	4	6	1	13	5		3				
Q Level G	3	3	3	9	2	8	6			1			
Q Level H	8	2		8	2	13	7					1	
Q Level I	1		3	6		5	15						
R Level H				7	1	7	3						
R Level I			3	2		6	2						
S Level G			3			2	2	1					
S Level I					2	2							
T Level G	3		1	3		2	2						
T Level I	2	2	1	10	2	9	6	1					
U Level G	2	1	2	11	1	4	8	1			4		
U Level H	6	7		2		5	2						
U Level I	1	1	1	6		13	4	1		1			
V Level G			1	2		4	1						
V Level H			2	3		1	3	1					
V Level I	1	1	2	8		4	6						
X Level G	5	2		4		4	1					1	
X Level H	5	2	2	6	1	8	7					1	
Y Levels H&I	8	10	9	25	1	24	23	2	1	2	1		
Z Level G		1	6	6	3	10	5	1					
Z Level H	4	1	6	6	2	11	8						
Entrance	30	20	17	52	6	73	48		3	1			
East, Level A-C	253	169	77	101	14	350	246	9	6	2	1		
West, Level A-C	70	53	18	69	12	129	82	8		2	1	1	
Features													
81													
83				10	1	3	3		3				
85	2		1	5	1	1	7		1				
86	5	8	1	3	1	14	4						
87		1	1	3		5							
88	3	1	2	7	1	8	6						
97	1	3		3	1	6	2						
				1						1			

*Data from Skinner 1974, cores not separated into types.

Table C.2. Numbered Ground-stone Artifacts

GS Number	Description	Provenience
1	Metate	Unknown
2	Metate	Pit House 1, Feature 81
3	Metate	Pit House 1, Feature 81
4	Metate	Room 12, Fill
5	Metate	N604 E505, Level 2
6	Metate	Unknown
7	Metate	Unknown
8	Metate	Unknown
9	Metate	Pit House 1, Feature 81
10	Mortar	Room 15, Level 4
11	Mortar	N610 E510, Level 5
12	Mortar	Pit House 1, Grid M, Level 3
13	Mano	Pit House 1, Grid V, Level 3
14	Mano	N630 E550, Level 4
15	Mano	Room 15, Level 1
16	Mano	Unknown
17	Mano	Pit House 1, Grid G, Level 3
18	Mano	Room 15, Level 6
19	Mano	Room 2(?)
20	Mano	Room 2A, Level 2
21	Mano	Room Block A, Surface
22	Mano	Room 15, Level 1
23	Mano	N640 E550, Level 4
24	Mano	Pit House 1, Level 1
25	Mano	Room A, Surface
26	Mano	Room 15, Surface
27	Mano	Room 15, Level 6
28	Mano	Room 15, Level 6
29	Mano	Pit House 3, Fill
30	Mano	Room 1, Floor
31	Mano	Room 4B, Floor
32	Mano	Pit House 1, Feature 87
33	Mano	Room 11, Level 2
34	Mano	Room 11, Level 4
35	Metate	Room 6 or 4, Fill
36	Mano	Pit House 1, Grid V, Level 1
37	Mano	Room 15, Level 2
38	Mano	Pit House 3, Fill
39	Mano	Room 12, Level 8
40	Metate	Room 12, Level 2
41	Mano	Room 11, Level 2
42	Mano	Room 12, Level 8
43	Mano	Room 12, Level 8
44	Mano	Room 12, Fill
45	Metate	Room 11, Level 1
46	Mano	Room 12, Floor 2
47	Mano	Room 12 or Room 13, Level 3
48	Mano	Room 12, Floor 2
50	Mano	Room 2A, Level 2
52	Mano	Room 14, Feature 69
53	Mano	Room 12, Level 3
54	Mano	Room 12, Level 3
55	Metate	Room 15, Level 3
56	Mano	Room 15, Level 2
57	Mano	Room 11, Level 4
58	Mano	Pit House 1, Grid S, Level 2

Table C.2. *(Continued)*

GS Number	Description	Provenience
59	Mano	Surface
60	Mano-chopper	Room 12, Level 4
61	Mano	Room 12, Surface
62	Mano	Unknown
63	Mano	Pit House 1, Level 1
64	Mano	Room 12, Feature 43
65	Mano	Room 15, Level 2
66	Mano	Room 11, Level 2
69	Mano	Pit House 3, Fill
70	Mano	N620 E540, Level 3
71	Mano	Room 11, Level 3
72	Mano	Pit House 1, Level 1
75	Mano	Pit House 1, Grid N, Level 4
76	Mano	Room 12, Fill
77	Mano	N620 E510, Level 4
78	Mano	Pit House 3, Fill
79	Mano	Pit House 3, Fill
80	Mano	Room 15, Surface
81	Mano	Room 12, Level 2
82	Mano	Unknown
83	Mano	Room 15, Level 3
84	Mano	Room 12, Fill
85	Metate	Room 6, Floor 1, Feature 22
86	Metate	Room 12, Feature 40
87	Metate	Room 6, Floor 1, Feature 22
88	Metate	Room 6, Floor 1, Feature 22
89	Metate	Pit House 1, Feature 81
90	Metate	Pit House 1, Feature 81
91	Mano	N620 E510, Level 2
92	Mano	Room 15, Level 2
93	Metate	Room 12, Level 1
94	Mortar	N620 E520, Level 2
95	Palette	Room 11, Level 2
96	Palette	Room 12, Level 7
97	Palette	N650 E550, Level 3
98	Palette	Room 4A, Feature 14
99	Pipe	Pit House 1, Grid N, Level 4
100	Pipe	N620 E510, Level 5
101	Pipe	N610 E510, Level 4
102*	Ax	Room 2A, Feature 5
103*	Ax	Room 2A, Feature 5
104*	Turtle Vessel	Room 12, Feature 43
105*	Metate	Room 12, Level 2
106*	Metate	Pit House 3, Level 7
K1*	Mortar	N620 E510, Level 1
K2*	Mortar	N650 E550, Level 3
K4*	Mortar	Room 12, Level 1
K6*	Polishing stone	Room 12, Level 5
K7*	Mano	Room 12, Level 3
K8*	Mano	Room 12, Level 3
K13*	Mano	Room 14, Feature 69
K17*	Mano	Room 13, Level 2
K19*	Mano	Room 12, Level 5
K20*	Mano	Room 12, Feature 43
K21*	Mano	Room 12, Fill

*Not present in the collections, data from photographs.

Table C.3. Data for Manos

Provenience	GS	MAT	TYPE XSEC	SHP	SUR1	STR1	SUR2	STR2	2nd EXT	cm			POR
										LEN	WID	THI	
Unknown	16	VBAS	TUR	R/S	FL	X				9+	10+	4+	1/2
Unknown	82	BAS?	WEG	O/I	SC	X				11+	12+	6.5	1/2
Surface	59	RHY?	TUR	R/S	SC	X	C	A		13+	8.0	2.1	4/5
Room Block A, Surface	25	BAS	TAB	?	SC	A				9+	7+	3+	1/4
Room Block A, Surface	21	RHY	TAB	R/S	FL	XY	FL	A		12+	10.0	4.2	1/2
ROOM													
1, Floor	30	RHY	TAB	R/S	FL	X				6+	9+	3.0	1/3?
2(?)	19	VBAS	TUR	O/I	FL	A				13+	10+	4+	1/2
2A, Level 1	20	RHY	TUR	R/S	FL	X				9+	11.5	4+	1/3
2A, Level 2	50	RHY?	TUR	R/S	FL	X				11+	7.9	2.8	1/2
4B, Floor	31	VBAS	TAB	O/C	FL	A				9+	16+	5.2	?
N620 E540, Level 3	70	BAS	WEG	?	FL	A				6+	9+	4+	1/16
N630 E550, Level 4	14	BAS	TUR	O/I	SC	X				10+	6.5	4.0	3/4
N640 E550, Level 4	23	VBAS	?	?	SC	A				6+	6+	3.6	?
11, Level 2	41	VBAS	TAB	R/S	FL	A				22.4	10.4	4.8	W
11, Level 2	33	VBAS	TUR	R/S	C	XY				18.6	11.2	3.8	W
11, Level 2	66	VBAS	TUR	?	FL	A				7+	9+	4.4	1/8?
11, Level 3	71	RHY	TAB	?	FL?	A				6+	4+	2.3	?
11, Level 4	57	SAN	TAB	R/S	FL	A	FL	A		11+	7.5	3.5	1/4
11, Level 4	34	BAS	TAB	R/S	SC	A	SC	A		19.0	8.6	3.0	W
12, Surface	61	BAS	TUR	O/I	A	A				13+	15+	6.8	1/2
12, Fill	K19	?	?	O/I	?	?	?	?		25.1	11.3	?	W
12, Fill	84	VBAS	WEG	R/S	SC	X				21.4	10.3	3.6	W
12, Fill	K21	VBAS?	TUR?	R/S	?	?	?	?		22.1	11.3	?	W
12, Fill	44	VBAS	TAB	R/S	FL	A	SC	A		22.0	10.2	4.8	W
12, Level 2	76	RHY?	WEG	O/C?	FL	XY				10+	9+	3+	1/3
12, Level 2	81	VBAS	TUR	R/S	FL	A				12+	11.0	6.2	1/2
12, Level 3	K7	?	?	O/I	?	?	?	?		15+	10.1	?	1/2
12, Level 3	K8	?	?	O/I	?	?	?	?		17+	12.9	?	1/2
12, Level 3	54	VBAS	TUR	O/C?	FL	A				9+	11+	4+	1/3
12, Level 3	53	VBAS	TUR	R/S	FL	X				16.4	12.6	4.2	W
12, Level 3	47	RHY?	TAB	O/C	FL	R				12.6	9.2	3.3	W
12, Level 4	60	RHY?	TAB	O/I	FL	XY	FL	A	ED	13.6	8.6	2.3	W
12, Feature 43	64	BAS	TAB	?	SC	X	SC	A		11+	8+	5.0	1/16
12, Feature 43	K20	?	BAS?	R/S	?	?	?	?		25.7	11.0	?	W
12, Floor 2	48	VBAS	TUR	R/S	SC	X				13+	11+	3.8	1/4
12, Floor 2	46	BAS	TAB	O/C	FL	R	FL	XY		11.2	0.2	3.2	W
12, Level 8	39	BAS	WEG	O/I	C	X				16.3	10.0	3.0	W
12, Level 8	43	BAS	TUR	O/I	FL	A				13.3	12.8	5.0	W
12, Level 8	42	RHY?	TAB	O/I	FL	X	FL	X		22.3	13.4	4.8	W
13, Level 2	K17	?	?	R/S	?	?	?	?		21.7	9.8	?	W
14, Feature 69	52	VBAS	?	R/S	FL	A				11+	11+	3+	1/4
14, Feature 69	K13	?	?	O/I	?	?	?	?		16+	13.5	?	1/2
15, surface	80	VBAS	TUR	O/I	SC	A				13+	11+	6.4	1/4
15, surface	26	VBAS	?	O/I	C					7+	13+	5+	1/4
15, Level 1	22	BAS	TUR	O/C	FL	XY				12+	14+	4.4	1/2
15, Level 1	15	RHY	TUR	O/C	SC	X	C	X	HS	9+	8.0	5.5	1/2
15, Level 2	37	VBAS	TUR?	O/C	SC	A				12+	8+	5.3	1/4?
15, Level 2	65	VBAS	WEG	O/I	FL	X				11+	12.2	6.4	1/2
15, Level 2	56	VBAS	WEG	?	FL	A				7+	11.2	4.4	1/8
15, Level 2	92	VBAS	TUR	R/S	FL	A	C	A		10+	10.2	3.2	1/2
15, Level 3	83	VBAS	TUR	R/S	FL	A				16.2	10.5	5.2	W
15, Level 6	18	BAS	TUR	?	FL	A	C	A		10+	10+	5.4	1/2
15, Level 6	27	?	TUR?	?	A	A				11+	6+	5+	?
15, Level 6	28	VBAS	TUR?	?	FL	X				9+	8+	4.8	1/8
PIT HOUSE 1													
N620 E510, Level 2	91	RHY?	WEG	?	FL	A				10+	8+	4+	1/16
N620 E510, Level 4	77	VBAS	TUR?	?	FL?	A				9+	6+	4+	?
Levels A-C	24	BAS	TUR	R/S	FL	A				11+	10.0	3.7	1/2
Levels A-C	72	RHY?	TAB	?	FL	A				6+	10+	3.2	1/8
Levels A-C	63	VBAS	TAB?	R/S?	FL	A				9+	8+	3.8	1/8
Levels A-C	74	BAS	TUR	?	SC	X	SC	A		7+	6.4	1.8	1/3
Grid G, Level I	17	RHY	TUR	?	FL	A				10+	9+	4.3	1/2
Grid N, Level I	75	BAS	TUR	O/I?	SC	X				8+	9.3	3.6	1/3
Grid S, Level G	58	RHY?	TUR	R/S	FL	X				11+	11.0	3.0	1/2
Grid V, Level G	36	VBAS	TUR	?	FL	A				10+	14+	4.2	1/3
Grid V, Level I	13	VBAS	TAB	O/C	FL	A	FL	A		10.0	9.0	2.9	W
Feature 87	32	VBAS	TAB	O/C?	FL	A	FL	A		9+	9+	4.3	1/4
PIT HOUSE 3													
Fill(?)	29	VBAS	TUR	R/S?	FL	A				10+	13+	4.9	1/3
Fill(?)	38	VBAS	TUR	?	FL	A				11+	9.0	3.6	1/3
Fill(?)	69	VBAS	TAB	?	FL	A	FL	A		10+	8+	3.0	1/4?
Fill(?)	79	RHY	TAB	O/I	SC	X				8+	9.0	4.3	1/2
Fill(?)	78	BAS	TUR?	?	SC	A				5+	5+	4.8	1/16
Fill(?)	38	RHY	TUR	O/C	SC	A			A	8+	12+	4+	1/3

Table C.4. Data for Metates

Provenience	GS	MAT	TYPE XSEC	SHP	SUR	STR	2nd EXT	cm LEN	cm WID	cm THI	POR	cm GSD	cm GSW
Unknown	1	VB	IT	?	C	A	A	15+	17+	11.5	1/4	3.0	13+
Unknown	8	G?	T	O/C	C	Y	A	42+	38+	6.5	W	2.4	21+
Unknown	7	VB	?	?	SC	A	R	35+	10+	8.5	1/4	?	?
Unknown	6	VB	IT	O/C	C	Y	P	23+	12+	11+	1/4	3.2	6+
ROOM													
4, Level 1	35	SA	S?	O/C	FL	A	P/G	18+	16+	3+	1/4	?	?
6, Feature 22	87	VB	IT	?	C	A	?	13+	10+	8+	1/4	1+	5+
6, Feature 22	85	VB	IT	?	C	Y	?	15+	9+	6+	1/4	1+	9+
6, Feature 22	88	VB	IT	?	C?	A	?	8+	8+	6+	1/4	?	8+
11, Level 1	45	BA	E	O/C	SC	XY	A	16.3	12.4	3.8	W	0.3	8.0
12, Level 1	4	AN?	B?	O/C	C	A	P/G	25+	28+	14.0	1/4	10	22+
12, Level 1	93	SA	?	?	FL?	A	A	12+	6+	4.3	1/4	?	?
12, Level 2	40	AN	E	O/I	SC	Y	A	18.2	8.8	5.8	W	0.2	5.5
12, Feature 43	86	SA	IT	?	B	XY	?	16+	15+	7+	1/4	3+	5+
15, Level 3	55	AN?	E	O/I	SC	XY	A	12+	11+	4.3	W	0.2	8.0
PIT HOUSE 1													
N604 E505, Level 2	5	BA	B?	O/C	C	Y	A	33+	31.2	13.0	1/2	4.4	24.0
Feature 81	9	VB	T	R/S	C	A	P	26+	20+	?	1/4	?	15+
Feature 81	3	VB	IT	?	C	A	?	17+	5+	10+	1/4	6+	17+
Feature 81	2	VB	IT	O/C	C	A	P/G	25+	23+	11+	1/4	7+	17+
Feature 81	89	VB	IT	?	C	A	P	8+	8+	5+	1/4	1+	8+
Feature 81	90	VB	?	?	C?	A	P	5+	9+	7+	1/4	?	?

References

Anderson, Keith M., Gloria J. Fenner, Don P. Morris, George A. Teague, and Charmion McKusick
  1986 The Archaeology of Gila Cliff Dwellings. *Publications in Anthropology* 36. Tucson: Western Archeological and Conservation Center.
Anyon, Roger
  1980 The Late Pit House Period. In *An Archaeological Synthesis of Southwestern and South-central New Mexico*, edited by Steven A. LeBlanc and Michael Whalen, pp. 143–204. Albuquerque: Office of Contract Archaeology.
  1984 Mogollon Settlement Patterns and Communal Architecture. MS, Master's thesis, Department of Anthropology, University of New Mexico, Albuquerque.
  1988 The Mangas Phase in Mimbres Archaeology. Paper presented at the Fifth Mogollon Conference, Las Cruces, New Mexico.
Anyon, Roger, and Steven A. LeBlanc
  1980 The Architectural Evolution of Mogollon-Mimbres Communal Structures. *The Kiva* 45(3): 253–277.
  1984 *The Galaz Ruin*. Albuquerque: University of New Mexico Press.
Anyon, Roger, Patricia Gilman, and Steven A. LeBlanc
  1981 A Reevaluation of the Mogollon-Mimbres Archaeological Sequence. *The Kiva* 46(4): 209–222.
Baker, Gayla S.
  1971 The Riverside Site, Grant County, New Mexico. *Southwestern New Mexico Research Reports* 7. Cleveland: Case Western Reserve University.
Bannister, Bryant, John W. Hannah, and William J. Robinson
  1970 *Tree-Ring Dates from New Mexico M-N, S, Z*. Tucson: Laboratory of Tree-Ring Research, University of Arizona.
Blake, Michael, Steven A. LeBlanc, and Paul E. Minnis
  1986 Changing Settlement and Population in the Mimbres Valley, SW New Mexico. *Journal of Field Archaeology* 13: 439–464.
Bradfield, Wesley
  1929 Cameron Creek Village, A Site in the Mimbres Area in Grant County, New Mexico. *School of American Research Monograph* 1. Santa Fe: School of American Research.
Brody, J. J.
  1977 *Mimbres Painted Pottery*. Santa Fe: School of American Research.
Brown, Kenneth
  1971 Saige-McFarland: Summer 1971 Excavations. MS on file, Laboratory of Anthropology, Santa Fe.
Brunett, Fel V.
  1972 Excavations at Blacks Bluff, Grant County, New Mexico. MS on file, Laboratory of Anthropology, Santa Fe.
  1986 Excavations at the DeFausell-Karshner-Lewis Site (LA 34779) at Gila, New Mexico. Paper presented at the Fourth Mogollon Conference, University of Arizona, Tucson.

Burns, Peter E.
  1972 The Heron Ruin, Grant County, New Mexico. *Southwestern New Mexico Research Reports* 7. Cleveland: Case Western Reserve University.
Bussey, Stanley D.
  1973 Late Mogollon Manifestations in the Mimbres Branch, Southwestern New Mexico. MS, Doctoral dissertation, University of Oregon, Eugene.
  1975 The Archaeology of Lee Village. *COAS Monograph* 2. Las Cruces: COAS Publishing and Research.
Chapman, Richard C., William Gossett, and Cye Gossett
  1985 Class II Cultural Resources Survey of the Upper Gila Water Supply Study Area. MS on file, Bureau of Reclamation, Phoenix.
Cosgrove, Hattie S., and C. Burton Cosgrove
  1932 The Swarts Ruin, A Typical Mimbres Site in Southwestern New Mexico. *Papers of the Peabody Museum of American Archaeology and Ethnology* 15(1). Cambridge: Harvard University.
Di Peso, Charles C., John B. Rinaldo, and Gloria J. Fenner
  1974 *Casas Grandes, A Fallen Trading Center of the Gran Chichimeca*. Vols. 4–8. Dragoon: Amerind Foundation.
Doyel, David E., and Emil W. Haury
  1976 The 1976 Salado Conference. *The Kiva* 42(1).
Draine, R. Patrick
  1971 Saige-McFarland: Pit House 3. MS on file, Laboratory of Anthropology, Santa Fe.
Fewkes, Jesse Walter
  1914 Archaeology of the Lower Mimbres Valley, New Mexico. *Smithsonian Miscellaneous Collections* 63(10).
Fitting, James E.
  1972a Chipped Stone from the 1967 Mimbres Area Survey. *Southwestern New Mexico Research Reports* 8. Cleveland: Case Western Reserve University.
  1972b Preliminary Notes on Cliff Valley Settlement Patterns. *The Artifact* 10(4): 15–30.
  1973 An Early Mogollon Community: A Preliminary Report on the Winn Canyon Site. *The Artifact* 11(1–2).
Fitting, James E., Claudia B. Hemphill, and Donald R. Abbe
  1982 *The Upper Gila Water Supply Study: A Class I Cultural Resources Overview*. Springfield: Hemphill Associates.
Fitting, James E., James L. Ross, and B. Thomas Gray
  1971 Preliminary Report on the 1971 Intersession Excavations at the Saige-McFarland Site. *Southwestern New Mexico Research Reports* 4. Cleveland: Case Western Reserve University.
Gillespie, William B.
  1987 Vertebrate Remains for LA 5421, the Saige-McFarland Site. MS on file, Laboratory of Anthropology, Santa Fe.
Gilman, Patricia A.
  1980 The Early Pueblo Period: Classic Mimbres. In *An Archaeological Synthesis of Southwestern and South-central New Mexico*, edited by Steven A. LeBlanc and Michael Whalen, pp. 206–270. Albuquerque: Office of Contract Archaeology.

Gladwin, Winifred, and Harold S. Gladwin
1934   A Method for Designation of Cultures and Their Variations. *Medallian Paper* 15. Globe: Gila Pueblo.

Gomolak, Andrew R., and Dabney Ford
1976   *Reclamation of a Vandalized Prehistoric Settlement Site, Berrenda Creek Project 1976.* Las Cruces: Department of Sociology and Anthropology, New Mexico State University.

Hammack, Laurens C., Stanley D. Bussey, and Ronald Ice
1966   *The Cliff Highway Salvage Project.* Santa Fe: Laboratory of Anthropology.

Haury, Emil W.
1936   The Mogollon Culture of Southwestern New Mexico. *Medallion Paper* 20. Globe: Gila Pueblo.

Hemphill, Claudia B.
1983   The Eaton Site: Late Archaic on the Upper Gila. MS, Master's thesis, University of Oregon, Eugene.

Klinger, Timothy C., and Stephen H. Lekson
1973   A Bead Cache from Saige-McFarland, a Mimbres Site in Southwestern New Mexico. *The Artifact* 11(4): 66–68.

Laumbach, Karl W.
1980   Emergency Survey and Excavation in Southwestern New Mexico. *Cultural Resource Management Division Report* 354. Las Cruces: New Mexico State University.
1982   Perennial Use of Late Mimbres Small House Sites in the Black Range. In *Mogollon Archaeology*, edited by Patrick H. Beckett, pp. 103–109. Ramona: Acoma Books.

LeBlanc, Steven A.
1975   *Mimbres Archaeological Center: Preliminary Report of the First Season of Excavation, 1974.* Los Angeles: The Institute of Archaeology, University of California.
1982   Temporal Change in Mogollon Ceramics. In "Southwestern Ceramics: A Comparative Review," edited by Albert H. Schroeder. *Arizona Archaeologist* 15: 107–127.
1983   *The Mimbres People.* London: Thames and Hudson.
1986   Development of Archaeological Thought on the Mimbres Mogollon. In *Emil W. Haury's Prehistory of the Southwest*, edited by J. Jefferson Reid and David E. Doyel, pp. 297–304. Tucson: University of Arizona Press.

LeBlanc, Steven A., and Carole L. Khalil
1976   Flare-rimmed Bowls: A Sub-type of Mimbres Classic Black- on-white. *The Kiva* 41(3–4): 289–298.

LeBlanc, Steven A., and Michael Whalen
1980   *An Archaeological Synthesis of Southwestern and South-central New Mexico.* Albuquerque: Office of Contract Archaeology.

Lekson, Stephen H.
1972   The Saige-McFarland Site: Excavation of Room 12. MS on file, Laboratory of Anthropology, Santa Fe.
1978a   Settlement Patterns in the Redrock Valley of the Gila River, New Mexico. MS, Master's thesis, Eastern New Mexico University, Portales.
1978b   The Villareal Sites, Grant County, New Mexico. MS on file, Laboratory of Anthropology, Santa Fe.
1982   Architecture and Settlement Plan in the Redrock Valley of the Gila River, Southwestern New Mexico. In *Mogollon Archaeology*, edited by Patrick H. Beckett, pp. 61–73. Ramona: Acoma Books.
1984a   Prehistoric Settlement Along the Palomas Drainage, Southern New Mexico. In *Prehistoric Use of the Eastern Slopes of the Black Range, New Mexico*, edited by Margaret C. Nelson, pp. 15–23. Albuquerque: Maxwell Museum of Anthropology.

1984b   Mimbres Settlement Size in Southwestern New Mexico. In "Recent Research in Mogollon Archaeology," edited by Steadman Upham, Fred Plog, David G. Batcho, and Barbara E. Kauffman, pp. 68–74. *University Museum Occasional Papers* 10. Las Cruces: New Mexico State University Museum.
1984c   Dating Casas Grandes. *The Kiva* 50(1): 55–60.
1986a   The Mimbres Region. In "Mogollon Variability," edited by Charlotte Benson and Steadman Upham, pp. 147–155. *University Museum Occasional Papers* 15. Las Cruces: New Mexico State University Museum.
1986b   Mimbres Riverine Adaptations. In "Mogollon Variability," edited by Charlotte Benson and Steadman Upham, pp. 181–189. *University Museum Occasional Papers* 15. Las Cruces: New Mexico State University Museum.
1988a   The Mangas Phase in Mimbres Archaeology. *The Kiva* 53 (2): 129–145.
1988b   Regional Systematics in the Later Prehistory of Southern New Mexico. In *Fourth Jornada Mogollon Conference Collected Papers*, edited by Meliha S. Duran and Karl W. Laumbach, pp. 1–37. Human Systems Research, Tularosa.
1988c   The Idea of the Kiva in Anasazi Archaeology. *The Kiva* 53 (3): 213–234.
1989   An Archaeological Reconnaissance of the Rio Grande Valley in Sierra County, New Mexico. *The Artifact* 27 (2).

Lekson, Stephen H., and Timothy C. Klinger
1973   A Mimbres Stone Effigy Vessel. *The Artifact* 11(4): 5–7.

Mills, Barbara J.
1986   Temporal Variablity in the Ceramic Assemblages of the Eastern Slopes of the Black Range, New Mexico. In "Mogollon Variability," edited by Charlotte Benson and Steadman Upham, pp. 169–180. *University Museum Occasional Papers* 15. Las Cruces: New Mexico State University Museum.

Mills, Jack P., and Vera M. Mills
1972   The Dinwiddie Site. *The Artifact* 10(2).

Nelson, Ben A., and Steven A. LeBlanc
1986   *Short Term Sedentism in the American Southwest: The Mimbres Valley Salado.* Albuquerque: University of New Mexico Press.

Nelson, Ben A., Margaret C. Rugge, and Steven A. LeBlanc
1978   LA 12109, A Small Classic Mimbres Ruin, Mimbres Valley. In "Limited Activity and Occupation Sites," edited by Albert E. Ward, pp. 191–206. *Contributions to Anthropological Studies* 1. Albuquerque: Center for Anthropological Studies.

Nesbitt, Paul H.
1931   The Ancient Mimbrenos, Based on Investigations at the Mattocks Ruin, Mimbres Valley. *Logan Museum Bulletin* 4. Beloit: Logan Museum.

Parsons, Francis B.
1955   A Small Mimbres Ruin near Silver City, New Mexico. *El Palacio* 62(10): 283–289.

Scott, Catherine J.
1983   The Evolution of Mimbres Pottery. In *Mimbres Pottery*, edited by J. J. Brody and others, pp. 39–67. New York: Hudson Hills Press.

Shafer, Harry J.
1982   Classic Mimbres Phase Household and Room Use Patterns. *The Kiva* 48(1–2): 17–37.
1986   The NAN Ranch Archaeology Project 1985 Interim Re-

port. *Special Report* 7. College Station: Anthropology Laboratory, Texas A&M University.

1987 *Explorations at the NAN Ruin (LA 15049), 1986 Interim Report*. College Station: Anthropology Laboratory, Texas A&M University.

1988 *Archaeology at the NAN Ranch Ruin, the 1987 Season*. College Station: Department of Anthropology, Texas A&M University.

Shafer, Harry J., and Anna J. Taylor
1986 Mimbres Mogollon Pueblo Dynamics and Ceramic Style Change. *Journal of Field Archaeology* 13(1): 43–68.

Skinner, Elizabeth
1974 Similarity of Lithic Industries in the Burro Mountains and the Cliff Valley of Southwestern New Mexico. *The Artifact* 12(3): 26–44.

Stuart, David E., and Rory P. Gauthier
1981 *Prehistoric New Mexico*. Santa Fe: State Historic Preservation Division.

Stuiver, Minze, and Bernard Becker
1986 High-Precision Decadal Calibration of the Radiocarbon Time Scale, A.D. 1950–2500 B.C. *Radiocarbon* 28(2B): 863–910.

Stuiver, Minze, and P. J. Reimer
1986 CALIB and DISPLAY (Programs). Quaternary Isotope Laboratory, University of Washington, Seattle.

Withers, Arnold
1985a Three Circle Red-on-white: An Alternative to Oblivion. In "Southwestern Culture History," edited by Charles H. Lange, pp. 15–26. *Papers of the Archaeological Society of New Mexico* 10. Santa Fe: Sunstone Press.

1985b The Short Happy Life of Mogollon Red-on-brown. In "Prehistory and History in the Southwest," edited by Nancy Fox, pp. 15–18. *Papers of the Archaeological Society of New Mexico* 11. Santa Fe: Sunstone Press.

Index

ABSTRACT

The Saige-McFarland Site is located on the Upper Gila River in the Mimbres area of southwestern New Mexico. Almost all previous information about the archaeological Mimbres culture has come from excavations in the Mimbres Valley, about 65 km east of the Upper Gila. It has long been known that Mimbres pottery occurs outside the Mimbres Valley, but very few sites have ever been excavated to clarify the nature of the Mimbres of the Upper Gila.

At Saige-McFarland an extensive pit house occupation is overlain by at least four small masonry pueblos. Partial excavation of the site reveals a sequence similar to that defined in the Mimbres Valley: a Three Circle phase pit house village with a Great Kiva dating to about A.D. 900, a small Mangas phase masonry room block dating to A.D. 950–1000, and a final Mimbres phase pueblo occupation ending about A.D. 1150. The architectural styles used over this 250-year span are identical to styles used in the Mimbres Valley and the ceramics associated with these structures reflect the developmental series of types first defined in the Mimbres Valley. The Saige-McFarland Site demonstrates that the Mimbres of the Upper Gila and the Mimbres of the Mimbres Valley are, for practical purposes, the same.

The Saige-McFarland Site offers new data on the evolution of Mimbres architecture. During the Mangas phase small masonry structures were built that developmentally are intermediate between earlier pit house villages and the later, large Mimbres phase pueblos. The Mangas phase room block at Saige-McFarland continued to be occupied through the Mimbres phase, but its initial form presents the best data to date on Mangas phase construction. Mangas phase architecture has not been identified in the Mimbres Valley.

Surveys of the Gila Valley above and below the Saige-McFarland site demonstrate that the patterns seen at Saige-McFarland characterize a 75-km length of this river. The Upper Gila area was a major locus of Mimbres culture, equal in most and perhaps all respects to the much better known Mimbres Valley locus.

RESUMEN

El sitio Saige-McFarland está localizado en el alto Río Gila en el área mimbres del suroeste de Nuevo México. La major parte de la información previa acerca de la arquelógica cultura mimbres nos ha venido de las excavaciones en el Valle Mimbres, como unos 65 km al este del Alto Gila. Se ha sabido por mucho tiempo que las cerámicas mimbres ocuren fuera del Valle Mimbres, pero muy pocos sitios se han excavado para clarificar el género de los mimbres del Alto Gila.

En Saige-McFarland una extensiva ocupación de casas de poso está sobrepuesta por no menos que cuatro pueblos de albañilería. Excavación parcial del sitio revela una sucesión parecida a la que se ha determinado en el Valle Mimbres: una aldea de casas de poso de la fase Three Circle con su Gran Kiva fechando hasta aproximadamente A.D. 900, un bloque de cuartos de albañilería de la fase Mangas fechando hasta A.D. 950 a 1000, y finalmente un pueblo de la fase Mimbres que se desocupó aproximadamente en 1150. Los estilos de arquitectura que fueron utilizados durante este lapso de 250 años son identicos a los estilos utilizados en el Valle Mimbres y la céramica relacionada con estas estructuras refleja la serie de desarrollo de tipos que fue primero determinada en el Valle Mimbres.

El sitio Saige-McFarland ofrece nuevos datos sobre la evolución de la arquitectura mimbres. Durante la fase Mangas se construyeron pequeñas estructuras de albañilería, que en el desarrollo de la cultura, son intermedias entre las más viejas aldeas de casas de poso y los más recientes, grandes pueblos de la fase mimbres. El bloque de cuartos de la fase Mangas del sitio Saige-McFarland continuo ser ocupado durante la fase Mimbres, pero su primera forma presenta los mejores datos sobre la construcción de la fase Mangas. No se ha identificado arquitectura de la fase Mangas en el Valle Mimbres.

Examenes del Valle Gila río arriba y río abajo del sitio Saige-McFarland muestran que los modelos que se ven en Saige-McFarland caracterizan un estrecho de algunos 75 km de este río. El area Alto Gila era un mayor punto de la cultura mimbres, el igual en casi todos, y quizá todos, respectos al mas conocido punto del Valle Mimbres.